BEFORE ENDEAVOURS FADE

A GUIDE TO THE BATTLEFIELDS OF
THE FIRST WORLD WAR

BY ROSE E. B. COOMBS, MBE

AN

AFTER THE BATTLE

PUBLICATION

Thiepval: the majestic Memorial to the Missing stands amid fields still scarred with the battle-lines of the Leipzig Redoubt.

Credits

© Rose E. B. Coombs, MBE, 1990

Paperback: ISBN 0 900913 61 4
Hardback: ISBN 0 900913 62 2

Printed in Great Britain

First Published August 1976
Second Edition November 1977
Third Edition November 1979
Fourth Edition March 1983
Fifth Edition July 1986
Sixth Edition April 1990

Designed and edited by Winston G. Ramsey
Editor *After the Battle* magazine

PUBLISHERS
Battle of Britain Prints International Ltd.
Church House, Church Street,
London, E15 3JA
Telephone 081-534 8833

PRINTERS
Plaistow Press Limited
Church House, Church Street,
London, E15 3JA

PHOTOGRAPHS
All photographs are the copyright of the author, except those from the Imperial War Museum archives (designated IWM) and the aerial photographs which were taken by *After the Battle* magazine.

MAPS
All maps are the copyright of the Michelin Company and are reproduced with their permission.

FRONT COVER
The 41st Division Memorial at Flèrs.

BACK COVER
Newfoundland Memorial at Gueudecourt.

ENDPAPERS
Trench maps of the period. **Front:** Hill 60 in the Ypres Salient from GSGS 3565, May 1917. **Rear:** The Somme battlefield in December 1916 reproduced from GSGS 3347.

PAGE 4
Dawn over Ypres.

PAGE 155
Desplanque Farm Cemetery located at La Chapelle d'Armentières.

ABOUT THE AUTHOR
'You haven't talked to THE expert on the Great War until you have talked to Miss Coombs.' So ran one letter received at the Imperial War Museum, London, where for 36 years, from 1946 until 1982, Rose Coombs worked — in latter years as Special Collections Officer.

Her interest in battlefields began at an early age, influenced largely by her father who served in the RAOC, but it was not until after the Second World War (in which she served as a Radar Operator with Nos. 10 and 11 Groups, RAF), that she was able to realise her ambition, through her position at the Imperial War Museum, to visit the battlefields of Europe.

During the years which followed she had the opportunity to make hundreds of visits to the Western Front of 1914-1918, on many occasions acting as guide to ex-Servicemen's groups returning to the battlefields. She has accompanied authors writing on the period and lectured groups of all ages, giving freely of her detailed knowledge of the terrain, its history, the units and personalities involved, and what remains today. Miss Coombs has now combined years of study, travel and research in this profusely illustrated publication.

Contents

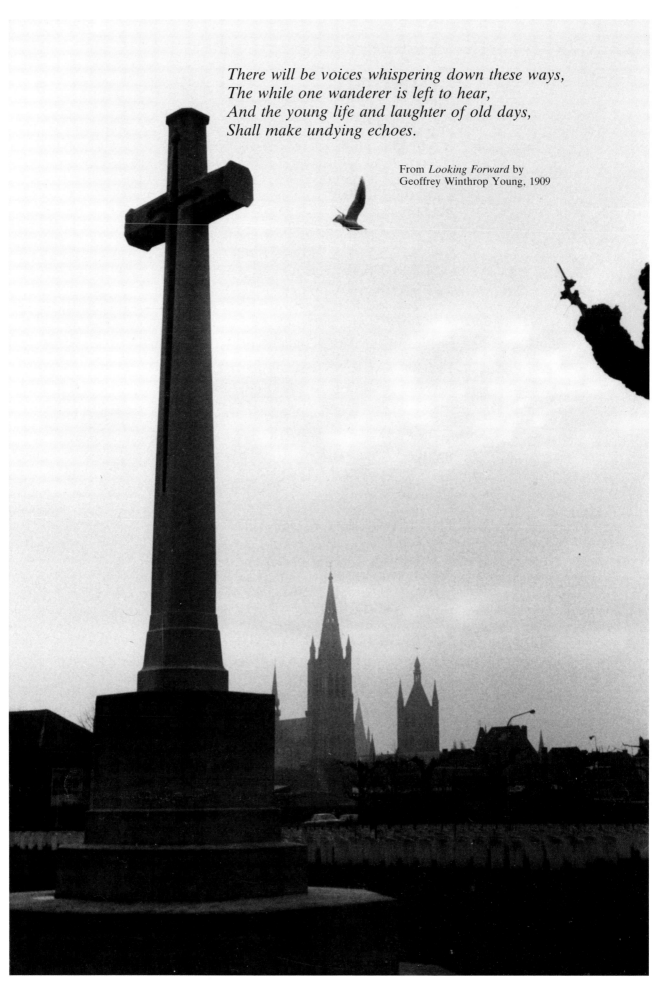

There will be voices whispering down these ways,
The while one wanderer is left to hear,
And the young life and laughter of old days,
Shall make undying echoes.

From *Looking Forward* by
Geoffrey Winthrop Young, 1909

Introduction by the Author

A visit to the battlefields should begin at one of the traditional entry ports for the BEF — Boulogne, Calais, Dieppe or Le Havre. However, today the modern traveller can also take advantage of the routes through Dunkerque, Ostend and Zeebrugge, by ferry or hovercraft. As it is the nearest port to the English coast, I have chosen Calais as the starting and departure point for this itinerary. The ports of Boulogne, Dunkirk, Ostend and Zeebrugge are included in the relevant routes.

I have travelled all the routes described in an ordinary saloon car. On the whole the main roads now have excellent surfaces but here and there the camber of the roads is not ideal and care should be taken to maintain a suitable speed to counter this.

The motorways which now crisscross the old front line have access points to many of the areas covered in this book and views of parts of the battle-front can be obtained from them, but to really see the country it is necessary to keep to the old roads — the Routes Nationales (N); the Chemin De-

partmentals (D) or (CD), and the Vicinaux Ordinaires (VO). Frequently I have found these latter two categories are better surfaced than those nationally maintained roads, although narrower. Distances throughout are quoted in kilometres.

Maps are a necessity for any tour. Whilst I have indicated the route to be taken on black and white extracts, I recommend the visitor to purchase the following Michelin 1:200000 maps: Belgium Sheets 213 and 214; France Sheets 51, 52, 53, 56 and 57.

The new area sheets 236, 237 and 241 — Nord and Ile de France and Champagne respectively — are useful for forward planning, if a little large for use in the car. The scale is 1cm to 2km (very approximately half-an-inch to one mile) and all the features are indicated in colour.

The text is correct to January 1990. The renumbering of roads in Belgium and France is complete, but variations may exist still. Those quoted in my text are based on 1989 issues of Michelin maps. Autoroutes and international roads now carry 'E' numbers. In Belgium all

MISS ROSE E. B. COOMBS, MBE

main and secondary roads are numbered or named.

Another problem for the visitor today has been caused by the changes in place names due to the recent adoption of modern Flemish as opposed to the traditional spellings used for Belgian towns and villages as they were known to the BEF. For ease of navigation, I have indicated the version which is now to be found on signposts.

About this book

It is now over sixty years since war raged here. Thousands of soldiers died daily. Their relatives have visited their graves, their comrades also. Pilgrims have come from all parts of the world to say a prayer or bring flowers. An old soldier has tried vainly to find the trench he knew so well. But the old warriors — the majority of them — have disappeared; as have their loved ones. History is made but who will remember it? From far off, the descendants of those who fought here come to visit the villages whose names, for some four years, made people hold their breath. School children come with their teachers, coaches of tourists with guides, and the casual visitor. To all this guide is indispensible.

The author spares no pains to

attract your attention but she does not go in for melodrama. You will find all the details you need with the historic background to the events. As for the itinerary you will find little is missed. All battle sites and monuments are included, even to the smallest or the most modest. Graves of the known and unknown are pointed out and this is done with the utmost respect for all.

When the author asked me to write an introduction to her work, she recalled our many trips over the battlefields of France and Flanders. I would like to thank her for this expression of friendship and wish this guidebook every success.

Dr Alfred A. Caenepeel, OBE

Vice-Chairman, Last Post Committee
Founder & Curator, Ypres Salient Museum

THE LATE DR A. A. CAENEPEEL, OBE

In September 1989, the DOCUMENTATIE-CENTRUM DR ALFRED CAENEPEEL was opened as a public reference library, as an adjunct to the Ypres Salient 1914-18 Museum. This unique archive comprises books, maps, documents and photographs relative to every aspect of the Salient and of all the armies which fought there.

Demarcation Stones

In the decade following the Armistice, 119 small monuments were erected in Belgium and France, at intervals along the 960 kilometres of the Western Front, to mark the limit of the German advance in 1918. The Touring Club de France and the Touring Club de Belgique were the prime movers of this scheme which caught the imagination of the public.

Of pink granite, the monuments were no more than a metre in height. They were designed by the sculptor Paul Moreau Vauthier who produced three basic types, differing mainly in the helmet of the capstone. These were either of the British tin helmet or the French and Belgian 'Poilu's' helmet design. On the side of the stones were decorations consisting of a soldier's equipment — gas mask case, water bottle, etc., and each bore the inscription. 'Here the Invader was brought to a standstill' in either French, Flemish or English. On the front

face, the name of the place they were to stand in or near was inscribed.

The stones which became known as Demarcation Bornes or Stones were placed in positions where the battle line crossed a road or street, in town or country, at points decided by Maréchal Pétain and the General Staffs of France, Belgium, and Britain.

Funds to help in the erection of the monuments came from many sources beside the two Touring Clubs, which bore the main charge, and local authorities, ex-Servicemen's organisations and private people all contributed to their cost.

The number of stones remaining in-situ today is much depleted as many were destroyed or lost during the Second World War or have become the victims of the motor vehicle. For instance, of the seven donated by the Ypres League and erected in the Salient, only two or three have survived. Others have been broken up by the explosion of old ammunition which had been placed against them by farmers.

Where our itinerary passes a stone, I have usually drawn attention to it.

The Poppy Legend

The poppy legend originated in China. A white flower from which a potent drug was distilled was called the Flower of Forgetfulness. Ghengis Khan brought some of the seed westward but after a battle the flower became red. In the centre of each was a cross.

It was found that on many battlefields, when everything else had been laid waste,

the landscape was soon ablaze with the blood-red blooms. On the Somme battlefield in 1917 (and again after the war was over) the land burst forth in a blaze of scarlet with patches of yellow charlock and white chamomile. Many graves of those buried near the front line were soon marked by the charlock due to the seeds being released when the grave was dug.

Lord Macauley drew attention to the strange link of the poppy with battle and put forward the suggestion it should be regarded as the flower of sacrifice and memorial.

Battlefield Debris

The colossal expenditure in shell and ammunition during the First World War has left a dangerous legacy for the careless visitor today. Often, as the battle areas are traversed, small piles of rusting shells will be seen on the verge. These neat piles of ammunition are usually the result of a field being ploughed the 'Iron Harvest' I call it — and still to this day, regular collections are made by the military authorities to take these dangerous objects away for safe demolition.

The sight of such things seems to turn many visitors into collectors and, with little thought of the danger of these seemingly inoffensive objects, they are bundled into the car. Please leave them where you see them — or if it is within any of the memorial parks draw the attention of the Superintendent to them. Explosives do not improve with age and many French children are still maimed and blinded by handling such objects.

Even the apparently innocent rusty bayonet or length of barbed wire carries with it the danger of tetanus if carelessly handled. Recently scientists have been working on one aspect of the spread of the deadly disease rabies, as it has been realised that the

old battle-torn woods and shrublands are breeding grounds of the most frequent carrier — the fox. The French medical authorities have been investigating some of the untouched regions and have found evidence that careless wandering through dirty infectious ground can be dangerous.

Remember also that the removal of anything from private land is stealing. It is often possible to acquire material quite safely and legally for a small sum. However, always bear in mind the strict customs regulations concerning the importation of weapons and ammunition.

Accommodation

The traveller should be warned that, for the most part, the regions through which these routes pass are off the normal tourist track and, therefore, hotels are often few and far between. Beyond the coastal resorts or the cities of Amiens, Reims, or Arras, there is not a great deal of choice. The French and Belgian National Tourist Offices can supply lists of approved hotels in the area but it will be found that few are of three or four star classification.

Ypres has a fairly good selection of moderately priced hotels and out in the country, within easy access, there are some more expensive (but not outrageously so), country house type hostelleries. Usually in the small towns there are cafés with a few rooms.

Nowhere in France is one far from a good restaurant. In my travels I have never failed to find the Buffets de la Gare of the larger or main line stations of very good value. Amiens, Lille, Arras and Reims — all are good. Some stations have more than one restaurant on the premises catering for differing tastes or pockets. Often if there is no

such café on the station, one will be found in the vicinity, for example, in Albert and Armentières.

For those doing their own catering there is no village in France where bread cannot be bought daily (except between the hours of 12.00 and 2.00 p.m.). For reasonable prices I can highly recommend the hypermarkets on the outskirts of all major towns, frequently near motorway intersections. Parking is ample. This is important as in most towns parking meters have now been installed, they are expensive and the regulations are rigidly monitored by meter maids.

Calais–Ypres

ROUTE I VIA BERGUES

Calais. Hôtel de Ville Belfry

Now a modern sprawling industrial area and busy port, **Calais** was a most important British base particularly for the ordnance services and the auxiliary units for the BEF. Hospitals, training camps and depots all grew up behind the town and, in February 1918, the train ferry link with the then new Richborough military harbour was established.

Little of the Calais the first BEF knew remains, and the new residential and industrial zones now spread over the flat land behind the sand dunes where the troops encamped. Here and there, however, little bungalows (originially temporary wooden huts) remain as residences.

During the Second World War, Calais was almost entirely destroyed in 1940; thereafter to be encircled by concrete bunkers of the German defences. Many of these were added to the old forts which had previously been its main defence. Gradually many of these have been removed to make way for new building. The huge modern complex of the ferry terminal, geared to the requirements of motor vehicles — cars, coaches and huge trucks — is surrounded by open areas for parking.

The recommended route to leave the terminal for destinations other than Calais centre now takes the coast road between the Bassin des Chasses and the old fort with the ruins of concrete bunkers scattered drunkenly as the demolition continues. The road hugs the old moat up to the roundabout where it is joined by the road from the hoverport. In the sand dunes around the hoverport a few bunkers remain.

To visit the town, follow the signs for 'Centre Ville' which lead across the Pont Mobile, through the Place de Suède, the rue Cdt Bonninque, the Place d'Armes and the rue Royale and Place Maréchal Foch, past the Parc Richelieu and the bridges — Pont George V and Pont Jacquard — and the Central Station to the Parc St Pierre and the famous Hôtel de Ville. Another route is from the Place de Suède, which leads down the rue de Moscou and the open railway.

In the **Parc St Pierre** is the **Musée de Guerre**. The exhibits are mainly related to the 1939-45 conflict. In front of the nearby **Hôtel de Ville**, a magnificent building in the Flemish Renaissance style with its famous Belfry, in the Place du Soldat Inconnu is the equally famous sculpture by Rodin of the Six Burghers of Calais.

From the roundabout the currently rather narrow road and poor surfaced rue de Nord connects with the access road for the wide bypass which now encircles Calais. The N1-E40 on the left leads towards Gravelines and Dunkerque through modern residential areas amid which the occasional large concrete bunker can be glimpsed, but most of these have now gone. The little single storey dwellings in the rue de Phaisbourg are replacements for the wooden bungalows already mentioned.

The N1 is straight and very uninteresting. The rather drab ribbon development gives way to the flat agricultural region of beet and corn fields, market gardens and the occasional old sugar factory standing idle now the crops are taken direct to the modern refineries outside Dunkerque.

A more interesting route to Dunkerque and Belgium is now signposted from the first turning to the left after the railway crosses the rue du Nord. This passes through part of the new industrial zone for about 1 km then a sharp right turn followed ½ km later by a left onto the D119. This road winds its way through the immediate hinterland of the sand dunes, through **Fort Vert** with a number of desolate bunkers, defences for the **airfield** at **Marck** which is on the right (8 kms), and for coastal artillery protecting both Calais and Fort Philippe, all of Second War vintage. Waldam is a small modern village passed through before the hamlets of Le Tap Cul and L'Etoile, part of Oye Plage where the road rejoins the N1 on the modern outskirts of Gravelines. The nuclear power station and oil refinery at Petit Fort Philippe have caused considerable extension of the residential areas of both Grand Fort Philippe on the west bank of the River Aa and Gravelines. The N1 now curves round to the south of the ancient town.

During the Great War **Gravelines** was a Belgian headquarters. It is possible to visualize the encampments located where light industry amid the workers' estates is now in view below the new road. There are still vestiges of the old fishing port with military connections dating back many centuries. Within the crumbling walls and ramparts, largely designed by Vauban, the narrow and busy streets follow a spider's-web pattern. It is a quaint place and can be approached by a continuation of the D119 instead of turning right and then left onto the N1. The old road through the town centre with its attractive church tower rejoins the N1 at a new crossroad on the eastern side. The main road makes a sharp right hand turn here. About 1 km further east is one of the **best preserved windmills** in Flanders, away to the right among the beet fields.

After 5 km, Loon Plage, a suburb of the ever spreading complex of Dunkerque, is bypassed to the north. New roads have been constructed to carry the heavy traffic the new docks have caused and several further access routes are proposed to form a complete ringroad for the old port.

In 5 kms, at a major crossroad, the N1 swings to the left to enter Dunkerque. Keep ahead on the N335 to the next major crossing where the N225, a fast dual carriageway, is the access road for the A25 autoroute. A short way along the N225 there is a lake for small craft and nearby there is a road sign which announces 'Zero altitude'.

The quickest route to Ypres is via the A25 to the Steenvoorde turn-off (28 kms) but if a visit to Dunkerque has been made, leave by the D916 which follows the Canal de Bergues for 9 kms, passing the old **Fort Vallières** about midway, to the quaint old town of Bergues. It can also be reached from the N225 by taking the left turn to Bierne and Bergues on the D352.

Bergues is a sleepy country town surrounded by fortifications designed in 1667 by one of France's illustrious sons, Sebastien Le

Above: **The Porte de Cassel at Bergues.** *Left:* **Until recent years, a Bailey Bridge, dating from the Second World War, straddled the moat at this spot.**

Reproduced from Michelin Sheet No. 51 29th Edition and 213 16th Edition 1989

8

ROUTE I ———
ROUTE II – – –
ROUTE III · · · · ·
ZEEBRUGGE-YPRES – · –

SCALE 1:200 000 1cm—2km

Proven. La Lovie Château, headquarters for many BEF units and a base for King George V for his visit to the Western Front in July 1917.

Abdij St Sixtus. A deserter from the Lancashire Fusiliers was shot here in 1915.

Prestre de Vauban, Marshal of France (1633-1707). He is remembered on the **Porte de Cassel** by a plain memorial plaque. This gate is one of the narrow gateways which gave entry to the town across the moat fed by the three canals whose junction is in the town. These canals were a vital asset to the BEF. The Inland Waterways Transportation units operated barges to carry stores and casualties over many miles through Flanders. Bergues was a staging post to and from the coast.

Belgian troops used the town as a rest centre during the Yser battles and being only 25 kms behind the front line, it was bombarded in 1915. In 1940 it was badly damaged and many of the old houses were destroyed. Vauban's walls survived, as did the Port de Cassel with the emblem of the Sun King (Louis XIV) on the outer side, although the bridge over the moat did not and was replaced by a Bailey Bridge in 1944; now this has gone too after many years' service.

The D916a, the road to the frontier at Oostcappel via Rexpoede, crosses the fertile agricultural plain with its tiny farmhouses set amid neat fields, and church spires of the villages dominate the landscape which was the southern boundary of the Belgian front.

After 13 kms we reach Oostcappel frontier post — a small uninteresting hamlet. Driving straight on, the road has become the N308. Then, 7 kms further on is **Proven** well known to the BEF as a rail centre which, by 1916, was vast. Training areas and hospitals were set up all over the commune. **Mendinghem British Cemetery** on the right of the road just before the village is one of a trio of cemeteries in the locality which served the hospitals and casualty clearing stations. The other two are **Dozinghem** and **Bandaghem**, all three names being coined by the British troops to sound like the local Flemish ones.

In the woods to the east of the village the divisions grouped prior to the Third Battle of Ypres and, at **La Lovie Château** 2½ kms down the road to Poperinge, was the Fifth Army Headquarters from June to November 1917. From May 1915, the house was commandeered as an Army headquarters. At that date the VI Corps took the house over and the base set up by them remained until February 1916 when XIV Corps took over. In July the VIII Corps took their place, being in residence until the advent of the Fifth Army, who were followed by II Corps, and from April 1918 the 34th, 41st and 49th Divisions each used the house until August when II Corps returned. In July 1917 King George V stayed here during his visit to the Front.

Halfway between Proven and Westvleteren is the **Abdij St Sixtus**, a Trappist monastery where the monks brew a strong beer with mead from their bees to improve

the taste and aroma. A casualty clearing station and other military establishments were housed in the Abbey grounds. In May 1940, General Montgomery paused here

briefly with his 3rd Division Headquarters prior to Dunkerque, leaving some personal belongings with the Abbot until his return in 1944.

The Germans captured Poperinge on October 4, 1914 but were driven out eleven days later. The photo of Scottish troops in the Grand Place was taken in 1917.

Transport of another age in the square, since renamed Groot Markt, with the graceful Stadhuis in the background.

Toc H, Everyman's Club in Poperinge. Over 25,000 used the attic chapel.

In 7 kms **Poperinge**. 'Pop' to every British soldier was the forward base for the Ypres Salient from the autumn of 1914 onwards. The town, briefly occupied by the Germans in October 1914, was recaptured on the 15th and soon became the venue for the military. Training camps, depots and hospitals sprang up amid the hop fields. Refugees from Ypres crowded in and the station became one of the most important behind the lines, as almost all troops going up to the front or returning on leave entered the area from its platforms.

The main square bustled with transport, horses, mules and men with lorries of all shapes converged here, as all the roads leading from it led to one facility or another. Restaurants and estaminets did a roaring trade despite frequent bombardments among the thousands who sought relief and relaxation from the rigours of trench life.

Follow the signs for the centre and you will arrive in the pleasant **Grote Markt** with the elegant Gothic **Stadhuis** at the eastern end and nearby St Bertin's church. Gassthuistraat curves away on the western side of the square with the old chapel which gives it the name on the right, a doorway beside it leads to the hospital. Further along a tall white house, perhaps the most famous in 'Pop', comes in view. The beautiful iron doors are the entrance to **Talbot House**.

The Reverend Neville Talbot, senior chaplain of 6th Division, had been searching for a house which he could open as a church club for the division in 1915 when by chance the owner of No. 10 rue de l'Hôpital (as the street was then called) left to find less dangerous quarters — the house had been hit several times by artillery shells — and the Padre persuaded the Army to rent the house for the duration. In charge of the project he placed an old friend, the Reverend Philip Byard Clayton. A rotund little man in 'specs' with a contagious sense of devotion and fun, he had been padre at No. 16 General Hospital in Le Tréport earlier in 1915 and in November arrived at GHQ Montreuil expecting to be sent to the Guards Brigade but his tall friend (Talbot stood 6 foot 7 inches) asked for him. And so 'Tubby' arrived in Pop and the house was opened on December 11, 1915 as a club for Everyman with rooms where men could relax and enjoy comparative comfort and a delightful garden, but the most important place in the house was the Upper Room — the chapel in the old hop and fruit attic. It was named **Talbot House** after Neville Talbot's brother Lieutenant

Gilbert Talbot who had been killed at Hooge on July 30, 1915 and who lies in Sanctuary Wood Cemetery.

The house remained open with few interruptions until, in May 1918, enemy bombardment forced its closure for a few months before re-opening on September 27, 1918. In January 1919 the owner reclaimed his house and the Club had to close but the spirit which had been born there did not die. In 1919, the Christian Movement Toc H was founded to help men and women who in the harsh days of peace searched vainly for employment and the 'brotherhood of the trenches'. Thus the name was perpetuated and the organisation grew worldwide. Branches sprang up in almost every country, all working to aid people through their life 'to think fairly, to love widely, to witness humbly and to build bravely'. This their founder did throughout his long life, travelling extensively from his base near the Tower of London until his death in December 1972. Each branch on formation was presented with a lamp, similar to those used in the time of Christ, to recall that which burned in the Upper Room at Pop.

In the years after the war, Tubby and other Toc H members made pilgrimages to the Salient but it was not until 1926 that they could persuade the owner of the Old House to allow visits. However, Lord Wakefield, who in 1928 had purchased the mine crater at Spanbroekmolen, the Pool of Peace, bought the house in 1929 and soon once more its doors were open wide. During the German Occupation from 1940 to 1944 the people of Poperinge hid the treasures from the house which they had stripped as the Germans came; all were back in their familiar places when Tubby made his first post-war visit. It is still a venue for pilgrims, not necessarily Toc H members, and is presided over by a Warden and a small band of volunteers to help him and his wife. There is always a cheerful welcome.

Further along the street, following the curve, you will see another famous building. Now a private house, it was known the world over as **Skindles** — the sign is still proudly worn above the front door. Originally the **Café de la Commerce des Houblons**, it was opened under the direction of Madame Beutin and her two daughters. Their friendly welcome made it an extremely popular venue for the young army officers who crowded into Poperinge right throughout the war. When the Beutins opened at the then **No. 43 rue de l'Hôpital**, one young blade from Oxfordshire was reminded forcibly of a similar establishment at Maidenhead, Berkshire — Skindles Hotel — and in time this name was adopted by Madame Beutin. It has been recorded that General Plumer was there the night before the Battle of Messines began and legend has it that ten seconds before the great arc of mines was detonated, he ordered a Vermouth!

Hotel Skindles, the famous Officers' Club, now a private house.

Immediately after passing Skindles take the next turn to the left and turn back into the Grote Markt skirting St Bertin's church. To the right in St Bertinstraat is the **College Stanislas**, an episcopal establishment used as a hospital by the Friends Ambulance Unit for civilian casualties from Ypres in 1915. Although the 1915 and 1918 bombardments caused much damage, there are many old houses in the town and, in spite of modern building going on everywhere, there is much of the town recognisable to those who knew it over sixty years ago.

Leave Poperinge by the N308 Ieperstraat and pass the real target for the enemy artillery — **the station**. It has been written that whenever a leave train was due to depart, the enemy artillery interfered; but this did not prevent the place being the most popular and the most loathed spot in the vicinity; always thronged with travellers waiting for the trains. Returning men, however, did not loiter with the same indifference. A rumour which took a great deal of scotching was that the stationmaster of Pop had been shot as a spy due to the suspicious regularity of the shelling.

The twelve kilometres along the straight road to Ypres were travelled by all not using the railway running parallel to it. The road was lined by encampments, hutted and tented, hospitals, dumps and offices. Today, all sign of these has gone with the passage of time. Across the railway now runs a great new highway which eventually will encircle the town as a bypass. Only the cemeteries

The forecourt of 'Pop' station was rarely devoid of soldiers during the war.

Red Farm Military Cemetery, Brandhoek, with a headstone to a civilian on the left.

Brandhoek New British Cemetery.

remain to remind us of the thousands who passed this way. Even the tall trees which survived the bombardments have been felled to make way for the four-lane road and replenished with saplings.

On the outskirts of the town the N308 crosses the ring-road which is now connected to Ieper (Ypres) by a fast dual carriageway bypass N38 which avoids Brandhoek and Vlamertinge and links with the motorway north of Ieper. The old road narrows at **Brandhoek** 3½ kms. On the left is **Red Farm Cemetery**, one of the smallest in the Salient. Here in April-May 1918 46 British soldiers and three civilians were buried. A right turn in the centre of Brandhoek leads to the new highway and across it some of the cemeteries made when the hamlet was the centre of hospitals and casualty clearing stations. Cross the railway and the new road and immediately go right and bear left and, in a few metres, two cemeteries are reached. In that on the right, **Brandhoek New British Cemetery**, lies Captain N. G. Chavasse, VC and Bar, MC, RAMC, who died from wounds on August 4, 1917 (Plot III, Grave B15). Medical Officer to the 1st Bn. Liverpool Scottish, he went to France with the battalion in November 1914. He was awarded the Military Cross in 1915 in recognition of his gallantry at Hooge, and for his devotion to duty and his self-sacrifice and extraordinary energy and inspiration at Guillemont in August 1916, the Victoria Cross. For similar services in July and August 1917 he was awarded posthumously the Bar to the VC. He died two days after his action in Brandhoek Military Hospital. His headstone is unique, for it bears two small representations of the VC in place of the usual large one.

Returning to the crossroads, the third cemetery of Brandhoek is seen on the right. Turn right on to the N308 again. About 2 kms further along on the north side of the road stands a tall red brick building, the **Hop Store**. Just beyond the trees behind it is the **Hop Store Cemetery** recalling the casualty clearing station there. Until they were rebuilt recently, against the wall of the abutting cottage was a water pump from which men and horses going to and from Ypres were refreshed.

Another kilometre and **Vlamertinge** is reached. Almost totally destroyed in artillery barrages, the village was held by the Germans between October 7-10, 1914. All around, the BEF built camps and stores and the inevitable hospitals and casualty clearing

stations. By 1918 only the battered tower of the church remained. Behind the church is **Vlamertinge Military Cemetery** which is entered by a pair of unusual gates. These are of special design in memory of Lieutenant Mitford who lies within this cemetery, also it is the last resting place of Captain Francis Grenfell, VC (Plot II, Grave B14).

In the second Vlamertinge cemetery, the **New British Cemetery** on the Ouderdom road to the south of the village, there lies another VC — CSM John Skinner, VC, DCM, King's Own Scottish Borderers. He won his award in 1917 for bravery in the Third Battle of Ypres when he put three blockhouses out of action in one continuous battle in August. He returned to England for the investiture by King George V and the customary fourteen days leave. At the end of this time, when he reached Folkstone, he was sent to hospital and posted to the Reserve Battalion in Edinburgh. However, a

few days later he was seen with his company back in the Salient. He had refused to go to Edinburgh and, having his return leave warrant in his pocket, after two days in hospital he had risked a court-martial to return to his men. He also had a bet with a pal. QSM Ross. Both had been wounded eight times and the wager was: who would get the ninth first. Skinner won the bet on March 17, 1918 when he was shot between the eyes when trying to rescue a wounded man.

His funeral was remarkable. The South Wales Borderers' Padre, the Rev. Kenelm Swallow, officiated at the ceremony in the pouring rain when his body was brought to the cemetery in Vlamertinge on a gun carriage drawn by a magnificent team of horses and then carried to the grave (Plot XIII, Grave H15) by six brother VCs of the 29th Division. The ceremony took place on March 19, 1918 and is unique in military history.

The hop store near Vlamertinge — once a casualty clearing station.

The grave of a VC. John Skinner in Vlamertinge New British Cemetery.

Totally destroyed, the Asylum on Poperingseweg was rebuilt in identical style and flourishes today as a psychiatric centre.

Another 2 kms along the N9 and the spires of **Ypres** are in full view ahead as the straight road bends and is crossed by the railway. In the trees, before the crossing, once stood a solitary house. Set in a pleasant garden with ponds before the front door, this was **Rossières Château**, or better known as 'Goldfish Château'. It was hardly damaged during the war, despite its occupation by many formations' headquarters including V Corps, the Canadians and other divisions, and the proximity of the railway and enormous stores dumps nearby. Then, in 1920, it was entirely destroyed when an ammunition dump blew up. It was said that the German General von Bissing, who occupied it briefly in October 1914, was enchanted by it and stated then that he wanted it as his 'prix de guerre' and therefore the German artillery carefully

avoided it! Today a bungalow occupies the site.

Another kilometre and Ypres is entered. On the left a red brick wall encloses the famous **Asylum**. This Victorian-style building has been rebuilt in almost identical form as it was completely destroyed during the bombardments. In 1915, the Friends' Ambulance Unit, which had established itself there in December 1914, was driven to the cellars before it and the nuns who assisted, evacuated it in May 1915. At a ceremony in 1965, three of these gallant ladies were present although all have now passed away, the last in 1979. Sister Marguerite became famous for her work with the wounded and wrote a book about her experiences. Now, new quarters for the patients have been erected in the gardens.

A few hundred metres further on, the road crosses the old canal and the level crossing known as **Bridge No. 10** or 'Devil's Bridge'. Turning right towards the station, because of the one-way traffic system it is not possible to go ahead into Elverdingestraat where the **headquarters of the Commonwealth War Graves Commission** is to be found at No. 82. This is the office of the Superintendent of the north-west Europe area.

Also along this street is the **prison** in whose cellars many British soldiers found refuge, including the Guards and, I believe, on occasion the Town Major. Taking the first main turning on the left, Botterstraat, the main shopping street, the Grand Place is reached and the Cloth Hall comes into view.

The rebuilt Cloth Hall, Ypres.

ROUTE II VIA CASSEL

The vista seen today over Flanders from Cassel.

Leave Calais by the N1-E40. In 22 kms the outskirts of Gravelines are reached. Turn right onto the D11 from the ring-road signposted Bourbourg-Cassel. The road crosses the flat meadows and small fields with their attendant farms to the country town of Bourbourg astride a canal. Follow the signs for Cassel (8 kms) through the town, having crossed the canal and railway, and continue onwards over the Canal de la Haute Colme at Loobergue and thence through the Erkelsbrugge road junction to Arneke.

After 21 kms we reach **Arneke**, a sleepy village belying the fact that it was a busy railway centre surrounded by training depots and reinforcement camps. Ahead the solitary hill of Cassel rises above the gently undulating landscape. The road climbs up and around the wooded slopes of the steep hill and joins the N42 from St Omer after 7 kms at the entry to the town.

Cassel. As the narrow street rises, a square, until recently Place General Plumer, now Place Général Vandamme, opens on the left. Immediately thereafter, the main road, even narrower, proceeds downhill to the Grand Place. The town clings to the crest and slopes of the 156-metre-high **Mont Cassel** which, since Roman times, has been an important road junction as major highways converge from each cardinal point.

The scene of many sieges through the centuries, it had been burnt and devastated no less than nine times when, in 1914, once more it became an important military centre. Once more the medieval streets, houses and cellars rang with the voices of soldiers and, not for the first time either, English accents were heard. An earlier occupation placed it forever in the nursery literature of British

children, for here it was that the Grand Old Duke of York marched his 10,000 men up the hill only to march them down again. This was during the 1793-1794 campaign in Flanders mounted by the Duke of Coburg when the Duke of York led the English contingent against the French revolutionary army and was soundly beaten in a nearby battle.

In October 1914, Sir John French set up a base in Cassel for the period of October 11-24, but it is as the headquarters of Maréchal Foch (from October 1914 to April 1915 and again in April 1918) and as that of General Plumer's Second Army (from 1916 to 1918) that Cassel will be remembered.

Although the town suffered considerable

The Castel Yvonne in Cassel was once occupied by General Plumer.

damage in the Second World War, in many aspects it still appears much the same as 70 years ago as the rebuilding has been in character.

On the summit of the Mont de Cassel are the **Jardin du Publique**, once the **Place de Castel Moulin** now the Terrasse du Château, which can easily be reached from the square below, up the narrow winding street passing the tall red brick house, **Castel Yvonne**, where Lord Plumer lived. His rooms overlooked the great plateau with Ypres and the grey mass of the Messines Ridge in the distance.

The Jardin du Publique is dominated by a wooden windmill of the type which, until the early years of this century, were found throughout this part of Flanders. This mill, which is open to the public, is a reconstruction based on a mill salvaged from Arneke.

Nearby is the equestrian statue by Georges Malissard of Maréchal Foch, a copy of which is in Grosvenor Gardens, close to Victoria Station, London. The statue, on a pedestal of Soignies and Breton granite, was unveiled by Raymond Poincaré in the presence of the Maréchal on July 7, 1928 and looks out over the battlefields of the Yser, Ypres and Messines. The square face of the pedestal represents the stubborn resistance of the Allied armies. An arc of trees frames the statue which is set on the spot from where Foch was given to watching the smoke of battle rise from the trenches in the distance.

Beneath the gardens are the cellars of the old castle which stood here and were used by the military in both wars. Second Army Headquarters also used the large building (now a café), as well as other houses in the town. In front of the café, in the centre of the car park, is a memorial to the three major battles of Cassel, 1071, 1328 and 1677. An

Above: **Cassel. A surviving bunker on the summit in the Jardin du Publique. Beneath were underground offices.** *Right:* **Maréchal Foch surveys the battlefields.**

archway leads from the garden direct to the main square by an extremely steep path and road. Near the path leading to the gateway is a concrete bunker and an entrance to the cellars.

At various strategic points around the park orientation tables are set into the tops of the balustrades. Distance and directions for towns all over the globe are etched in slate. From these viewpoints the magnificent panorama unfolds. In bygone times it was said that from the summit of the Mont de Cassel could be viewed five kingdoms: those of France, England, Belgium, Holland, and of God. Certainly on a clear day the view encompasses the hills of Kemmel and the Mont de Cats, Vimy Ridge and the lighthouse of Dunkerque. With the aid of binoculars the spires of Ypres, or the pillars of the Vimy Ridge memorial, can be discerned. Closer at hand, the old Roman roads and those built by Napoleon's engineers like spokes from a wheel can be determined. The roofs of the Renaissance-style buildings straggle immediately below the park, among them the Hôtel de Ville with its many dormer windows, each said to represent one of the cantons in the province of Flandres Maritime of which Cassel was the capital.

In the **Hôtel de Ville**, the erstwhile Hôtel de la Noble Cour set on the Grand Place, Maréchal Foch had his office. It is preserved as a **museum** with photographs and documents displayed together with the Maréchal's furniture and other treasures. More exhibits relating to the war effort of Cassel are on show in the **Town Museum** with relics of past glories in the same building. The museum is open on Sundays from mid-June to mid-September, 2.00 p.m. to 6.00 p.m.

The rue d'Ypres, now renamed **rue du Maréchal Foch**, leads from the Grand Place eastwards. At **No. 32-34**, the **Hôtel de Schoeberque** was the residence of the Maréchal during his tour of duty and it was here he received notabilities and where King George V, the Prince of Wales, the King of the Belgians and Sir Douglas Haig stayed on different occasions. A plaque on the wall of the modern hotel commemorates these dates and visits.

The road bends past the white buildings at the end of the street as it begins its tortuous descent to the valley. At the corner is an old archway, the ancient Porte d'Ypres. The town cemetery is on the precipitous slopes in between two very dangerous hairpin bends.

At the foot of the hill, the road to Poperinge and Ypres crosses the D916 for Bailleul. Just off this road, some 2 kms away, is the hilltop village of **St Marie Cappel** below which are the fields where the **Royal Flying Corps aerodrome** was established. Today; little or no sign of the aerodrome can be traced.

The Hôtel de Schoeberque was used by King George V and other notable visitors.

After crossing the D916 the road (D948) enters the wooded slopes of the Mont des Recollets and some further dangerous corners have to be negotiated before the long straight road to Steenvoorde (6 kms).

Among the copses on the right of the road just before **Steenvoorde** is the hunting lodge so vividly described by R. H. Mottram in his *Spanish Farm* trilogy. Steenvorde is a dusty market town with an unusual church spire. The D948 now bypasses the town but it is quite simple to bear left and drive through and rejoin the main road before it crosses the Dunkerque-Lille autoroute.

For 4 kms the D948 runs dead straight to the frontier station and customs post where the juggernaut lorries queue for clearance. One road on the right leads across the beet and wheat fields to the village of **Godewaersvelde** — this name defeated the Tommies who referred to it always as 'Gertie wore velvet'. Now the direct road to Poperinge, 4 kms from the frontier, avoids the tortuous narrow road through Abeele leaving it to tractors and local traffic, easing the burden on the Belgian customs post on the northern edge of the town, on the N333.

The road up from the frontier post is international, France lying on the right, Belgium to the left. A little way along, the new road is joined by the old one to **Abeele** on the left. It is also the way to gain access to the small **Abeele Military Cemetery** near the site of the **RFC aerodrome**. The Cross of Sacrifice can be seen above the shrubs along the road.

Using the new road, in 1 km take a small road on the right — GR5a — and then left and the beautiful **Lijssenthoek British Cemetery**, the second largest in Flanders, is reached. Here men of many nationalities lie amid beautiful gardens and trees. Begun in 1914 by the French (who had established a casualty clearing station at **Remi Farm**, on the boundary of the cemetery, to which a railway spur was laid from the Poperinge line), the cemetery bears the unusual dates 1914-1920. In these peaceful surroundings Frenchmen are the earliest burials but close by lies the last officer to die in the Salient — Lieutenant-Colonel Beatty Pownall — together with his comrades who lost their lives in September and October 1918. Men from the Commonwealth and the Chinese Labour Corps, Algerians and the only Americans to be buried in the Salient lie close to a large German plot.

Remi Farm has changed little over the years. In the great barn, where men were sheltered during the war of 1914-1918, the beams bear signs of earlier military occupations. Etched on them and on the walls are initials and dates of soldiers' visits of a previous century. Graffiti of Poilu and Tommy are intermingled.

To the south of the cemetery is a **nursery garden** where shrubs and plants are propagated for use in the cemeteries of the region.

Poperinge is reached by continuing through the hopfields and then turning left at the crossroad and rejoining the main road, going right.

A casualty clearing station was established by the French Army at Remi Farm *(left)* beside which a burial ground was laid out which was to become the second largest cemetery in the Ypres Salient — Lijssenhoek British Military Cemetery.

15

ROUTE III VIA ST OMER

Now that the autoroute A26-E15 has connected with the outskirts of Calais, it is possible to use it for a fast journey to St Omer, but the more attractive and interesting route is the N43. This road runs close to two major canals of the region. Both played important rôles in the Great War carrying supply barges up to the back areas and depots.

Pont d'Ardres (12 kms) was a bustling base bristling with soldiers working on the barges and in the dockside establishments. Today it is little more than a village near the new bridges which span the canals on whose banks new industries are springing up.

Ardres (5 kms). A quaint little town through which the road climbs as it leaves the flat plain for the more undulating country before St Omer. In these fields the training camps and ranges were built. The occasional rough mound and bramble-strewn ditch may be the remnants of practice trenches and the full-size replica of sectors of the front line which were made in 1916 and 1917.

St Omer (23 kms). A quiet and attractive town set on hills between the canals. From October 12, 1914 to April 31, 1916 the British General Headquarters was based here. In 1917 it became the Royal Flying Corps and Royal Air Force Headquarters until the end of the war. In 1917 it also began to become a regular target for enemy air raids and, with the opening of the German Spring Offensive in 1918, it came within easy artillery range. Evidence of the destruction can be noted now only in a few isolated buildings, as much of the town has been repaired or rebuilt. In the Second World War, the town was a German Luftwaffe base and was raided by the Allied air forces more than twenty times, inflicting further damage now made good.

The arrival of the BEF in 1914 was far from being the first time that contact with England had been felt. This started in Saxon times, when Hereward the Wake stayed here and later during the sieges of the Middle Ages and the 18th Century wars of Marlborough. In the **Jardin Publique** remnants of the Vauban ramparts are preserved below the eminence on which stands the Basilica of Notre Dame. This large 13th Century church is crowded with reminders of the town's historic past and still bears witness to the attacks of both wars.

Among the few remaining signs of the British presence in 1914-18 is a small, faded, bluish-green circular plaque, similar to those

St Omer. Place du Maréchal Foch, scene of Lord Roberts' funeral in November 1914.

seen around London, on the crumbling walls of **No. 50 Avenue Carnot**. It records the death in this house of Field-Marshal Lord Roberts on November 14, 1914. The grand old man had been visiting the Indian Corps when he returned to Sir John French's headquarters with a chill which turned to pneumonia. On November 17 his body was moved in military state to the Hôtel de Ville, the streets being lined by troops from every unit in France. A large number attended the short service held in the **Place Gambetta** (as the Place du Maréchal Foch was then known) before the cortège moved to the station through troop-lined streets.

Also in the Avenue Carnot is the **Hôtel Sandelin**, a beautiful 18th Century house which is an excellent provincial museum and art gallery. **No. 37 rue St Bertin** bears no marks to recall it being the residence of Sir John French and later Sir Douglas Haig. Further down this street, which leads to the ruins of the **Abbey of St Bertin**, are the old buildings of the **Hôpital Militaire**, previously a school solely for the education of Roman Catholic boys from Britain. Opened in 1592 it was moved firstly to Bruges and later, in the 18th Century, Liege, before going to Stoneyhurst in Lancashire in 1794 where it still flourishes.

St Omer was a very popular leave town as it provided many amenities for leisure not readily available closer to the front. In the

unique marshes to the north and eastern outskirts called the **Watergangs** (from the curious labyrinths of canals and drains of this reclaimed region), many estaminets were opened for the officers and men who enjoyed the fishing or boating. In the forest of Clairmarais were huge camps and supply depots and special facilities for the men on leave. Within the walls of the ancient farms whole battalions could be accommodated and several of these are situated at the forest edge. Near one farm rises the ruined tower of the **Abbey of St Omer** — a refuge where Thomas à Becket sought shelter after his contretemps with Henry II.

Taking the N42 eastward through the new suburbs and industrial complex growing up on the dried marshes, **Arques** is reached in 4 kms. The road crosses the major Canal de la Haute Colme, and at **Les Fontinettes** it was connected by a remarkable hydraulic barge lift to the Canal de Neuf Fosse. The lift transported the barges up and down the 50ft difference in levels. It was built in 1887 and was in use without a break until recently replaced by a slope, as in both wars there was an unwritten agreement between belligerents not to bomb it. Beside the new facilities the old Assenseur des Fontinettes can still be seen with a barge in the lift.

Just beyond the crest of the rise outside Arques, a wide flat plateau is reached and the **site of the aerodrome** comes into view.

No. 50, Avenue Carnot, where Field-Marshal Roberts died.

No. 37, rue St Bertin — used by both French and Haig.

The roads were lined with concrete shelters but these are now crumbling and gradually disappearing amid the beet fields.

To the south of St Omer is the residential suburb of **Blendeques** in whose pleasant valleys and woods are a number of elegant homes, many being classifed as châteaux. Here HM King George and Queen Mary resided during their visits to the troops. Some of the châteaux still bear military placards on their walls proclaiming the offices which they once housed. The **Château de l'Eminence** proudly displays a fire point notice by its crumbling front door; another, the **Château Bellevue**, was the main office of an officer school.

To the west of St Omer on the Boulogne road (N42) at the **Wisques** crossroad is the **Abbey of St Paul**, and, a short distance up the road to Wisques village, its sister convent. To these were brought the typhoid victims from Ypres in 1915 and here were established schools for the evacuated children. Between here and **Wizernes** to the south was a complex for the V2 missiles of 1944.

After 2 kms the road forks; take the N42 for Hazebrouck, passing through **Renescure**, a railway station well known to the BEF, and **Ebblinghem**, a village with associations with the training camps.

Hazebrouck (18 kms). A name known to every British soldier. Thousands passed through the station en route for Ypres or the Somme. From the outbreak of war, the name of this quiet market town and vital junction for road and rail communications was rarely out of the news, having become an Army headquarters in October 1914.

In the first German drive westwards, the town was surrendered peacefully by the Abbé Deputy, Lemire, to avoid destruction, but the British Cavalry Corps cleared the town and nearby Forest of Nieppe and the I British Corps set up its headquarters here. Once again a British Army, the First Army, was based in the town, and in 1815 Wellington used it as one of his major bases. In 1915 the Second Army took over. General French resided in one of the graceful houses in the then Grand Place but now, as the traveller enters from the rue Warein, it will be noticed the name has changed to **Place General de Gaulle**.

This huge rectangular market place, with its unusual classical Hôtel de Ville, was always bustling with troops and is still the hub of a thriving town. Here and there uneven cobblestones survive from earlier times to shake the unwary driver. In another square — **Place de la Victoires** — is the town war memorial and one of the few ancient buildings remaining — the church of St Eloi dating from the 16th Century.

Château de l'Eminence where the King and Queen resided during tours of the front.

Hazebrouck was a major advance base, there being ordnance, signals, engineer, medical and transport depots crowded around this important railway junction. Army workshops, where all manner of equipment was produced from odds and ends, opened in the town. Administrative offices occupied the large halls and other requisitioned buildings. Training areas and reinforcement camps opened in the surrounding countryside; to the south-west were sited the hospitals and casualty clearing stations.

Towards the end of 1917, the town, which had previously suffered occasional bombardments, was seriously damaged by shellfire. One gun operating from near Lille was said to be a British high velocity piece captured during the Battle of Cambrai. The Forest of Nieppe, the scene of the British cavalry action in October 1914 which cleared the advancing German troops, was threatened again in the Spring Offensive from the south-east and heavy fighting ensued in April 1918. Hazebrouck was menaced and the civilian population was evacuated but the stands of the 29th, 31st and Guards Divisions and the 1st Australian Division which stemmed the onslaught saved the town. Casualty clearing stations which had operated from 1916 to 1917 returned in the summer of 1918 as did No. 9 Field Hospital.

In the Second World War the town was again very badly damaged but, in many aspects, it is still very recognisable as the soldiers' centre of rest and leisure and of the base works and junction for the front which

it was for so long. Many of the billets and buildings the military used have been repaired in the old style.

Leave Hazebrouck by the rue de Bailleul (N42) out into the area of the 1918 battles for Hazebrouck, now once more a peaceful agricultural region which becomes slightly more undulating as the road approaches **Strazeele**, 7 kms away.

This village was the Germans' first objective in their attack on Hazebrouck from the east in April 1918, but the 33rd Division and the Australians stood in their way and held on. The nearby villages of **Méteren** (to the north-east) and Merris (to the south) were overrun but were recaptured by the 9th Scottish Division and 1st Australian Division respectively on July 9 and 19. In 1914, the German advance on Méteren was the scene of a bayonet charge by 2nd Bn. Seaforth Highlanders in III British Corps (General Poultney) checking and clearing action.

Four kilometres south of Méteren, the N42 crosses the Dunkerque-Lille motorway before entering **Bailleul** in 3 kms as the D944. A picturesque market town, famed since ancient times for its lacemaking which, with linen, is still one of the major industries. Bailleul was a military base for much of the war — a real front line town. It fell briefly to the Germans but was recaptured by the British on October 14, 1914 and thereafter, for three-and-a-half years, it was to act as a forward base for the British and French before being almost totally destroyed in the savage fighting of the Battle of the Lys in the spring of 1918. Bailleul provided a welcome

Hazebrouck's magnificent town hall overlooks the Grand Place.

This chapel was signals HQ.

Bailleul. The reconstructed Hôtel de Ville beside the Belfry.

The memorial to the 25th Division which recaptured the ruins on August 30, 1918.

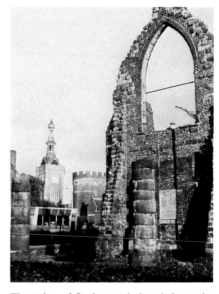

The ruins of St Armand church form the backcloth for the town's war memorial.

'A good reputation endures for ever' . . . 'faithful unto death'. So are the Chinese Labour casualties remembered in Bailleul British Cemetery Extension.

respite to the fighting forces and a haven for the wounded in the hospital facilities of its well known asylum and clinic. Troops thronged its pleasant market square above which the **Belfry of the Hôtel de Ville** rose defiantly. Cafés and estaminets flourished and one in particular, 'Tina's', in the rue de Dunkerque, became a famous and popular officers' haunt.

The town had hardly suffered from artillery bombardment but in July 1917 the relative peace was shattered by heavy shells which caused much damage. Then the almost complete destruction of the town came when the Germans advanced to capture the ruins on April 15, 1918 after the heroic defence of the British 34th and 59th Divisions which were forced to retire exhausted. For four months the town was in German hands and then on August 30 the British 25th Division regained possession of the ruins.

Today, the old market square once more is the centre of a charming busy little town; the Hôtel de Ville and the Belfry have been rebuilt in warm red brick and the cafés and shops welcome both resident and visitor.

The road enters the centre of the town at a roundabout, in the centre of which is the **obelisk memorial to the 25th Division**, and, turning left, the square is reached. In the street behind the Hôtel de Ville can be seen the ruins of the **Church of St Amand** now forming an integral part of the town's **War Memorial**.

The road to Belgium, the D23, leaves the square at the opposite end and almost immediately a green CWGC sign can be seen indicating the way, down a small street on the right, to the **Bailleul Communal Cemetery and Extension**. The entrance to these cemeteries is just beyond the main gates to the town cemetery, after which the road deteriorates into a muddy track. Whilst the Communal Cemetery is relatively small, the Communal Cemetery Extension provides the last resting place of over 4,000 men of many nationalities. Alongside their British and Commonwealth comrades lie French, Russian, Chinese, and many Germans. From the cemetery walls a panoramic view of the Monts de Flandres provides a background to the **site of the old Royal Flying Corps base and aerodrome**. Among those buried here is Sergeant Mottershead, VC.

Returning to the D23, turn right on to the Loker (Locre) road for about a kilometre, passing round the walls of the **old asylum** and the hospital which was so vital to the troops. I understand the present-day aspect resembles very closely that of 60 years ago.

Ahead now rise the hills of Flanders — Mont Noir, Mont Rouge and Mont Kemmel with the Mont des Cats far over to the left. At the first road junction keep to the Loker road but, a short distance beyond, take the left fork, the D223 for **Mont Noir**. As the road approaches the village one of the 1939-45 concrete bunkers which surround the hill comes into view on the right, and almost immediately on the left is the entrance to a **small cemetery** where British and French soldiers who died in 1918 lie together. Between April and September 1918 there was heavy fighting in this area when, having secured Kemmel, the Germans were thrown back by the 34th British Division.

The Bailleul Asylum and hospital cared for great numbers of casualties.

The wooded slopes of Scherpenberg today hide the dugouts built into its sides.

The 34th Division Memorial, Mont Noir. Note the divisional chequerboard sign.

Further up the hill, actually on the crest, is the **34th Division Memorial**. For many years this was known locally as Nurse Cavell for who else could be the Angel of Victory!

The customs post is at the main crossroads just below the summit. Around it now are cafés, hotels and souvenir shops. Between Mont Noir and Mont Rouge, across the valley and the lower Mont Vidaigne, is a téléphérique. On the slopes of both hills are sports facilities of many kinds with camp sites and caravan parks nestling amid the trees.

Three kilometres further on is **Loker (Locre)**. This village was almost entirely destroyed in the battles for Mont Kemmel. On the wall of the **Hôtel de Ville**, opposite the church, there are three memorial plaques commemorating French units which participated in the 1918 operations.

The direct route to Ypres, the N375, passes beneath the **Scherpenberg** rising on the right of the road. As it is approached, the entrance to a series of dugouts can be seen above the tree-line. Scherpenberg was heavily defended by the French and the British 21st, 25th and 49th Divisions when it was attacked on April 29, 1918 but it was not captured. A kilometre further along is the hamlet of La Clytte (De Klijte) where the Poperinge-Kemmel road crosses.

After 4 kms, **Dickebush** (Dikkebus) is reached, a familiar name to all who served in the Salient. The artificial lake was lined with trenches and hutments. Access to the lake is gained from the first crossroad after the village when, taking the right-hand road, the white brewery (which was a delousing station and bath centre) is passed. It is difficult today, as one sits on the terrace of the café overlooking the peaceful waters, to envisage the devastation and mud and the appalling conditions which prevailed in 1917 and 1918 along the banks, but, with the right light, traces of the revetments can be clearly discerned. After a further 5 kms, Ypres is reached by way of the modern station, now flanked by the bypass.

Sunset over the peaceful waters of Dickebush Lake.

Zeebrugge-Ypres

The old armoured cruiser HMS *Vindictive* alongside the outer wall of the mole. Special gangplanks were provided for the raiding party to reach the raised parapet and ladders enabled the troops to descend the other side (Charles de Lacey).

An interesting route to Ypres is via **Zeebrugge** — the port where the 3rd Cavalry Division disembarked in October 1914. They had been sent there to cover the Belgian retreat from Antwerp, but five days later the Germans occupied the town. They set about converting the port into a front line naval and seaplane base and by December it was operational.

The modern ferry terminal is part of a huge new dock complex catering for container ships, tankers, freighters and ferries. To the west of the **old mole** great areas of once open seas have been reclaimed and a new sea wall has been erected enclosing an enormous area for future port facilities and expansion. The old mole is still discernible along the new road — Leopold II Dam — which leads to and beyond the North Sea Ferry Terminal. Doverlaan, the road from the Dover-Felixstowe terminal, filters into Leopold II Dam, and the spacious roundabout before the major traffic junction of Kustlaan (Ostend to Knokke Heist) and Baron de Maerelaan, the new road to Brugge connecting with the motorways.

From St George to Sir Galahad. In September 1979, the author took this historic photograph of the Royal Fleet Auxiliary rounding the end of the old mole. Little did anyone then know the tragedy to befall her in another war nearly three years later 8,000 miles from home.

The damaged wall, where *Vindictive* went alongside on April 23, 1918. (IWM)

This plaque once marked the spot.

Left: 'In memory of St George's Day, 1918 when every moment had its deed and every deed its hero.' So read the inscription on the original memorial at Zeebrugge unveiled in 1925. In 1942, German forces destroyed the monument — all that was salved were a few of the stones which were set in the pavement after the war in front of a new memorial *(right)*. In the background stands the old Palace Hotel, demolished after it was closed in 1978.

To the west of the ferry port access road there is a new pedestrian promenade from the eastern end of the Zeedijk. There is a car park between Troostlaan and Maerelaan. The new footway is called Sint George's Day Wandeling and is at present 1 km long.

The old mole, built in 1895-1907, was 2½ kms in length and protected the entrance to the harbour and the Bruges canal. For much of its length it was some 150 feet wide with the esplanade being on the seaward side right up to the narrower extremity and the light-house. Near the place where HMS *Vindictive* with the tiny *Daffodil* and *Iris* came along-side on St George's Day, 1918, there was once a weatherbeaten bronze plaque, but gone are the quay over which the Marines and sailors swarmed and fought and the bridge which connected the mole to the shore, penetrated by the old submarine *C3* under Lieutenant Sandford. The site of the Lübeck Battery has disappeared in the new complex as has the place where in 1925 an elegant monument, some 46 feet high, was erected. It was surmounted by a bronze sculpture of St George and the Dragon and was the scene of an annual ceremony during the pilgrimage of the men of the Zeebrugge Association. In 1942 the Germans destroyed the memorial and melted down the bronze.

On April 23, 1983 an attractive **memorial** to the events of April 1918 was dedicated. It stands at the landward end of Sint George's Day Wandeling and incorporates the memo-rial which replaced the original column erected in 1925 and destroyed in 1942 by the German occupation forces, with fragments salvaged from the original column and the plaques from the old mole which marked the site where HMS *Vindictive* went alongside and the breach in the mole made by Lieute-nant Sandford, VC, and his submarine, *C3*.

Previously in the basement of the **Palace Hotel**, demolished in the modernization of the port and its access road, the **Zeebrugge Museum** was housed. The future of this museum is still in the balance and at present the exhibits are in store in Brugge (Bruges). Plans exist for the rebuilding and use as a museum. The building had been the German headquarters and the museum included re-productions of the murals they had used to decorate the walls of various rooms. Relics of the men and ships (Captain Fryatt and the SS *Brussels* included), the uniforms and medals, badges and equipment, photographs and documents of the naval actions were displayed together with artefacts relating to civilians and to the Second World War and the two occupations of the port. Actual portions of the ships, life-size dioramas and

models depicting St George's Day 1918 and coastal defence were shown. One unusual item was a replica of a full-size small Belgian sitting room demonstrating many types of

booby-trap. Facilities for lectures were pro-vided and school parties welcomed.

Leaving the terminal, turn left at the traffic lights onto N34, Kustlaan, and in 1½

With the reclamation of a large area of the former harbour for new dock facilities, the memorial has been resited and re-erected with new stonework which incorporates the plaque from the mole and fragments from the original monument.

German and British casualties from the raid were buried together in Zeebrugge churchyard overlooked by the Salvage Corps Memorial.

kms, having crossed the locks to the inner harbour, **Zeebrugge church** will be seen off to the right between the new highway bounded on the left by the sprawling new container port works and the old main road, the Heiststraat, to the left of St Donaasplein. Here in the **small cemetery**, originally a German burial ground (note the inscription over the gateway), British seamen and Royal Marines are buried alongside 173 German dead. Here also is the smallest of the **Memorials to the Missing**, a small stone panel set in the wall commemorating three officers and one mechanic who had lost their lives on that memorable day and have no known grave, among them Lieutenant-Commander A. L. Harrison, VC, killed whilst leading one of the storming parties from HMS *Vindictive*. There is also a simple memorial erected in 1920 to the British Salvage Corps.

Return to the N34 for **Blankenberge** in about 5 kms. In the **Communal Cemetery**

The smallest Memorial to the Missing — to four men lost during the attack.

Above: **HMS *Vindictive* alongside Ostend mole, October 1918 (IWM), and *right* the bow of the ship preserved today.**

The Nieuwpoort Memorial to the Missing, remembering those who lost their lives at Antwerp in 1914 and along the coast between 1914-18 and have no known grave.

The Memorial to King Albert beside the lock gates at Nieuwpoort. These were the sluices opened by the lock-keeper in 1914 to flood the surrounding countryside.

Lieutenant-Commander G. N. Bradford, VC, of the *Iris* lies buried.

Another 21 kms and Ostend is reached. At various places along the road will be seen bunkers of the Atlantic Wall but none of the old 1914-18 fortifications or gun sites remain.

Ostend (Oostende) is one of the main holiday resorts on this long sandy coastline as well as being a major port for ferries to the UK. A railway terminus for the long distance continental trains and an airport add to its importance. The N34 enters Ostend over a series of bridges crossing the locks into the inner harbour and the canal to Bruges (Brugge). As the road rises and turns to the left over the outer end of the lock leading into the dry dock, a small park will be noticed laid out beside the basin. It can be reached by turning left (one-way traffic). There, amid the flower beds, rests the **bow section of the *Vindictive* and the masts of the *Intrepid* and *Thetis*.** The upper sections of the mast of HMS *Thetis* (nearest the road) is fairly new as the original fell to pieces with wood-rot. (I know for I gave a section of it to the Imperial War Museum, London!)

On August 27, 1914, a small force of Royal Marines landed in Ostend to protect the evacuation of thousands of refugees to England. On October 4, the Royal Naval Division disembarked for the ill-fated expedition to Antwerp and two days later the 7th Division landed to proceed to the front.

When the Belgian Government and King Albert had to evacuate Antwerp, they made their HQ in Ostend. However on October 13, the Government left for Le Havre and the King went to lead his army on the Yser. Ostend was occupied by the Germans on the 15th.

Here, as at Zeebrugge, the Germans constructed a naval base for their submarines but, because it was constantly under attack from both the air and sea, the repair shops and stores were moved to Brugge and Zeebrugge. Ostend then became a secondary port for small craft only and Zeebrugge took precedence both as a destroyer and submarine base.

On April 23, 1918, at the same time as the major attack on Zeebrugge, an attempt was made to block the canal and harbour entrances using two old cruisers, the *Brilliant* and *Sirius*. This was unsuccessful and on May 9-10 another attempt was made, this time with HMS *Vindictive* which had been filled with concrete and was sunk between the piers in the harbour entrance sealing the large craft in the basins. After doing a great deal of demolition, the Germans left Ostend on October 17, 1918.

There is a choice of roads from Ostend to Nieuwpoort: the N34 runs close on the coast along the dunes past large modern blocks of flats through the busy streets of the resorts, whilst the N318 runs behind the built-up area

passing the airfield and gives views over to the left of the Yser battlefields.

In 16 kms, the roads converge close by the huge circular **Memorial to King Albert** erected above the multiple sluices for the canals at the inland end of **Nieuwpoort**. The striking brick archways surround a mounted statue of the King; on one wall is a small bronze plaque to his wife, Queen Elizabeth, who died in 1968. A lift takes visitors to the balcony at the top of the arch, giving magnificent views of the Yser, the canals, Nieuwpoort and Lombardsijde. This was the western end of the front line which ran 600 miles to the Swiss border; the whole region was utterly devastated.

This end of the line was usually in the hands of the French and Belgians but in June 1917 the British XV Corps took over the line with men of the 1st and 32nd Divisions and, later, the 66th Division. They held the line from St Georges, Ramskapelle to the sea at Nieuwpoort and withstood the onslaught of the major German attack of July 10, 1917. Although the battalions were cut off, they held on until the battle eased on July 17, when they were relieved by the 49th and 33rd Divisions after having suffered very heavy casualties. The 41st and 42nd Divisions came in September but the other divisions left the area which was now a stagnating front and, in November, these last two divisions were relieved by the French.

In a triangular plot beside the road, beneath the gaze of King Albert, three lions guard the cenotaph of the **British Memorial to the Missing**, Nieuwpoort. This memorial is to the 566 officers and men who died in the operations at Antwerp in 1914 and later actions on the Belgian coast, particularly those in 1917.

The **six sluices** over which runs the road to Ramskapelle, control the canals to Veurne and Dunkerque, the Canal de Paschendaele (to Brugge) and two regulate the Yser. These were opened by the lock-keeper during the Battle of the Yser in 1914 thereby flooding the lower reaches of the Yser and stemming the German advance. The garrison in Nieuwpoort was aided by British naval machine-gunners.

Take the N367 for a short distance and then the N356 to the right for **Ramskapelle** with the **British Cemetery** on the right. Here are buried men from scattered graves in the region including a group of Russians who died in 1919 and some Czechs and Belgians who died in October 1944. Shortly, the new autoroute A18-E40 crosses our road and we reach the village in 3 kms.

Graves of British, Czechs and Russians in Ramskapelle St George's Road.

The Franco-Belgian memorial in the centre of Ramskapelle village.

Ramskapelle was a vital position on the railway to Dixmude in the Yser battles of 1914 and was on the edge of the flooded areas. Go straight through the village and join the N355, noticing the **Franco-Belgian memorial** on the churchyard wall in the centre of the village. On the edge of the village, just before joining the main road, on the right will be seen a **Demarcation Stone** with behind it across the lawn a model windmill, actually a transformer station. The Demarcation Stone was damaged in the fighting here in 1944 and has been moved from its original site in road improvements. A ceremony is held here each year on October 31 in memory of the battle of 1914.

Take the N355 to the left and travel 5 kms through the rich pasture of this fen and marshland to **Pervijze**. An observation post used during the 1914 actions was situated in **a tower** in the village.

A tower in Pervijze used as an OP.

Keep with the N355 for 2 kms then turn left onto a small road and almost immediately another left. After 1 km take a right turn by a café to reach, by a very narrow road, the **Belgian Army Memorial Chapel**. This is set in a remote point on the Belgian front line at **Oud-Stuivekenskerke** (it is shown on the map as O.L. Vrouwhoekje). The modern chapel is built close to the ruins of the old one which was fortified and defended by the Belgian Army during the Yser battles of 1914 and October 1918.

Around the chapel are tablets bearing the badges of many Belgian regiments and several memorials including **a Demarcation Stone** bearing the name Dixmuide. In the porch of the chapel are maps of the actions. The chapel is worth visiting purely for the beauti-

The Demarcation Stone once marked the extent of the front line in 1918.

ful stained glass windows — portraits of the King and Queen of the Belgians and Belgian soldiers. Part of the old fortified chapel nearby remains with a memorial to a militant priest.

Return to the road and continue to Stuivekenskerke, keeping to the right in the village, and then right, along the banks of the canalised Yser. Dotted about the area will be seen concrete shelters, mostly of French origin but some German and a few Belgian.

In 5 kms we reach the **Boyau du Mort** — the Trench of Death. This is a section of trench along the river bank which is preserved, somewhat artificially but based on genuine Belgian trenches. They were repaired by Belgian Army Engineers in 1974. The trenches are entered through a small museum, and nearby are the ruins of a blockhouse and the old mill which was here when the trenches were built. Within the trench area is another **Demarcation Stone**.

Dixmude (Diksmuide), 2 kms further on, is once again the sleepy market town it was when the war came in October 1914. It was defended to the death by the French troops of Général Jacques, the French Marines of Admiral Ronar'ch and the Belgian Army. Fighting against a much stronger opponent, who bombarded the town incessantly, it fell

on November 10. Many artillery batteries were then emplaced in and around the town. It was not recaptured until the end of September 1918 when it fell to the Belgians.

Our road actually arrives in Dixmude close to the **Ysertoren**, the huge memorial tower of the **Free Flemish — VVK-AVV** (standing for 'All for Flanders — Flanders for Christ'). This memorial has been an object of political strife and the original was blown up in 1946. The present tower stands a little behind the site of its predecessor which is in ruins near the entrance to the park. In the crypt are various memorials to the Flemish patriots. In the new tower is a museum which has some quite interesting and varied exhibits, including a comprehensive collection of the work of the Belgian artist, Joe English. There is a good explanation of the battles involving Dixmude and collections of papers and other relics. There is a lift to the top where the windows look out over the surrounding countryside.

In the main square of Dixmude is a **statue of Général Jacques** and in the local park, a **Memorial to the French Marines and Admiral Ronar'ch**. The town hall is in the old Flemish style (as are the other houses in the square) and was rebuilt in the late 1920s. The war relics once housed in the town hall were, until quite recently, on view in a house in Wilgendijkstraat on the corner of G. B.

Oud-Stuivekenskerke. This is the Memorial Chapel of the Belgian Army built close to the ruins of the old one defended by the Belgians in 1914.

The huge Free Flemish VVK-AVV tower in Dixmude — an earlier memorial was blown up in 1946.

This is the Boyau du Mort — the Trench of Death. Situated near Stuivekenskerke, it is a section of Belgian trench which has been preserved, rather artificially, with concrete. There is a blockhouse and old mill nearby, all dating from the First War.

Jacquesstraat. For a time, the collection was then displayed excellently at **Eesen Château** on Woumnesweg (N369) but in 1989 it was closed. Hopefully the museum will re-open in 1990. The château is a large and gracious building set amid a small park on the outskirts of the town. Ypres is 23 kms distant. The road crosses much of the region that was flooded and the 1914 battlefield. Now it is once more a rich agricultural plain with a large nature reserve at Blankaert.

Not far north-east of Diksmuide is the large **German Cemetery of Vladslo** famous for the Kollwitz sculptures. These can be seen in the distance from the entrance (which houses an information room) and consist of two granite figures representing Mourning Parents. The famous German artist and sculptress, Käthy Kollwitz, gave them in memory of her son, Peter Kollwitz, killed October 21, 1914, whose grave is in front of them. To reach the cemetery, take the N369 from Diksmuide for 3½ kms and turn right at Beerst on N363 for 1¾ kms. It is then found on the left.

The Kollwitz sculptures representing Mourning Parents watch over the 25,000 German soldiers who lie in Vladslo Cemetery.

This is the skeleton of Ypres as seen from the air in 1918. The ruins of St Peter's church are visible. The ramparts in the foreground lie either side of the Lille Gate. (IWM)

YPRES

Ypres — Ieper — Ypern — there are said to be at least 27 different ways in which the name has been spelled over the centuries — dates from about 962. Centuries earlier there had been a settlement on the site, vestiges of which can still be seen beneath the Lille Gate.

By the Middle Ages the town had become one of the strongest and wealthiest in all Flanders and was the centre of a flourishing textile trade. Only Bruges and Ghent rivalled it and the inter-city squabbles were frequent and warlike. In the 13th Century, Ypres reached its zenith with a population of 40,000 in the city and some 150,000 in the surrounding region. In 1260 its most famous building — the Cloth Hall — the largest of its type, was begun when the Belfry and east wing were built. By 1286 the west and side wings were completed and in 1304 the whole magnificent hall was finished. The building was a covered market and store where ships could moor alongside and load and discharge cargoes onto the covered quay along the banks of the Yperlee. Forty-eight doors led from the street direct to the vaulted sale area, with store rooms on the upper floor. No great additions were made until 1619 when the Nieuwerck was constructed along the eastern walls.

In 1383 the town was besieged by the English under the Bishop of Norwich assisted by 20,000 troops from Ghent. Ypres withstood the siege but the flourishing trade was severely affected as the weavers in the neighbourhood left rather than starve, taking the livelihood of the town with them. The importance and influence of Ypres then continually diminished until two centuries later the population had been reduced to 5,000.

Commercially, the position of Ypres may have waned, but never so its strategic importance. Since the 14th Century it has undergone many sieges and been vassal to several princes. The centre of resistance to Spanish domination, it was sacked by the Duke of Parma in 1584 and throughout the next ninety years was constantly fought over by the French and Spaniards. Each left their mark on the fortifications and outlying defences. By the Peace of Nijmegen in 1678, Ypres became French and Vauban was entrusted with the defence works. Previously there had been six gates, a wall and moat beyond which the Spanish had formed defences of demi-lunes. On the eastern front, where the Antwerp gate had stood, they built a pentagonal-shaped citadel. This Vauban removed and replaced with a strong work — the Corne d'Anvers. Between it and the Corne de Thourot to the north, a passage led to the Menin Road. Crenellated stone walls were replaced by stone and brick finished ramparts and bastions. Casemates in the ramparts behind St Jacques church were constructed in 1690. Vauban also reduced the number of gates to the town to four, three of which had ornate façades. The Antwerp gate was the most beautiful and bore on its inner face a long Latin inscription to the glory of Ludovicus Magnus dated 1688. These defences withstood the wars of 1689-1712 when Ypres was not taken. However, in 1713 the Dutch took the city and held it until 1744 when King Louis XV forced the surrender.

In 1792, Ypres was taken and retaken several times during the war between France and Austria. In 1793, the Austrians entered the town again and rebuilt some of the earlier defences which had been dismantled by Emperor Joseph II. These were in their turn levelled in 1794 after the French regained the city.

In 1804 Napoleon visited Ypres and the main gate was named after him, having an imperial eagle carved into the stonework.

Thus, in name at least, the Antwerp gate disappeared.

In 1815, prior to Waterloo, all the exterior works were hastily rebuilt under Colonel Carmichael Smyth of the Royal Engineers and were manned by British troops from Ostend and Nieuwpoort.

After Waterloo, when Belgium was united with Holland, Ypres was again strongly fortified against any possible French invasion and, at this time, the Napoleon Gate was renamed the Menin Gate. With the grant of independence to Belgium in 1838, Ypres became Belgian. The Belgian government in 1852 decided that Ypres no longer required to be a fortified town and levelled all the outer works and pulled down the Vauban walls on the north front. A year later the western ramparts were removed to make room for the railway and the old gates demolished to give wider passage for the roads. Only the Lille Gate was retained.

In 1914 Ypres once again lay in the path of the warring nations and, during the advance of the German IV Cavalry Corps, was entered by their 3rd Cavalry Division on October 13. They requisitioned 75,000 BFr and held the Burgomaster to ransom. The BEF reached the town on the next day and occupied it entirely.

Then began the first agony of Ypres; the great artillery barrage started on November 22 wreaking great damage to the ancient buildings and setting the Cloth Hall on fire. The civilian population suffered considerable casualties and the names of the Abbé Delaere and Sister Marquerite are remembered to this day for the gallant work they did among the homeless and wounded. Not until May 9, 1915, during the month-long barrages of the Second Battle of Ypres, when the Cloth Hall together with the Collegiate Church of St Martin and many other important houses and buildings, were destroyed, were the civilians finally and compulsorily evacuated and Ypres left to the military. This was the second agony of Ypres and lasted until after the Third Battle of Ypres in 1917. However, during the comparative quiet of 1916 many people briefly returned to the ruins of their homes.

In the spring of 1918 Ypres came perilously near to falling to the Germans but, although they reached the outskirts on the eastern and south-eastern flanks, the British lines held and, in the final Allied advance Ypres was relieved when the last German troops were ousted from the Salient on September 28.

The **Grote Markt** — the Grand Place, one of the most impressive in Flanders, is dominated by the reconstructed **Cloth Hall**. Under the guidance of architects J. Coomans and P. A. Pauwels, this great building was rebuilt in its original form externally between 1920 and 1962. Internally the great halls on the first floor were constructed much as they had been but, for the most part, the other rooms — offices, council chambers, etc. — are of modern aspect. In 1967 King Baudouin unveiled a stone in the main foyer to commemorate the actual completion and reoccupation of the Nieuwerck as the offices of the Burgomaster and his staff. The main entrance is in the eastern arcade. Here is the Tourist Office, where in addition to the excellent leaflets issued by the town a variety of guide-books can be purchased. The most important Council Chamber — the **Raadszaal** — is on the first floor. It is lit by a huge modern stained glass window, the design tracing the history of Ypres, its traditions, legends and industries, in vivid colours. Here are held all major receptions and functions.

Another doorway leads to the **Salient 1914-1918 War Museum** (Entrance fee 30 BFr). Open from April 1 to November 15. Modernized in 1984 this excellent museum is concerned with every aspect of the Great War, its causes and aftermath in West Flanders. Elegantly displayed in sequence, dioramas and models, equipment, weapons, uniforms and badges, medals, documents, photographs, pictures, maps and posters tell the story as it concerns the Belgian, British, French, American and German forces and the civilians. Every item has been found either in the area or is similar to that used or worn here. Relics of some of the personalities connected with the war are included: Sir John French, later the Earl of Ypres, is represented by his banner and a pair of shining boots; Lord Plumer's hat rests nearby; the travelling tea service presented by Lady Haig in memory of her husband, and the sword of Prince Maurice of Battenburg presented by his sorrowing mother. Fragments of the old buildings are to be found, including the façade of the last example extant of a King Albert House, a type of temporary residence provided immediately after hostilities ceased; a door from the old Cloth Hall stands close by in a new section of the display. Specimens of grave markers of the British, Belgian, French and German cemeteries with photographs and pictures of the memorials and cemeteries can be seen beside examples of children's artwork of their view of the war and the graves. The dioramas include a representation of the battlefield in 1917, a typical airfield of 1917-18, the old Menin Gate and Lille Gate, and the town as it was in 1918. Near the entrance desk at the head of the stairs is a full-size trench section with some of the fine collection of trench signs. Examples of trench art are shown in cases alongside the shell-cases from which they were made. Guide-books and a small selection of appropriate literature are on sale at the desk.

The **Belfry** is open to the public and access is obtained by application to the museum custodian. From the museum the upper chambers are reached by a narrow winding stairway. Fine views of the town and country beyond are gained from the galleries. On a clear day the coast can be seen across the flat plain. The bell chamber houses the famous carillon which plays each day at set hours and the chiming bells which toll the hours half-an-hour before their due time. It is not advised to visit this chamber when the hour of midday is tolled as the reverberations and vibrations can be injurious.

Of the original Cloth Hall of 1260, only the lower portals of the Belfry around the 'Donkerpoort' and a few pillars in the Tourist Office and halls beyond it remain. On the walls above the Donkerpoort are the municipal coat-of-arms and flanking the passage are the statues of Earl Baldwin IX and his Queen, Margaret of Champagne, King Albert and Queen Elizabeth. Above is the statue to Our Lady of Thuyne, the patroness of Ypres since the siege of 1383. A plaque commemorating the dedication of the town to the Sacred Heart (on the Jubilee feast of Our Lady of Thuyne in 1933) is to the left of the gateway, and on the right is the **Memorial to the French killed during 1914-1918 in the Salient**.

The present-day aspect of the Grote Markt closely resembles that which it held in the 18th Century as most of the houses are, externally at least, copies of those destroyed. Among them is the old house of the canteen of the Cloth Hall, now the **Klein Stadhuis restaurant** which dated from 1624. A near neighbour, now another café '**Den Anker**' was a copy of its 1611 counterpart. Further along beyond the Diksmuidestraat is the old **Kasseirij** building which until 1967 officially housed the Burgomaster and served as Hôtel de Ville during the years of the reconstruction of the Cloth Hall. Opposite between Meensestraat and K. Torhoutstraat is the **Court of Justice** which was formerly the Hospital of Our Lady. On the southern side the hotels are close copies of earlier houses but, as the years go by, the modern shop fronts are detracting somewhat from the grace of the Renaissance façades.

Almost an exact match . . . Taken from a little higher altitude, in the centre of the city we see the restored Cloth Hall.

Through the Donkerpoort beneath which is a large shell and the entrance to an inner courtyard of the Cloth Hall (where remnants of the old buildings are stored) — access to **St Martin's Cathedral** is reached, across some of the few remaining old cobblestones of Ypres. High above the south door is the magnificent **Rose Window** which is the **British Army and RAF Memorial to King Albert**. During the design process for the window, it was discovered that there was no official crest for the British Army and one had to be created and approved by King George V. This is to be found in the upper segment of the window opposite those of the RAF and the Fifth Dragoon Guards.

The church was completely destroyed during the war and, when it was rebuilt, the design included the present spire, which, although included in the pre-1914 plans, had never been built. The original cathedral was built in the 13th Century on the site of an earlier church founded in 1073 and was the seat of a bishop until it became the collegiate church under the administration of a dean in the 19th Century. The church is in Gothic style and is lofty and full of light from the many windows.

On the wall of the north transept is a **Memorial Plaque to the British Commonwealth War Dead in the Ypres Salient**. It is one of several placed in cathedrals all along the 1914-1918 front line. In 1973, archaeological excavations in the north aisle resulted in the discovery of the grave of Robert of Béthune — the Lion of Flanders — one of the greatest of the Counts of Flanders who died at Ypres in 1322. Long and widespread research led to this discovery and one of the most vital documents used was a photograph taken in early 1915 by Professor Barbour, then attached to the Friends' Ambulance Unit, which he took the day after one of the bombardments. This photograph showed a mural on the wall of the north aisle and, from a copy of the photograph made by the Imperial War Museum in 1972, it was possible to read the inscription which identified the figure as being Robert of Béthune and referred to his tomb being close by. After the bombardments nothing was left of the wall and no other photographs were known.

Behind the cathedral are the remains of the old cloisters, now a repository of fragments from the ruined church. In the garden to the south-east of the church is the **Munster Memorial** — a beautiful Celtic Cross com-

The magnificent Cloth Hall is the home of the Salient War Museum.

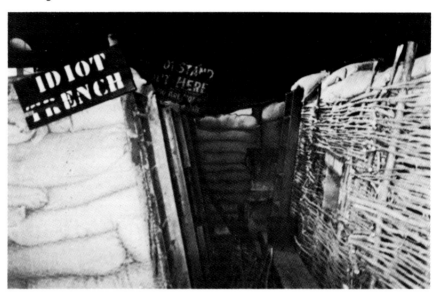

The Museum has preserved a large number of trench signs from the Salient.

memorating the men of the Munster Regiments who died in the Great War.

Across the Vandenpereboomplein — once partly a waterway to the Cloth Hall — is **St**

George's Memorial Church. The main door is in Elverdingestraat which carries the traffic to the west. The church was designed by Sir Reginald Blomfield and was built in 1928-29

The spire of St Martin's Collegiate Church . . . a pre-war dream fulfilled.

A typical CWGC British Memorial plaque; this one in St Martin's, Ypres.

The memorial commemorating the men of the Munster Regiments.

as part of the British settlement. The idea came from Earl Haig who suggested that a church should be founded for use as the place of worship for the British colony (which was quite large immediately after the Great War) and for pilgrims to the Salient. The site also included the Eton Memorial School for the children of the gardeners and other officials working in the region and the community centre for them.

Today, the church, a memorial to all who died in the Salient, and the old schoolroom, now the Parish Hall, are all that remain of the settlement. The school closed after the Second World War and the community buildings were sold. The church foundation stone was laid by Field-Marshal Lord Plumer on July 24, 1927. Almost every item contained within the precincts is a memorial. The windows, the furnishings and the decorations all commemorate a unit or an individual. Recent additions include memorials to Sir Winston Churchill, Field-Marshal Montgomery and a number of officers and men. Services are held regularly each Sunday evening and the Chaplain is in attendance on certain other occasions. The vigorous Friends of St George's Memorial Church, Ypres, who are always glad to welcome new members, keep it in repair; their meetings are held usually in London under the auspices of the Bishop of Gibraltar in Europe.

The offices of the **Commonwealth War Graves Commission** are to be found at the other end of **Elverdlingestraat** at **No. 82** which lies on the right-hand side beyond the town prison. In a street behind the Grote Markt — Merghelynkstraat — is the **reconstructed town house of an 18th Century gentleman** and it is well worth a visit as it depicts the pure French style of the period. From the gracious exterior in the Louis XV and Louis XVI style to the beautifully proportioned interior and period furnishings, one gains a fair idea of the way people of the upper classes lived in this merchant town.

By far the most important edifice in Ypres to the British visitor is the **Menin Gate**. Built on the site of the original Hangoart Gate (later the Antwerp Gate) this magnificent archway was also designed by Sir Reginald Blomfield and was inaugurated by Field-Marshal Plumer on July 24, 1927 in the presence of King Albert. At the time of the Great War, there was no actual gate on the site. It was indicated by the presence of two lions, one on each side of the roadway which cut through the walls. These lions are now in Canberra, Australia. Through this cutting, many thousands of men wended their way to the Salient. A tag line at the time was, 'Tell the last man through to bolt the Menin Gate'.

Although Vauban's original gate no longer stood, virtually every man who fell in the Salient would have passed the twin lions which guarded the spot in 1914.

It was only fitting therefore that this was the location chosen for the Memorial to the Missing, designed by Sir Reginald Blomfield, surmounted by a lion, now at rest, looking out over the Salient.

Some of the 'Old Contemptibles' return to Ypres . . . and the memorial, in August 1982. All around them are the inscribed names of fellow soldiers . . . over 54,000 of them . . . who fought and died in the Salient and yet have no known grave. The missing who fell subsequent to August 16, 1917 are commemorated at Tyne Cot.

29

operated with the police chief and early in the summer of 1928 the nightly ceremony began. In October of that year it was discontinued until the following spring. The Last Post Committee was formed and soon afterwards the Brussels and Antwerp Branch of the British Legion announced their wish to present to Ypres four silver bugles. In 1935, the British Legion of the County of Surrey subscribed £400 to go towards a fund to fulfil the aims of the Committee:

'. . . to ensure the sounding of the Last Post each evening for all time at the British Memorial at the Menin Gate in honour of the soldiers of the British Empire who fell at Ypres or in the neighbourhood during the war of 1914-1918 and in addition to do everything . . . that could increase the significance of this tribute to the Armies of the British Empire.'

Thus was born a tradition. For ever since November 11, 1929, except for the break during the German occupation of Ypres (from May 20, 1940 to September 6, 1944) it has continued. The day the Germans left Ypres, the Call sounded out that evening.

Two more silver bugles were presented by the Old Contemptibles' Association of Blackpool and Fleetwood and, in 1959, Colonel I. Whitaker presented two silver trumpets in memory of former Cavalry and Artillerymen and himself who served in the Salient. Each night, two of the firemen in civilian dress take up their positions in the centre of the road beneath the Salient face of the Memorial and the police halt the flow of traffic through the gateway. Then, in a simple ceremony, the pure tones of the silver bugles ring out and echo away, never to a completely deserted scene. On major anniversaries and ceremonies involving the British or Ypres Municipal celebrations, up to six firemen in full dress blow the Call and often Reveille. The Chaplain of St George's and perhaps the Dean will say prayers before a congregation of hundreds and wreaths will be laid on the stairways.

The **ramparts**, which to this day encircle the eastern and southern sectors of the town, can provide a most pleasant promenade, from north of the Menin Gate to west of the Lille Gate. Refacing of the walls and rebuilding of the Lille Gate has finally removed the sections which for fifty years still bore signs of war damage. Beneath the massive fortifications was the best shelter the troops could wish for in the devastated town. For many years since a number of the casemates have served a variety of useful purposes as workshops, stores and garages. Until relatively

Now the archway forms the **British Memorial to the Missing** and bears the names of 54,896 of those who died between 1914 and August 15, 1917 and who have no known grave. Their names are engraved on panels which form the walls both inside the archway and on the walls on the terraces and stairways to them. Over the archway, a British lion broods above the inscription detailing the purpose of the memorial. On either side of the arch, the Commission maintains a quiet garden of green lawns and shrubs. Incorporated into the foundations of the memorial is one of the bastions of the old ramparts with one of the sallyports on the northern side.

Immediately after the conclusion of the inauguration ceremony in 1927, the buglers of the Somerset Light Infantry sounded the Last Post, and pipers of the Scots Guards played a lament. The simple ceremony of sounding the Last Post each and every night at 8.00 p.m. was conceived by Mr P. Vandenbraambussche, the then-Superintendent of the Ypres Police, soon after the unveiling. The buglers of the Ypres Fire Brigade co-

The shell-scarred Lille Gate was the main route for leaving Ypres.

Where *Wipers Times* was printed.

recently those along Bolingstraat from the Menin Gate contained relics dating from their usage as a signal headquarters and alterations made by the German Army during their occupation from 1940-44. In one of the casemates between Aalmoezenierstraat and the Lille Gate, the famous trench journal *Wipers Times* was once printed and published by the Sherwood Foresters. In 1989 this section of the inner façade of the ramparts was refurbished and the interiors renovated in the original Vauban style. Now it is proposed that this particular casemate will be on public view under the auspices of the '14-'18 Museum. It is in this eastern flank of the ramparts that the trees reflect the devastation wreaked by the August 1985 hurricane.

The **Lille Gate (Rijselpoort)**, with its medieval round bastions was called the Messines Gate for centuries. In his defence works. Vauban retained the two main bastions of the old gate and these remain although refaced in the recent refurbishing. The balcony above the gate and the roadway over the Kasteel Gracht have been modified. The Lille Gate was perhaps even more familiar to the BEF than the Menin Gate as, due to the extremely exposed position of the latter, the more sheltered southern exit was used as the main route to the front by the troops leaving Ypres.

Within the gateway on the eastern bastion is a doorway from which entry is gained to the **vaulted chambers** within. For many years this was a museum and called 'Plumer's Headquarters'. The inner room was very

probably used as a signals office and was frequented by officers and men from Plumer's staff, but I have it on the authority of his secretary that never was it his headquarters. The outer bastion walls are pierced by loopholes from which machine guns were trained. The late Sergeant Back told me that on the night before the attack on the Messines Ridge there were staff officers here and that some of the orders for the attack were given from this site. This chamber can also be viewed by application to the Salient Museum. Inside the western postern are traces of the old Roman-style walls and from here the Yperlee rises.

The old **'Wooden House'**, just inside the gate, is a replica of a similar building destroyed in 1917; at that time it was one of the oldest in the town.

Just across the Lille Gate is the **British Military Cemetery, Ramparts Cemetery**. This is the only one within the old walls of the town. From it is a very beautiful view over the moat.

The other cemetery in the town is the **Reservoir Cemetery** which lies on Plumerlaan, a road running parallel to Elverdingestraat, in the region of the Plaine d'Amour.

Beyond the Menin Gate, alongside the town cemetery, is the **Ypres Town BMC** and **Ypres Town Cemetery Extension**, the entrance to both being on Zonnebekeweg.

To return to the Ramparts and the moat, just beyond the cemetery the walks meander over the corner bastion known as the **Lion Tower** which like the Lille Gate dates from 1383. From here a view of the two half-moon (demi-lune) defences erected by Vauban in 1678 can be seen across the moat. Incidentally, the moat is fed by three rivers — the Zillebeke, the Bollaertbeke and the Vyverbeke (Dickebush Lake), and this part of it is known as the Majoor Gracht. Around the next corner within the walls, is the local deer park and just a little way further along under the trees is the cupola of a machine gun post.

On the town side of the walls slope the esplanade gardens where various sports can be played. Standing in this area is the **old powder magazine** built in 1818 on the foundations of an even older magazine built before Vauban's time. It is now the oldest building in Ypres. It was said to be bomb-proof and it seems this was true as it survived all the bombardments. The ramparts promenade ends in the square in front of the station — René Colaert Plein.

In addition to the churches already mentioned, there are in Ypres three others, **St Pieters, St Jacques** and **St Nicholas**. The oldest of these is St Pieters in Rijselstraat

Little Toc N stands in the rue de Lille alternatively named Rijselstraat.

(Rue de Lille). All three were almost totally destroyed but in St Pieters there are vestiges of the original 12th Century church and fragments of later embellishments.

In Rijselstraat there are several other interesting buildings. One of these is **No. 38 — the Belle Alms House**. The present building incorporates some of the original 16th and 17th Century portions of the chapel to the Belle Institution founded in about 1276. On the wall in the side street is a plaque to the memory of Master Jan Yperman, the father of Flemish surgery, who was closely connected with this almshouse from 1304-1329. The building now houses the Public Assistance Organisations Museum.

At **No. 70 is the Post Office**. This building is a replica of one of the stone-built houses of 14th Century Ypres. It may have been owned by the Templars. Off Rijselstraat is the old St John's Alms House which was founded by a rich local family, the Broederlaans, in 1277. Here now is the Municipal Art Gallery. A short distance further down the street on the opposite side is the building which once housed **Little Toc H** — the Ypres branch of the famous Poperinge club. In the Oude Vismarkt there are other replicas of the old architecture of Ypres.

Its wartime wounds were healed in a restoration programme in 1985.

Battles of the Ypres Salient 1914-1918

A BRIEF OUTLINE SUMMARY

First Battle of Ypres, October-November 1914

October: The front line extended from Langemark — Zonnebeke — Gheluvelt — Zandevoorde — Messines to Armentières. British Army held the line in the eastern and southern sectors with the French on their left and the Belgian Army to the north.

7: German Cavalry enter Ypres but remain only briefly.

13: Northumberland Hussars enter.

14: British and French troops enter and occupy Ypres entirely. The British force was IV Corps led by 7th Division. Their Divisional Headquarters was at the Château, later called Stirling Castle, on the Menin Road. IV Corps had their HQ in the convent in Poperinge, Advance HQ was set up in the Hôtel de Ville in Ypres with the overflow on the upper floor of the Cloth Hall. Below were the French Cuiraissiers who used the ground floor level as stables. General Rawlinson was billeted at No. 10 rue de Lille (Rijselstraat). In the 7th Division were the first members of the Territorial Army to see action, the Northumberland Hussars, a Yeomanry regiment. They were in Bruges on October 6 and in action on the 12th. The London Scottish and the Oxford Hussars, another Yeomanry regiment, were first in action on October 31.

22: German concentrated bombardment and attack on Ypres commences and they advance westward.

29-30: The front had contracted onto Ypres despite many gallant charges and stands by the British cavalry and infantry who were well outnumbered. The line now ran from Langemark — Broodseinde — Kleine Zillebeke — Hollebeke — Messines.

31: Germans pushed back to Gheluvelt.

November 1: Messines-Wytschaete Ridge captured by Germans who reach Wulvergem and Neuve Eglise.

2: French X1V Corps recapture the Ridge and British I Corps held furious attack on Gheluvelt.

10: German second bombardment of Ypres commences,

22: Cloth Hall, St Martin's church and many other buildings destroyed or badly damaged.

1915

Front line stabilised from Bixschote — Langemark — St Julien — Broodseinde — Hooge — Zillebeke — St Eloi — Wytschaete — Ploegsteert. Line remained almost unchanged without much gain or loss although there was continuous activity.

March: Heavy fighting on the Lys front. St Eloi changed hands on two occasions. The civilian population who had fled Ypres during the bombardments trickled back to their ruined homes.

Second Battle of Ypres, April-June 1915

April 14: Battle opens. Germans commence bombardment of Ypres which continued for nearly a month, completely destroying the town.

17: British capture Hill 60.

22: First gas attack on French territorial and colonial troops holding the line near Bikschote. The Belgian Corps were on the French left and the Canadian 3rd Brigade on their right. The French were pushed back to Steenstraat but the Canadians held the line at St Julien.

25: Main thrust of the German attack on British line. By the end of the month the front line ran south from Steenstraat to Zuideschoote — Boesinge — Hill 60 — Hollebeke — Wytschaete — Ploegsteert.

May: Heavy fighting with severe casualties to both sides continued.

5: Hill 60 attacked. British line pushed back on 3rd/4th from St Julien and Frezenberg and to Hooge later. Hooge Château fell but was recaptured on June 2.

July 22-26: British advance along Menin road near Hooge.

29-30: First use of liquid fire by Germans.
August 7: Gas attack on Hooge.

1915-1917

Front line remained almost static with artillery activity punctuated by infantry attacks on varying scales by both armies. Mining in certain areas constantly undertaken by both sides. St Eloi and Hill 60 were scenes of perpetual engagements.

1916

Hill 62 captured by the Canadian Corps who also stemmed the German advance in the direction of Zillebeke and Hooge, fighting over Sanctuary Wood and across the open country beyond to within 1,000 yards of Hill 60. The front line extended from Steenstraat and Lizerne to Zuidschoote and Pilkem to Weiltje and Frezenberg, Zillebeke and Hill 60 and Hill 62, St Eloi and Hollebeke, Kemmel and Wytschaete, Wulvergem and Messines, Ploegsteert Wood and St Yvon. Gains and losses fluctuating on either side.

1917

June: Battle of Messines.
1-7: British offensive heralded by unusually heavy and prolonged artillery bombardment obliterating Messines and Wytschaete.
7: In the early hours of the morning, 19 mines extending along the whole curve of the front line from Hill 60 and St Eloi to Messines were exploded. The New Zealand Division captured the highest point on the Ridge and advanced to beyond Messines village.
11: The advance along two miles of the front had continued and consolidated east and north of Messines. German counterattacks in the St Yvon—St Eloi regions were abandoned by June 14.
July: At the end of the month, the line ran from Dixmude along the Yser Canal to Lizerne, Het Sas and Boesinge, then down the Ypres-Bruges railway to Quatre Chemins crossroads on to the Pilkem road. It continued west of Wieltje village to Verlorenhoek, then west of Hooge skirting Sanctuary Wood passing west of Hollebeke and to the east of Ploegsteert Wood.

Third Battle of Ypres, July-November 1917

July 31: The Allied offensive began in bad weather in the early morning. In the region of Bikschote the enemy trenches were overcome to a depth of nearly two miles.

August 1: St Julien, Frezenberg, Pilkem, Westhoek were captured and Sanctuary Wood and Hooge fell after very severe fighting.

16: After a lull the Allied offensive resumed all along the line. Despite desperate fighting, the advance continued until September 20.

September 20: Langemark and Zonnebeke attacked and many fortified farms and trenches captured. Polygon Wood was the scene of heavy fighting by the Australians and Tower Hamlets also under attack.

26: Polygon Wood fell to the Australians and Tower Hamlets to the British infantry divisions.

October 4: The offensive was maintained along the front from Langemark to Tower Hamlets against increasingly determined resistance, the Germans defending the Passchendaele Ridge with every means possible.

9: British front extended now some seven miles from Poelkappelle to Broodseinde with the right flank on the slope of the Ridge. Casualties continued to be extremely heavy on both sides.

30: Passchendaele Ridge finally cleared of the enemy after the bloodiest battle in history. Ypres relieved completely. November 6 Passchendaele taken.

1918
German Spring Offensive
April 9-20: The Spring Offensive broke through the lines south of Ypres and the British and Portuguese forces withdrew on an arc from Neuve Eglise, Bailleul, Meteren, Vieux-Berquin, Festubert and La Bassée.

22-24: Germans attack and capture Mont Kemmel. Locre changed hands several times.

29: Severe German attacks between La Clytte and Zillebeke were repulsed and Mont Kemmel recaptured. Later the British division was forced to withdraw to Kemmel village.

Fourth Battle of Ypres, July-October, 1918

July 19: Battle of the Lys begins. The British attack.

September 1: The Allied advance begun in August had by this date reached La Bassée, Laventie, Neuve Eglise, Mont Kemmel, Wulvergem and Voormezele.

October: Ploegsteert, Messines, Warneton, Gheluvelt, Houthulst Forest, etc., had all been recaptured.

14: Last shell dropped on Ypres town, as the last German forces were chased out of the Ypres Salient.

16: Menin occupied by British Second Army.

At the end of the war, the honours of the British Military Cross and the French Croix de Guerre were conferred on the town of Ypres. These decorations can be seen together with the documents relating to them on permanent exhibition in the Salient Museum.

Zonnebeke then

YPRES SALIENT BATTLEFIELD TOUR

Zonnebeke now

Essex Farm Cemetery with the 49th Division Memorial. Close to the entrance stands the memorial to John McCrae.

ROUTE I

Leave by the Diksmuidestraat (N369) on the north side of the Grand Place shortly crossing the Wieltjegracht, a narrow weed-covered waterway at the site of the **Old Dixmude Gate**, and bear left at the fork almost immediately thereafter. Reaching the canal basin at the Kaaie, known to the BEF as **Tattenham Corner**, turn left with the road

Tattenham Corner, also called Dead End.

and after crossing the canal bear right at the next major turning. This is **Salvation Corner**, so called from the hut which the Salvation Army ran here for troops going up the line.

No Sally Army now at Salvation Corner.

The road runs parallel to the little Yperlee and the canal. Amid the modern residential area on the right is **Duhallow A.D.S. Cemetery** which was used in 1917 during the Pilkem Ridge battles. About ½ km further along, after leaving the built-up area and passing beneath the new road bridge, the canal bank rises to the right and the obelisk of the **49th Division Memorial** comes into view. Access is through **Essex Farm Cemetery** before it. Recent road improvements have included a new lay-by which now enables visitors to park off the busy road. In November 1985 a memorial was erected by the cemetery entrance to Lieutenant-Colonel John M. McCrae, Royal Canadian Army Medical Corps, close to the track which leads down to the canal and the towpath. This lane crosses a small bridge on the far side of which

is a **group of British dugouts** recently repaired and restored. The bridge was at the west end of Bridge No. 4, **Brielen Bridge**, and it was here, between the bridge and the memorial, that was the site of the dressing station above which Colonel McCrae in 1915 wrote his famous poem 'In Flanders fields the poppies blow. . . . ' Dugouts used by British divisions once stretched along both sides of the bridge in the canal bank.

SCALE 1:100 000 1cm–1km

Reproduced from Michelin Sheet No. 51 29th Edition 1989

Waterlogged British dressing station bunkers at Brielen Bridge.

village is entered is a **Demarcation Stone** and in a garden is a **concrete blockhouse** surmounted by a German mortar — a Minenwerfer known as Kleine Berta.

To gain the eastern flank of the canal and to cross the **Pilkem Ridge** we now turn right, soon crossing the bypass and the canal, taking the Langemark road. The canal has changed greatly as previously the only lock was at **Het Sas** further north. Since 1918 a southern lock has been added and the banks raised.

One km later, **Carrefour de la Rose** is reached. On the left is one of the most unusual and attractive memorials in the whole Salient. It is the **French 87th and 45th Divisions' Memorial** and is in the form of a Breton calvary and dolmen with a most useful and interesting orientation table and map. The map shows the stand made by the two divisions in the gas attack in April 1915. The calvary is a genuine one from Plouagat in Brittany and the dolmen was brought from Henanbiken. The small park is protected from the road by concrete posts like the wooden ones which held up barbed wire defences before the introduction of iron pickets.

A short way down the road on the left lies

One of the youngest casualties to die in the Salient — Private Strudwick, aged 15.

Behind Boezinge Demarcation Stone, a 'Kleine Berta' rests on a German bunker.

The Breton Memorial to the French 87th and 45th Divisions at the Carrefour de la Rose. The map nearby shows their stand in the April 1915 gas attack.

In the cemetery are buried over 1,000 soldiers from the British and Commonwealth Forces and one German. Among the British graves are those of Private T. Barratt, VC, of the South Staffordshire Regiment, and Private Strudwick, who, at the age of 15 years, was one of the youngest casualties to be buried here.

Continuing on towards Boesinge, remains of other canal bank dugouts can be seen to the right whilst on the left, a little further up, is **Bard Cottage Cemetery**.

After 4 kms leave the modern highway to enter **Boezinge** by the old road on the left. Burned by the Germans during their brief stay here in October 1914, it was for the next three years the most northerly boundary of the British sector. New housing development surrounds the area of the ditch which was the actual boundary close to a farm on the right which remains. Beyond this point the French held the line joining with the Belgian Army near Dixmude. Fierce battles were fought in the region in 1915 during the Second Battle of Ypres and again in the Third Battle in 1917, during which the French made a successful attack and crossed the canal to the eastern bank. On the left-hand side as the

Artillery Wood Cemetery, named after the small copse which was here, but continue straight on to reach **Pilkem** village. Turn left into Bikshootsestraat. Across the railway there is a road junction, the left turning, Slaaktestraat, takes you by the **largest German bunker** remaining (built as a signal station), while the right fork passes two bunkers on the right and one on the left. Both roads join the Bikschote road with two

more bunkers. These are, like others in the area, part of the chain of defences built by the Germans in the winter of 1915-16. They form a huge arc across the northern and eastern sectors of the Salient. At the next fork go left past **Bikschote Mill** burnt down in 1977 but now rebuilt.

The largest German bunker remaining in the Salient near Pilkem Road.

After 1 km turn left at the crossroads for Steenstraat. Two more bunkers can be seen along the road to the left. The road crosses over the path of the A19, the Veurne to Kortrijk autoroute, which now sweeps down to the south-east, cleaving its way across the Salient below St Julien and Zonnebeke, skirting Polygon Wood and Nonneboschen to Gheluvelt. In 1½ kms turn left to join the N369 and **Steenstraat**. This village, lying amid the rich fields, was at the western end of the French line on April 22, 1915. Their line ran eastwards to a point south of Poelcapelle where it joined the sector held by the Canadian Corps with the British 27th and 28th Divisions beyond them east of Zonnebeke and Polygon Wood.

April 22 had been a beautiful sunny day when, at about 5.00 p.m., a greenish-yellow cloud began to appear on either side of Langemark and slowly creep towards the French lines. Soon the whole four-mile length of the front held by the 87th and 45th (Algerian) Divisions was shrouded in the noxious cloud of chlorine gas. Within an hour the whole front had given way as the French and their colonial troops took the brunt of the unexpected horror which now hid their sector completely from view and they fell back to the canal. The Canadians on their right flank were, at the outset, beyond the field of the gas but, as they went to fill in the gap they were drawn into it, falling back to St Julien. The French recaptured Steenstraat on May 15 and some 2,000 Germans were found dead on the battlefield. On July 31, 1917, the French recrossed the canal by night with the aid of many pontoon bridges.

Cross of Reconciliation near Steenstraat.

Having crossed the canal (1 km), the tall, graceful aluminium **Cross of Reconciliation** will he seen up the slightly rising ground on the right-hand side. This is a French memorial which replaced the original cross which had been erected to the memory of those who were gassed in April 1915. It was destroyed in 1942 by the occupation forces who objected to the reference in the inscription to the Germans as barbarians.

It was in this area that the French and Belgian lines joined during the 1915 battles and the short circuit from here through **Lizerne** (turning right at the crossroads) and then taking the first right will bring you back to the great Cross. There are several Belgian memorials in this district recalling the various attacks made here.

The Belgian Cemetery in Houthulst Forest with its distinctive headstones.

Turning left now onto the N369 again, continue for 5 kms to the hamlet of **Kippe**. Bikschote, which was one of the centres of the gas attack of April 1915, lies over to the right. Kippe is the northern extremity of the Ypres Salient; to the left is the small town of Merckem, but we turn right for Houthulst, passing **Jokehoven** 3 kms further on.

Houthulst is reached in 3 kms. Turn right onto N301 at the crossroad. The road soon comes to the edge of **Houthulst Forest** whose western side it skirts for 3 kms. This forest was described by Napoleon as the key to the Low Countries. After a bitter defence by the Belgian Army, with support by French cavalry and territorial troops, it fell to the Germans on October 21, 1914. In the Allied advance during the Third Battle of Ypres, the southern extremities were reached. The whole region was subjected to gas attacks and, although the defending Germans suffered very heavy casualties, all attempts to outflank the forest were defeated by their holding the Spriet Ridge. It was not until September 28, 1918 that the Belgians finally recaptured it. During their occupation the Germans had converted the entire forest into a fortress. From here their heavy artillery bombarded the Allied lines to the south. When the forest was captured, the Belgians took 150 guns and over 6,000 prisoners.

On the edge of the forest is the **Belgian Military Cemetery**. As the Belgian Army did not hold a sector in the Salient, this is their only cemetery in the immediate area. Besides the 1,704 Belgian dead, there are also some French and Italians buried here.

Access to parts of the forest is restricted for in its depths the Belgian Army bomb disposal unit has a base. Here are brought the large numbers of shells, bombs, grenades and other ammunition still found in the Salient (and elsewhere in this part of Belgium) to be detonated and destroyed. Farmers still find dangerous relics as they till the land; the spring and autumn ploughing particularly bring forth the 'iron harvest'. This local hazard — builders and developers are affected also — is faced with phlegmatic acceptance with the Belgian Army constantly on call making regular patrols, yet each year casualties, often fatal, still occur.

In 4 kms **Velhoek**, a hamlet on the furthest edge of the Allied advance in October 1917. **Poelkapelle** is another 3 kms. This small town was briefly in the British Cavalry area in October 1914 after which (until 1917) it was well inside the German line and became a fortress. It was ravaged by bombardment and reduced to ruins in the latter stages of the autumn 1917 attacks. The 53rd Brigade of 18th Division captured it on October 23. Among the other divisions involved were the 29th, 4th and 11th. One of the tanks which was in support of the 11th was knocked out

and bogged down in the centre of the town and was still there when the **Memorial to Georges Guynemer** was unveiled in July 1923.

The great French air ace was killed on September 11, 1917 during a combat with an Aviatik. His flight companion, Lieutenant Benjamin Bozon-Verduraz, did not see his Spad fall as at the vital moment he was busy attending to another group of enemy machines. It was later reported that the German infantry in Poelkappelle had found the wrecked machine and the dead pilot (who

The Guynemer Memorial, Poelkappelle.

had been shot through the head), and had moved his body to a dugout, but that an artillery barrage had almost immediately destroyed the trench and the aircraft. I have been told that the flying stork — emblem of his squadron — flies in the direction of his crash.

About 1 km to the east of the town on the N313 Westrozebeke road lies **Poelkappelle British Cemetery**, the third largest in the region. It was created after the war from battlefield graves. Over 7,000 men lie here. Amongst them is Private J. Condon, Royal Irish Regiment, at 14 perhaps the youngest to die here. Another is 2nd Lieutenant H. G. Langton, 4th Bn. London Regiment, whose headstone is unusual for its musical inscription.

Poelkapelle British Cemetery. *Left:* **Private Condon at 14 is believed to be the youngest to die in the Salient.** *Right:* **A good example of a 'special memorial' where the original grave has been lost.**

locations of the other German graveyards. The cemetery is in two almost distinct sections. The **Alter Friedhof**, the old cemetery, is under the shade of the great oak trees, which stand like enormous Imperial Guardsmen above the greensward, and has grey slatish stones with the names of the dead picked out in white-painted lettering. Here lie 10,143, of whom 3,836 are unknown. Here and there groups of small basalt crosses break the serried ranks of stones. Immediately through the entrance is the **Kameradengrab** — the mass grave of 24,834 men. Bronze pillars bearing their names flank the grave, with memorials to the regiments of various parts of Germany. Away over the far side of the cemetery stand the brooding figures of mourning comrades.

The northern end of the cemetery, beyond the protection of the oak trees and behind the three concrete bunkers and their linking memorial stones, which are part of the fortifications of the Langemark Line, is the **Einbettungsfriedhof-Nord** where 9,475 men lie buried. Divisional memorials are to be found on the slabs of stone between the bunkers. A quiet pool marks the boundary of

Blockhouses of the Einbettungsfriedhof-Nord in Langemark German Cemetery.

At the Guynemer crossroad turn right for **Langemark**, 2½ kms. This town was attacked by the Germans on October 23, 1914 but the untried divisions were no match for either the 2nd British Division or the French, and the student troops suffered heavy casualties. In the wake of the gas attack of April 22, 1915, Langemark was occupied by the German 51st Reserve Division and it remained in German hands until August 16, 1917 when 20th Light Division recaptured the ruined town and 2,000 prisoners. In April 1918 the Allies withdrew in the face of the Spring Offensive and it was not until September 28 that the town was finally recaptured by X Corps supporting the Belgian Army. By this time there was not a building left standing — all had been pulverized in the bombardments.

At the main crossroads turn right, passing the square and the modern church on the left, and cross the railway. After a short distance the houses give way to beet fields (on the right) whilst, on the left of the road, is the sombre **German Military Cemetery, the Soldatenfriedhof**. A long, low, dark red granite building houses the gateway and incorporates the student memorial. This is a small room containing the Registers of those who are known to be buried between the tall oak trees and in the newer section to the

north of the entrance. A visitors' book is also provided. Both chapels are entered through magnificent cast-iron doors of intricate design. The chapel walls are covered with the names of the students who died and on the wall of the second is a map depicting the

the graveyard in which is reflected the Teutonic cross. This is a forbidding place with its subdued colours and gloomy atmosphere heightened by the very neatness and trimness of the lawns, hedges, walls and trees.

Away in the distance the mourning comrades overlook the huge mass grave.

In the distance beyond the cemetery, a little way along the road behind the Broenbeek, is another large bunker of the same line as those in the cemetery. In front of it is the **Memorial to the Royal Artillery and Royal Engineers of the 34th Division**. After the bunker was captured in September 1918, it was used as an advanced dressing station under the command of Robert Lawrence, a brother of T. E. Lawrence. He described to me the frightful conditions in this region in 1917 and 1918. There were no trenches, just a sea of mud across which duck-boards led from shell-hole to shell-hole right back to Velhoek and Koekuit. The concrete pill-boxes were the only stable buildings remaining. At certain times more men were lost by drowning than by the bullet.

Return to the centre of the town, the church being on the right, and at the traffic lights go right on the Boezinge road. A short distance along the road, now flanked by modern villas, is the stark grey **Memorial to the 20th Light Division**. Over the Steenbeek, and in the yard of a large farm, is a square pillbox, **Cement House**. Next door to the farm is the large **British Cemetery** which bears this name. Until recently all bodies found in the Salient and identified as British were buried here. Some time ago, a tiny cemetery near Mons had to be closed due to roadworks at Maisières and the eighteen or so officers and men (who had died in August 1914) were transferred here. Among them is Captain Knowles, one of the first British officers to lose his life.

The 34th Division RA and RE Memorial stands in front of a German bunker.

The 20th Light Division's Memorial now surrounded by modern houses.

Cement House, a German bunker next door to the British Cemetery.

Here lies Captain J. E. Knowles, Middlesex Regiment, killed near Mons on August 23. 1914. His grave and those of his men were moved from Maisières.

At the next crossroads, known as **Iron Cross** — a heavily bombarded spot as it was a main crossing of the transport routes to Langemark — turn left and in about ½ km turn right. thereby crossing the eastern side of the **Pilkem Ridge**. On the right, 2 kms further on, is a large and most interesting concrete bunker. It is a fortified Belgian farmhouse, **Goumier Farm**. On some British maps it is called Gournier Farm. Although it has been in almost constant use by farmers as a cattle shelter or pigsty in the years since the war, it remains in fair condition. The Germans were the first to fortify it, enclosing the brick walls in concrete, and in places it is possible to discern the imprint of the shuttering. As a strong point with excellent visibility, it was under frequent attack and changed hands on many occasions until the end of July 1917 when the 38th Welsh Division captured Pilkem. The Royal Engineers added further strengthening and blast walls

to Goumier and thus it is one place where the two differing styles of work can be studied closely. After again falling into enemy hands, it was finally recaptured by the Black Watch. Some years ago a **plaque, in memory of the 38th Welsh Division**, was placed on the bunker and, with the farmer's permission, visitors can inspect it.

Keep to the right at the fork just beyond the farm and continue for about 2 kms along this road across the ridge, passing between small farms often with a blockhouse or concrete observation post now incorporated in their buildings, until a five-way cross is

reached. Take the second right and, after a couple of bunkers have been passed, a panorama unfolds. Proceed along this, the old **Boundary Road**, for a km and over a small crossroad, once known as **Hammond's Corner**, and the large **New Irish Farm Cemetery** is on the right. Among over 4,500 British and Commonwealth graves are a number of Chinese Labour Corps casualties. In a short distance the N38 (the Ypres bypass) is crossed and the descent into Ypres is made through the suburb of De Brieke. Take the right-hand fork and enter Ypres at the site of the old **Diksmuide Gate**.

Goumier Farm blockhouse with British and German concrete reinforcement and a memorial plaque to the 38th Welsh Division.

SCALE 1:100 000 1cm–1km

Reproduced from Michelin Sheet No. 51 29th Edition 1989

The 1st Bn. Monmouthshire Regiment.

ROUTE II

Leave Ypres by Brugseweg (N313) soon passing the large **White House Cemetery** on the rising ground above the little **Bellewaerdbeek** at **St Jan** (St Jean). The village was the site of forward dressing stations, all housed in cellars in 1915. By 1917 the village had been completely destroyed.

About ½ km on the left is **Wieltje Farm Cemetery**. Take the right fork shortly after to drive on **Oxford Road**. The **cemetery** of this name is on the right and beyond the lane is the **50th Northumbrian Divisional Memorial**. After the Second World War, an inscription relative to the division's effort in 1939-1945 was added to the column. In the fields behind the memorial, two lines of bunkers and emplacements, some of which are now only barely visible above the ground, mark the line of the **Cambrai redoubt** of 1917.

Returning to the main road, pass under the motorway and take the right-hand road, Roselaarstraat, for **Fortuinehoek**. It leads to Passchendaele and it was built shortly after the war. Soon after the turning on the right (note the bunkers in the fields), is the **grey limestone memorial** to the memory of Lieutenant H. A. Birrell Anthony and the officers and men of the **1st Monmouthshire Regiment** who fell in the Second Battle of Ypres on May 1, 1915. The memorial, set in a small stone-walled enclosure, is cared for by the Commonwealth War Graves Commission.

The 50th Northumbrian Div. Memorial.

However, return to the N313, and turn right along the highway, greatly widened here as it joins the Ypres ring-road. Off to the far side of this highway, from Wieltje village still runs the straight road to **Pilkem Ridge** known as **Admiral's Road**. The name derives from 1915 when an unnamed captain of the 6th Division used to charge up and down it in an armoured car of the Royal Naval Division. Regrettably when the motorway is completed it may be diverted.

A little way along the N313 now is the site of the notorious **Mousetrap Farm**. Originally known as Shelltrap or Death Farm, the present house is nearer to the road. These names were considered too ominous and so the famous name was acquired. It was the headquarters of the 3rd Canadian Brigade during the gas attack and, in the ensuing battle of St Julien, came into the line.

Soon after joining the main road, the little cemetery on the left is **Seaforth Cemetery**. Here lie 101 men of the 2nd Bn. Seaforth Highlanders who were killed near here on April 25-26, 1915. Almost next door is a farm in which is incorporated a large bunker, **Cheddar Villa**. As the cost of demolishing this typical German bunker would have been exorbitant, the farmer has designed his extension around it. It was captured in July 1917, and was utilised first as an aid post and then as a battalion headquarters by 1/4th Oxford and Buckinghamshire Light Infantry. The wide entrance of this bunker was the scene of a disastrous shelling on the night of August 7, 1917 when a platoon of the 1st Bn. Buckinghamshire Battalion was sheltering within it; direct hits killed many and all were wounded. It will be noted that the bunker, although set on the crest of a slope giving a wide field of vision, is also unsheltered.

In the distance to the north-east another bunker comes into view. This formed part of the German second line in front of **Kitcheners Wood** — now an open field — around which there was very heavy fighting in 1915.

After 1 km we come to **St Julien** (St Juliaan). This village was captured by the Germans on April 24, 1915 after the gas attack and the gallant defence by the Canadians. By July 1917, the Germans had completed their lines of concrete blockhouses in the area. The heavy bombardments which preceded the Allied attack, and the thunderstorms of the last few days of the month, turned the area into a sea of stinking, yellowish, slimy mud. These strong points were the only firm places left and the battle was a series of actions from one strong point to another, and it was disastrous in the extremely heavy casualties which it cost. St Julien was finally captured on August 3 by the 39th Division, whose casualties were 145 officers and 3,716 other ranks killed, wounded or missing.

Kerselaar — **Vancouver Corner** — is 1 km further on. This crossroad is dominated by the **Canadian Memorial**, a pillar surmounted by the head and shoulders of a soldier resting on his arms reversed, set amid green lawns, conifer trees and juniper bushes. Originally the trees were clipped close to represent shell tops and the juniper to resemble shell-holes. New trees have replaced the old in recent years. Until about two years ago, the inscription on the pillar misleadingly stated that '2000 fell and here lie buried' when in fact they lie in many cemeteries across the area of the April 1915 gas attack and not within the confines of the memorial park. The memorial faces the notorious **Triangle** of which the old road junction formed part.

The Canadian Memorial at Vancouver Corner. The new plaque was erected in 1986.

THIS·COLUMN·MARKS·THE BATTLEFIELD·WHERE·18,000 CANADIANS·ON·THE·BRITISH LEFT·WITHSTOOD·THE·FIRST GERMAN·GAS·ATTACKS·THE 22-24 APRIL 1915·2,000·FELL AND·LIE·BURIED·NEARBY

A modern mill stands on the site of the Totenmühle, a German observation post.

s'Graventafel New Zealand Memorial on the road to Passchendaele.

In the village church can be seen the 66th Division memorial window.

Turn right. Take either the first or second left turning. The first will, if the left fork is taken, lead past the mill built on the highest point in the sector. The Germans called it the **Totenmühle** — the mill of the dead — for it was one of their observation points constantly under attack. The present mill is a reproduction of the actual mill of 1915 and is often open to the public. From it can be gained a 360-degree view. After the mill, continue to the road junction and turn left. This road is a continuation of the second turning on the left from Vancouver Corner down to the Zonnebeke road. The name of the second corner is **Winnipeg**, a vital strong point in 1915 and 1917.

Travel 2 kms across the now peaceful meadows with small farms scattered beside clumps of trees and the inevitable pond. In 1917 this was completely torn up and many feet deep in Flanders mud. Only duck-board tracks were safe to use from one trench to another as few roads remained. The artillery was bogged down by the sticky, glutinous mud and many trenches were two or more feet deep in the slime. Crossing the region from east to west are the several small rivers or streams which, due to the continuous rain which followed the dry spell of July 1917, flooded the countryside. It did not drain off due to the destruction of the ground by bombardment and entrenching.

The next crossroad, s'Graventafel, is marked by the **New Zealand Memorial** to their dead in the Passchendaele battles. Turn

left before the memorial and cross the area where the New Zealand Expeditionary Force made their stand.

In 3 kms **Passchendaele New British Cemetery** with the new marker recalling the end of the 1918 battles is on the left. At the main road (½ km) go right into **Passchendaele** (Passendale). The village sprawls across the ridge at this point and, even though there has been much building beyond the old boundary of the village, it can be seen just what a valuable position it commands. For over three years the Germans held the ridge until, on November 6, 1917, in the culmination of the Third Ypres, the rubble which had been the village was captured by the Canadian Corps. Behind them were the gentle slopes of the western side of the ridge, a terrible scene of mud and blood, whilst ahead lay the green fields of an almost peaceful country hardly touched by war. In April 1918, following the German Spring Offensive, the Allied Command withdrew from the ridge and the Germans were once more in possession. On October 14, the Belgian Army drove the last of the enemy from the ridge.

In the centre of the village is the church, whose north windows form the **Memorial to the 66th Division**. From the porch it is possible to look down the slope and across the shallow valley to the rise of **Crest Farm** where the **Canadian Memorial** to the capture of Passchendaele Ridge stands. On the wall of the **Stadhuis** are several **memorials** to the **Belgian regiments** which took the village.

Continue along the N303 on the crest of the ridge, now a modern highway, to **Broodseinde**. On the left, a short way out of the village, will be seen a small obelisk set in the beet fields. This is the **Memorial to the 85th Canadian Infantry Battalion**, the Nova Scotia Highlanders who participated in the capture of the ridge in 1917.

The 85th Canadian Infantry Bn. Memorial now stands on the crest of the Ridge.

Modern marker just outside Passchendaele New British Cemetery.

The Canadians crossed the valley — then a treacherous morass — to capture and hold Crest Farm on Passchendaele Ridge.

The Tyne Cot British Cemetery and Memorial. Flanked by over 11,500 head-stones, the original graves cluster below the Cross of Sacrifice.

One of the original bunkers which have been retained within the cemetery.

After 2 kms along the ridge, take the right-hand road, signposted to **Tyne Cot British Military Cemetery and Memorial to the Missing**, noting bunkers behind the houses. Here, within a kilometre of the farthest point in Belgium reached by the British forces, lie the greatest number to be buried in any Commonwealth war cemetery. There are 11,908 graves in this quiet place of beauty. The entrance is a flintstone lych-gate and the view up the gentle slope to the Great Cross and the arc of the Memorial to the Missing, which curves between the two domed pavilions in the background, is a never-to-be-forgotten experience.

Tyne Cot was so named by the men of the 50th Northumbrian Division, who were among the many who fought to capture the complex of bunkers and pillboxes which surrounded the old barn which stood about 50 metres west of the level-crossing on the Passchendaele to Broodseinde road. It was captured by the 2nd Australian Division on October 4, 1917. The five bunkers which formed the redoubt were part of the German Flanders I Line. The largest of the bunkers was then used as a dressing station by the 33rd and 50th Divisions and two Canadian formations, burying their dead around it. The station and the cemetery were in use until the end of March 1918 when, after the Allied withdrawal, the area fell again into enemy hands.

After the war, over 11,500 dead were brought here from the surrounding battle-field; many of the missing listed on the panels of the memorial will be among them. The cemetery was designed by Sir Herbert Baker who wished to create the appearance of a huge English churchyard, and the flint walls and gate were laid out with the walls of the precincts of Winchester College in mind. In May 1922 King George V included a visit to this cemetery in his pilgrimage. It was then in course of construction and, at the King's suggestion, the Great Cross was built above the largest of the remaining blockhouses, leaving a small section exposed to show the concrete. A plaque recalls its capture by the 2nd Australian Division. Thus, this Cross of Sacrifice differs from all others with its pyramid of gleaming white Nimy stone 'pierre romaine de Lens', lifting it above the serried ranks of headstones and the many varieties of flowers, shrubs and trees. From the base of the cross, all the Salient stretching away to the south-west can be seen — a view right to Kemmel and beyond. On a bright, clear, sunny day the cross can be identified from the Dunkerque lighthouse. Tall trees guard the other two blockhouses retained within the cemetery.

Behind the Cross of Sacrifice are the original graves, well over 300 of them, which remain as they were found after the Armistice. Beyond them is the Stone of Remembrance and the terrace, raised up a few steps. At this level the graves are in fan-like sections in front of the flint and Portland stone memorial panels. At intervals the wall is broken by groups of Tuscan pillars behind which open two circular cloisters on either side of a central apse which is the **New Zealand Memorial to their Missing**. From it iron gates open into quiet greenswards shaded by cedars.

There are 34,888 names on the panels of the memorial which covers the period from August 16, 1917 to the end of the war. Six recipients of the Victoria Cross are either buried or listed on the panels. Two of these lie buried close to the site of their heroic action — the spot where they lost their lives. They are Sergeant L. McGee, 40th Bn., AIF, and Captain Jeffries, 34th Bn. AIF.

Return to the main road. Before taking the right turn at the Broodseinde crossroads for Zonnebeke, carry on a short distance in the Beselare direction to the **7th Division Memorial**. One of the earliest monuments to be erected in the Salient, it commemorates the action of the division in the early days of 1914 and in 1917. It stands on a field battery position with views over the ridge to the east, and down the slopes to the west the tower of Zonnebeke church rises between the trees. Sergeant Nick Keating, then a spritely 90-year-old, described to me in August 1982 how his battery suffered its first casualty here in October 1914, when a cow objected to being milked inexpertly by the battery sergeant. He was laid out by a well-delivered kick. At the crossroads a modern **memorial** recalls the French participation in the battles for **Broodseinde Ridge**.

Ex-Sergeant Nick Keating, RA, poses in August 1982 (then aged 90) beside the 7th Division Memorial on the site of his battery position in October 1914.

Left: **A really remarkable sight at the Zonnebeke brickworks quarry where the excavations have sliced through a cross-section of the battlefield and exposed the former trenches** 'end on'. This is the view from the dugout. *Right:* **Below ground, the author steps back in time to where men once rested in what is believed to have been an Australian dugout.**

Turning down the hill (N332) known to the troops as Devil's Hill (one of many) **Zonnebeke** is entered. This large prosperous village was completely destroyed, being the focal point of many actions, and was reduced to an ocean of mud. In the First Battle of Ypres, it was successfully defended when Gheluvelt fell in October 1914, and then it was captured by the Germans in May 1915. It was recaptured by the 3rd British Division in September 1917. Once again, in April 1918, Zonnebeke was overwhelmed in the German advance westward, but in September, when the Second Army began their great push eastward, Zonnebeke was recaptured on the first day, September 28 *(see photographs on page 33).* On the southern wall of the church

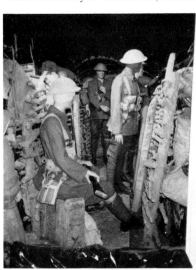

is a small bronze **plaque commemorating D21 Battery, Canadian Field Artillery**, which had a position amid the ruins in 1917.

Beside the church is the arched gateway to the present **Zonnebeke Château**, set in a pleasant park, the **Kasteldomein**. The château houses the excellent **Streekmuseum** where the history of Zonnebeke, Beselare,

Gheluvelt, Passchendaele and Zandvoorde is displayed. Alongside artefacts from ancient times is a detailed display of the events of the war together with relics and the fine collection of maps, photographs, models and explanatory graphs produced for the 1987 exhibition at Passchendaele. The museum is open from May to September. Recently a deep dugout system thought to be of Australian origin has been excavated near the church; hopefully this will be opened to the public in due course.

Continue through the village heading for **Frezenberg**. The road runs down the northern edge of the ridge to which the village gave its name, and which was so vital in 1915 and 1917. The artillery, the 122nd Heavy and the 37th Howitzer Batteries being among those positioned here, stemmed the advance on April 24, 1915. On May 8 the 28th Division was holding the ridge but was forced to withdraw after very heavy bombardments. One battalion, the 1st Suffolk, was almost destroyed, there being only seven men left alive at the end of the day. By July 1917 Frezenberg was a virtual fortress. It was attacked by the 15th Division through the mud and, with the aid of tanks, in particular one called 'Challenger', the village was taken.

However, just before Frezenberg, on the right rises the flourishing Zonnebeke brickworks — **Vanbiervliet Steenbakkerij**. The clay is excavated from a huge quarry at the rear and it is interesting to note in the slope of the walls the layer of blue — London — clay clearly visible some 20 feet down and the variations in colour above caused by trenches and shell holes. In 1984 the diggers found a large dugout close to the rear of the works almost beneath the rail on which the trucks operate. It proved to be an L-shaped complex, possibly a forward post or a field dressing station and is thought to be of Australian origin from the style of work. There was provision for over 120 men with bunks in three tiers and an officer's quarter. The management of the brickworks has thoughtfully preserved it in its entirety, installing electric lighting, a concrete covering and an access path to a solid door to enable visitors to taste the flavour of subterranean life. Much of the rusting wire of the bunks and the debris of occupation has been cleared but there still remains the damp atmosphere, the decaying corrugated iron, the original mud and cement steps, the makeshift wooden ladder and a few remnants of British gasmasks. When I saw it first shortly after discovery, all manner of bits and pieces were strewn around, including a few grenades and ammo, and from up above one of the lintels a petrified rat glared down. Visits can be arranged with permission gained by applying to the office at present

but it is hoped regular viewing hours will be made in the near future. This may be possible after working hours as access is dangerous whilst the trucks and other vehicles are operating.

Crossing the motorway, **Verlorenhoek**, involved in the 1915 and 1917 actions, is reached and in ½ km on the left, set back in the fields is **Aeroplane British Cemetery**, so named from the wreck of a machine close by. The **French National Cemetery of St Charles de Potize** and the mass graves is then on the left. Near the roadside is the **Crucifix and Mourning Women** erected in 1968 as a memorial.

The French National Cemetery at Potize. There are 3,748 graves and also the mass grave at St Charles de Potize.

Incidentally, the road to the right just before the cemetery is **Oxford Road**, leading to Wieltje, whilst the one on the left which we now take is **Cambridge Road**. In ½ km, at the junction of a farm lane on the left, is a lone **cross** — the memorial of Captain Henry L. Skrine, 6th Bn. Somerset Light Infantry, killed here and buried near the site on September 25, 1915. It is also the memorial of his battalion. Up the lane a few yards is another **cross**; this is to the memory of Captain Geoffrey V. S. Bowlby of The Royal Horse Guards killed near here on May 11, 1915. Ahead on the left is **Railway Wood**. The embankment of the old railway from Ypres can be seen to the right; in its banks are still vestiges of dugouts.

In ½ km, at the junction turn right. However, up to the left on the ridge is the lone cross of the **RE Grave**. This unusual memorial marks the grave of one officer and eleven NCOs and men of the 177th Mining Company, RE, who were killed in the mining operations in this area 1915-1917. It can be reached by a track further up the road to the left which leads off into the woods behind Hooge and Bellewaerde. Remains of craters made by the many mines exploded around here can be discerned along the ridge behind the cross. In the Second World War the Germans attempted unsuccessfully to build a V1 site between two of the larger craters.

Our road now dips down to cross the little Bellewaerdebeke, with away to the left the site of **Y Wood** and the trees of Hooge (Hoge). In 1½ km we join the Menin Road at **Birr Crossroads**, so named by the Leinster Regiment in action here in April 1915, and the **British Cemetery** of the same name is on the left. Another ½ km or so, having turned right, we arrive at the most notorious spot in the entire Salient — **Hellfire Corner** — the position on the Menin Road where the Zillebeke-Potize road crosses it and the railway. Almost hidden under the wall of the house on the right is a **British Demarcation**

This is the lonely RE Grave, Railway Wood. Here lie one officer and eleven NCOs and men from the 177th Mining Company, all killed in the area.

Stone marking the limit of the German advance in 1918. Possibly new building here may change its present location.

Turn right, reaching **Potize** (Potyze) in 1½ kms. At the edge of the village on the right

This was once called the hottest spot on earth — Hellfire Corner. Here the Menin Road, the Potize-Zillebeke Road and railway all meet. Nearby is a British Demarcation Stone recording the furthest advance of the Germans in 1918.

Hussar Farm was a British observation post which was fortified by the Royal Monmouthshire Royal Engineers.

Just a few dozen yards apart, the memorials to Captain Skrine (in the foreground) and Captain Bowlby in the distance mark the spots where they fell in 1915. Although both are commemorated as missing on the Menin Gate, could these crosses actually mark their last resting place?

will be seen one of the best preserved British observation posts remaining — **Hussar Farm**. The Royal Monmouthshire Royal Engineers constructed the strong point inside the old farmhouse. Despite four years exposure to enemy bombardment, the OP survived to provide useful storage for the farmer. As a result of various hits, it is possible to see the manner in which the strengthening was carried out, with lengths of railway line reinforcing the brickwork and concrete; even some of the original corrugated iron is in situ still.

Potize village figured significantly in the British lines, being a divisional headquarters. **Potize Château**, also known as the White Château (one of many) was used as an advanced dressing station but it was almost destroyed by shell-fire. Around its site now there are three cemeteries. At the crossroads turn left onto N332-Zonnebekseweg to arrive in Ypres just above the Menin Gate at a very dangerous crossroads. Shortly before reaching them, on the left is the entrance to **Ypres Town Cemetery and Extension**. Here are buried men who died in October 1914, the early months of 1915 and 1918, and today gardeners of the Commonwealth War Graves Commission. The grave of Prince Maurice of Battenberg is here. After the Armistice the Cemetery Extension was enlarged to provide graves for the many isolated and small groups of burials in the area and now some 600 lie here.

The grave of Prince Maurice of Battenberg, killed on October 27, 1914 when serving as a lieutenant with the King's Royal Rifle Corps. Son of Prince and Princess Henry of Battenberg, and a grandson of Queen Victoria, the British members of the family anglicised their name to Mountbatten in 1917.

Château Biebuyck. The modern house marks the site of General Haig's White Château HQ which stood here in 1914.

Zillebeke — totally destroyed but rebuilt in its original style. Some of the earliest British graves lie in its churchyard.

ROUTE III

Proceed through the Menin Gate into Maarschalk Frenchlaan, bearing right at the crossroads into the Menin Road. Soon **Menin Road South Cemetery** will be passed on the right, and just before reaching Hellfire Corner on the left is the site of **White Château** (another of them). General Haig's headquarters during the First Battle of Ypres, Château Biebuyck was in constant use even though badly damaged as the cellars provided shelter. Now the position is occupied by a yellow brick mansion set back amid the trees.

At the crossroads, just 1 km from Ypres, turn right to visit **Zillebeke**. On the crest of the rise to the left is **Perth (China Wall) British Cemetery** where over 2,700 men of the Commonwealth lie, having died in this front line area particularly in 1915, 1917 and 1918. It is not difficult to appreciate the significance of the rise, slight as it may be, as it overlooks such a panorama. Another ½ km down in the valley nestles the village at the eastern end of the lake bearing its name. From October 31, 1914 until September 28, 1918, Zillebeke was either in the front line or very close to it and was completely destroyed. It has been rebuilt on the old foundations, the church almost to the same design. Some of the earliest British burials are in the churchyard, others are in **Tuilleries Cemetery**, a little way before the church on the right. Nearby is the track to Hellblast Corner on the eastern extremity of the lake. Return up the hill to take the first right turn to reach Birr Crossroads in 1 km.

SCALE 1:100 000 1cm–1km

Reproduced from Michelin Sheet No. 51 29th Edition 1989

Turn right onto the Menin Road and in some 200 metres, at the end of the row of houses, turn right into **Canadalaan — Maple Avenue**. This road was built especially to make access easy to the Canadian Memorial on Hill 62 and Sanctuary Wood Cemetery. As it curves towards the woods and hill a magnificent view of Hooge Crater Cemetery can be gained. The gentle rise of the ridge is also very clear. **Sanctuary Wood Cemetery** is on the right in about ¾ km. In this graveyard lies Lieutenant Gilbert Talbot, MC, in whose memory Toc H was named. Here also lies

the German aviator Hans Roser, who was shot down by Major Lanoe G. Hawker, VC. Outside is the private grave of a friend of Lieutenant Talbot, Lieutenant Keith Rae.

A few metres further up Maple Avenue is a café behind which is a **Musée des Tranchées**. Admission fee. The family Schier, who own the café, have preserved this small part of the wood as it was found at the end of the war and it is now the only really authentic sector of trenches remaining in the Salient. The trenches belong to the **Vince Street-Jam Row** system of front and support lines of

Sanctuary Wood Cemetery: this is Gilbert Talbot's grave.

Memorial to Lieutenant Keith Rae, a close friend of Talbot.

The grave of Hans Roser, shot down by Major Hawker, VC.

The author (right) shows ex-Corporal William Holbrook and his daughter around the former battlefield in Sanctuary Wood.

Sanctuary Wood lies behind Hooge Crater Cemetery with its symbolic crater.

1916. Battlefield debris of all kinds are strewn around the copse and the trench lines. In the little indoor museum, to which visitors are shown before walking through the trenches, are on display many items found in the Salient or nearby including two sea mines from the Nieuwpoort area and some early German gravestones.

Sanctuary Wood was so named because in October 1914, when this was a relatively quiet sector, stragglers were gathered together in the wood where they came under the orders of General E. S. Bulfin of the 2nd Infantry Brigade. His instructions were that they were in sanctuary and not to be employed without his permission. By 1915, the wood began to lose its original usage and was soon in the front line or close to it. The 16th Lancers were in action in Shrewsbury Forest in February 1915, as were the Leinsters. After the advance in May 1915, the Germans were in the eastern sectors of the wood and harrassed the British and French encamped on the western edges. June 1916 was the time of a violent German attack which lasted for four days. then came the Canadian counter-attack and assault on Tor Top, Mount Sorrel and ending with the Canadians regaining all the lost ground. The trees were shot to pieces and the ground was often a quagmire. Bunkers and strong points were built (of which a few remain in the private sector of the wood behind the children's playground), and a few shallow subways. or rather covered trenches, were dug to replace those of 1914. Two short lengths of these can be seen in the museum but are only passable during dry weather.

The summit of the slope is crowned with the **Canadian Memorial** commemorating the battles of 1916. Views of the immediate region can be enjoyed from the gardens which surround the memorial. The proximity of Ypres and Hill 60 can be well appreciated and on clear days Mont Kemmel appears very near indeed.

Return to the Menin Road and turn right for **Hooge** (Hoge) ½ km up the slope of the modern highway, once a mere muddy track, shell-torn and dangerous — or dusty and dangerous — but always busy. As we approach Hooge the private chapel of the château looms up on the left opposite **Hooge Crater Cemetery**. **Hooge Château** was a British headquarters in 1914 and from it Sir John French and Sir Douglas Haig watched the 1st Division rally and capture Gheluvelt. The château of the day was a red brick building with a large conservatory set at the end of a straight drive some distance away from the present mansion, its parkland

The Hill 62 Canadian Memorial commemorates the 1916 battles.

extending down to the lake and woodlands of Bellewaerde to the left of the Menin Road. Always under fire, it was captured in May 1915 by the Germans and it was the scene of fierce fighting in June and July and often changed hands. On July 30 the Germans used 'liquid fire' (burning petrol) for the first time and, not long before, the British fired a large mine, one of many to be used in the vicinity during the attacks. One was across the Menin Road and now a stylised crater forms the entrance to the cemetery. This slopes down the valley overlooking Sanctuary Wood. Nearly 6,000 men are buried or commemorated here.

In the grounds of the château are vestiges of two other craters. The late Baron de Vinckt preserved and landscaped these into a beautiful garden. He told me that the site of the old château, of which nothing was left, was marked by two trees which survived and the stump of a third. Since the Baron's death, the modern château has been sold and is now a hotel and the garden has been adapted to include a car park.

East of Hooge the Menin road was heavily fortified; the Germans built a subway beneath it which remains today an obstacle for the modern builders. Almost hidden at the edge of the road near the entrance to

Hooge Château, used by the British in 1914 and Germans in 1915, stood beyond the tree in the centre of the picture. Bellewaerde Lake is in the background.

The King's Royal Rifle Corps Memorial at Hooge.

Captain Brodie's private memorial in Glencorse Wood.

The Princess Patricia Canadian Light Infantry Memorial at Westhoek.

Bellewaerde Safari Park is the **KRRC Memorial** close to the site of their action.

Continue for 1 km up the Menin Road as it curves to the right and climbs upwards; it straddles the location of the **Tank Grave** where in 1917 fourteen tanks sank beneath the glutinous mud as they were disabled in the attack on Polygon Wood. At the crest is the famous **Clapham Junction**, another notorious position, with the woods of **Stirling Castle** on the right. Here also is the obelisk of the **18th Divisional Memorial**, whilst on the left is another, that of the **Gloucestershire Regiment**. Both obelisks mark positions of particular interest to the respective formations. The 18th Division was much involved here in 1917 operations; the 1st Bn. Gloucestershire Regiment participated in the 1914 battles for Gheluvelt and the 2nd Battalion was heavily engaged here in 1915. Stirling Castle was so named by the Argyll and Sutherland Highlanders in 1915 when they had a depot here. Further along the Menin Road we pass the woods of **Château Herentage**; on the right and behind them are those of **Dumbarton Lakes**, both hotly contested. For many years the memorial of the 2nd Bn. Worcestershire Regiment was on the façade of a small villa on the left. It marked their deeds here and at Gheluvelt. Then on the left is **Inverness Copse** with its mine craters, now pretty pools.

At the next crossroads at Veldhoek at the end of the woods, turn left and take the right fork almost immediately. The left fork goes across the eastern flank of the Bellewaerde Ridge and along the southern edges of Glencorse Wood on the left, passing the **site of Fitzclarence Farm** on the right, but it is a difficult, narrow road. The right fork runs through similar pleasant meadowland and beetfields to a road junction where you turn left and straight away right to skirt **Nonneboschen**, now with **Glencorse Wood** beyond it. Much of this region is being developed into a residential area with service roads to the houses in the woods. Both the roads described run into the direct road from Zandberg (just below Clapham Junction) to Polygon Wood. Nonneboschen and Glencorse Woods were the scene of heavy fighting in 1914 and 1917. Here on November 12, 1914 Brigadier Charles Fitzclarence, VC, was killed leading the survivors of the 1st Guards Brigade in the counter-attack on the Prussian Guard. This gallant soldier, after whom Fitzclarence Farm was named, was known to the troops as 'GOC Menin Road'; his name is on the Menin Gate Memorial right at the top of Panel 3.

Cart tracks and paths still pierce the woods

but are not suitable for cars. One path links the two woods and, after leaving the shelter of the southern fringe of Nonneboschen, gains the northern flank of Glencorse Wood on its right with the soft curves of the Bellewaerde Ridge in view. In this quiet, peaceful area, once the scene of hectic activity and devastation, is the lone **memorial to Captain Ewen J. Brodie** of the 1st Bn. Cameron Highlanders who was killed in Glencorse Wood on November 11. 1914.

Clapham Junction with the twin obelisks of the 18th Division and Gloucestershire Regiment Memorials.

In 1 km (with the motorway running parallel on the right) turn left into **Westhoek**, crossing the **Bellewaerde Ridge** and part of **Frezenberg Ridge**, scene of fierce fighting in 1915 and again in 1917. Here the trenches were obliterated by withering artillery fire, leaving a shell-pocked desert. Among the regiments which stubbornly defended this region was the famous Canadian unit — the **Princess Patricia's Canadian Light Infantry**.

At the road junction in the village turn right on to Grotemolenstraat and in ½ km left on to Patriciaslaan. A ½ km down this narrow lane on the left stands the unusual **memorial to the PPCLI** — a maple tree encircled by a stone seat. It was dedicated and unveiled in 1958.

Return to Westhoek and turn left in the village to cross the motorway and then turn right to approach **Polygon Wood** with **Black Watch Corner** on the south side of the motorway near a cluster of cottages close to the bridge bearing the road from Veldhoek. This was the site of the great fight of the Royal Highland Regiment and the Cameron Highlanders with the Prussian Guard in November 1914. Turn left into a long, straight, narrow road which clings to the edge of the famous wood. Before 1914, the Ypres Military Riding School — the Polygon — was situated here and also the Belgian Army's old firing range which ceased to be used in 1870. The old butts, a large mound on the north-east side of the wood, still remain.

In October 1914, the wood, as it lay in the front line, was the scene of very heavy fighting and was attacked by the Prussian Guard. On October 24, 1914, the Northum-

Polygon Wood. The Australian Memorial and New Buttes cemetery.

Left: **Gheluvelt Château, the Worcesters' battleground in October 1914.** *Right:* **Memorials beside the reproduction of the old mill.**

berland Hussars were in action here, the first Territorial unit to be engaged. Despite terrible casualties, the British held on and retained the area until May 3, 1915 when, in the wake of the gas attack, the Germans overran it. On September 27, 1917, the Australians retook the wood and the memorial obelisk of the 5th Australian Division now crowns the Butte.

In about ½ km along the edge of the wood, now a leisure park, will be seen the entrance to **Polygon Wood Cemetery** on the left and, on the right, the glade leading to the **Buttes New British Cemetery** and the **New Zealand Memorial to the Missing** and the **5th Australian Division Memorial**.

In the wood are the remains of several concrete shelters built by both sides during its occupation. The type of ground here made trenches difficult to dig and maintain and, by 1918, when the Australians evacuated it during the spring advance, only a few shattered tree trunks were left from the pulverising fire which had rained down on it. The bunkers were the only cover remaining.

Continue round the edge of the wood into open country, keeping to the right into **Reutel** (1 km), and take the left turn to **Beselare**, joining the N303, and turn right again for Gheluvelt (Geluveld). **Polderhoek Ridge** (Poezelhoek) rises to the right off this road. The **château** was razed to the ground in 1917 having served both armies as headquarters. Now the whole region has been altered by the access roads for the autoroute. Just before the road rises to cross the autoroute (Nieuwe Kruiseke), take the small road to the right signposted Geluveld to reach the village in 1 km along the edge of the château park. This road formed part of the route of 1st Division in 1914.

As **Gheluvelt** is approached, the **old windmill** can be seen on the left. A reproduction of the original, and itself in much need of repair, it shelters the **Memorial of the South Wales Borderers**. Here also is the **2nd Bn. Worcestershire Regiment Memorial** removed from the Menin Road. The entrance to the château is just to the right behind the church

beyond the small village square. Here the 2nd Bn. Worcester Regiment counter-attacked after the 2nd Bn. Welsh Regiment in front of the village and the 1st Bn. South Wales Borderers were driven out of their trenches and forced to withdraw into the château grounds. In the counter-attack, the 2nd Worcesters penetrated the captured village, driving the Bavarians before them and at the same time rescuing the South Wales Borderers in the park. The gallant actions of these men on October 31 stemmed the advance and barred the road to the west. Although the village was finally taken by the Germans, the stand of the division enabled the British line to be withdrawn without interference. The Worcesters' counter-attack from the château grounds was inspired by Brigadier-General FitzClarence. The château was hardly damaged during the war, even in the action recapturing the ruined village on September 28, 1918, and it is one of the few large mansions in the Salient which looks much as it did in 1914. It is now municipally owned and on occasion is open to the public. The interior is very gracious and beautiful, providing an elegant background to official events.

Continue to the crossroads with the Menin Road (a dangerous place still) and go straight over to descend the ridge to **Zandvoorde** (2½ kms). The importance of Gheluvelt, as it strides the main road at the highest point of the ridge, can be appreciated well from here. Zandvoorde, on a hill, commanded a vital crossroads in 1914. The slope up from Zillebeke was the site of the charge by the Household Cavalry on October 26, 1914. During the next few days, other squadrons of the Household Brigade manned trenches in the village and the outskirts despite massive artillery fire which plastered the slopes. When the German XV Corps took the village they found two complete British cavalry squadrons with their machine guns, dead or dying in one meadow. On the

eastern edge of the village (at the back of a garden on the right of the Ten Brielen road) is the tall column of the **Household Brigade Memorial** erected on the site of the place where Lord Worsley's body was found at the end of the war. This marks the centre of the position held on October 31, 1914.

The Household Brigade Memorial was erected on the spot where Lord Worsley's body had been found.

Some little way down the slope, nestling into the hillside on the right, is the **Ten Brielen** German bunker, for years the only example bearing still the original ground cover. It was built in 1916, and is engraved with the name of the unit and date.

The Ten Brielen bunker at Zandvoorde erected by the 3rd Company, Arm.Bttn. 27. Built in 1916, it was restored in 1988.

Return to Zandvoorde and take the left-hand road for **Hollebeke**. After descending the slope (2 kms) and crossing the Basseville-beek, a small stream, there is a cluster of bunkers on the left and, on the right, the small mound in an orchard near a farm is the site of **Hollebeke Château**. Hollebeke, on the railway line and Ypres—Comines canal, was another of the hotly-contested positions in 1914 and 1917.

At the crossroad before the railway embankment turn right. The road runs parallel to the railway and in the embankment are several **bunkers and concrete shelters**. After crossing the stream again, turn left under the railway. The modern village of Hollebeke is on the left on the Comines road. It was entirely destroyed and, unlike the château, it was rebuilt.

Turn right. Almost immediately on the left is the ruin of **Lock 6 bis** of the old canal. This is also the eastern entrance to the leisure area, **Palingbeek Park**. The woodland beyond the lock stretches away to the west, along the canal and the hills on either side, right through to the site of **The Bluff**. It is possible to walk from Lock 6 bis the length of the canal to Spoilbank, along Kingsway and into Ypres near the station. Little remains to record the many operations which took place

Hollebeke. This is the site of the château which was entirely destroyed by the war and never rebuilt.

The old ruin of Lock 6 bis on the Ypres—Comines Canal, Hollebeke.

These German bunkers and concrete shelters can still be seen today in the railway bank at Hollebeke.

along this part of the canal but towards the western end at the Bluff there are several mine craters, now duck ponds, which recall the protracted mining operations of 1915 and 1916. To reach the main entrance and car park continue up the road, with **Battle Wood** on the right, and take the first road on the left. This comparatively new road, which follows an avenue of trees, terminates in a large car park in the middle of the park. A short distance from the car park is now a modern complex of an information and study centre for the nature reserve and café where once were bunkers and trenches. Nothing remains of the bunker on which the iron railings from the White Château gates were used for reinforcement. In the ravine and along the crests there are some reminders of the war — old brickworks from the canal, mine craters which are now ponds, and broken hillsides. New paths take the visitor through this sanctuary today. Hidden beyond the woods on the southern flank is the **White Château**, for a long time a German base. Although the track remains, there is no public access to the château today and the Dammstrasse can no longer be reached from

the canal and so make connection with the Warneton road. Among the many trenches which crossed and re-crossed the canal be-

tween the car park and the Bluff were the famous **International, Impudence** and **Imperial trenches**.

Remains of a 1915 mine crater on the Bluff. Until recent years, the remains of German bunkers, one reinforced with the old White Château gates, were still visible.

Labels on image:
AUSTRALIAN TUNNELERS' MEMORIAL
1917 CRATER
QVR MEMORIAL
GERMAN BUNKER
1915/16 CRATERS
HILL 60
SITE OF 14th LIGHT DIVISION MEMORIAL
CATERPILLAR CRATER

The famous Hill 60 and the Caterpillar mine crater at Zwarteleen have been preserved more or less as they were left in 1918. Now overgrown, our photograph shows how they appeared from the air in April 1976.

Return to the main road and turn left. Take the next turn to the right. Signpost for Hill 60. On the right, in private grounds, is the **Caterpillar position**. Across the railway and on the right is **Hill 60**.

This hillock was created in the nineteenth century when the railway was built. The low mound formed from the spoil from the cutting, some 230 metres by 190 metres wide, was called 'Lovers' Knoll' or 'Côte des amants'. On top was rich, loamy clay; underneath came seven metres of firm, dry sand separated from the hard, underlying blue clay by a very wet two-metre layer of quicksand. This then was the problem which was to face the infantry, the artillery and, most important, the mining companies of the engineers of the French, British and German armies during four years of bitter fighting.

Early in November 1914, at the end of the battles of First Ypres, the cavalry under General Byng was dug in on the forward slopes, following the famous charge of the Household Cavalry at Zwarteleen on November 6. Then the French XVI Corps relieved the British and the French support troops on the hill until the German 39th Division captured it on December 10. It was then established as a strategic observation post, giving the Germans excellent views over the British lines to Ypres.

In the same month, preparations commenced to regain the summit and Lieutenant Bruyeat was ordered to undermine and blow up the enemy fortifications on the crest. The Royal Monmouthshire Royal Engineers were brought in to assist in the mining which was completed in the spring of 1915.

In February 1915, 28th Division, II Corps, took over the line from the French. The officer in charge, Major D. Norton Griffiths, was one of the most colourful characters of the period, an eccentric but brilliant officer. One of his quirks was to use his own Rolls-Royce, adapted for military purposes, to travel around the battle area. Special mining companies were only then in the process of being formed and when, in April, the 5th Division relieved the 28th, the original mining parties were retained and reinforced by the new 171st Tunnelling Company, RE.

Five chambers were excavated and charged; the northern pair with 2,000lbs of powder each, the central pair with 2,700lbs each, and the southern one with 500lbs of gun cotton. As this last mine was very close to the German workings, it was not fully completed in order to avoid detection by the enemy. The 13th Brigade, who relieved the 15th Brigade on the night of April 16-17, 1915 in the line directly opposite Hill 60, were to carry out the initial attack following the explosion of the mines.

At 7.05 p.m. on April 17, after a very quiet day, the mines were blown in two pairs followed by the single one at ten-second intervals. One hundred and fifty of the enemy and two REs were killed in the explosions. Immediately the first artillery barrage began by the 15th and 27th Field Artillery Brigades and the 9th Heavy Artillery Brigade, with two French and three Belgian batteries supporting them. At the same moment, 'C' Company, 1st Bn. Royal West Kent Regiment, stormed the hill followed by the 1st/2nd Home Counties Field Company, RE, and, with complete surprise, gained the crest of the slope and took the craters. Casualties to the storming party were light as the German garrison was overwhelmed. Another company of the West Kents and two from the 2nd Bn. King's Own Scottish Borderers came up and began to consolidate the position. At this time the 2nd Bn. Duke of Wellington's Regiment was in support near Zillebeke and the 2nd Bn. Yorkshire Light Infantry were in reserve. The machine gun section of the Queen Victoria's Rifles followed the first storming parties onto the crest.

A little after midnight, the KOSB began to relieve the West Kents, but before this task was completed, the Germans launched three counter-attacks. Previously there had been some wild artillery firing but, as these infantry attacks approached the craters in which the defenders were dug in, their fire became more accurate. Each counter-attack was repulsed by the extraordinary fine machine gun and rifle fire.

The remains of a Hill 60 bunker near the rim of a large crater.

The Duke of Wellington's Regiment relieved the West Kents and KOSB at 8.30 a.m. to face heavy shelling and close fighting all day. The attacks by the Germans had won the right-hand sector by the railway cutting, but the tiny salient on the crest remained in British hands. At 6.00 p.m. the Duke of Wellington's, supported by the KOYLI, counter-attacked and won back the whole hill. That night (18-19) the 15th Brigade relieved the 13th Brigade. The 15th Brigade (1st Bn. Norfolk Regiment, 1st Bn. Cheshire Regiment, 1st Bn. Bedfordshire Regiment and 1st Bn. Dorsetshire Regiment) with the 1st Bn. East Surrey Regiment (14th Brigade) was attacked and, with the Bedfordshires, were first in the front line.

On the evening of the 19th, the QVRs (13th Brigade) moved up in close support. It had been a fairly quiet day but on the 20th furious fighting broke out again and continued on the 21st. The 1st Bn. Devonshire Regiment (14th Brigade) relieved the two front line battalions that day. By now the hill was unrecognisable: the top gone in the mine explosion, the trenches had disappeared and the craters were a mass of debris and corpses.

On the 19th, the British accounts claim that the Germans used gas shells in the artillery bombardment although this is not confirmed in the German archives. The German Fourth Army records say it was on April 20 that sixty gas shells were fired at the hill. It is probable that the gas detected on the earlier date came from the cylinders dug into the hill ready for attack but, up to then, unused.

The hill remained in British hands until, on the evening of May 1, a gas attack was launched on the 1st Bn. Dorsetshire Regiment (15th Brigade) and the 1st Bn. Devonshires (14th Brigade) and the 1st Bn. Bedfordshires (15th Brigade). This was the first occasion that a gas attack failed to achieve its object for the British battalions, although suffering heavy casualties, held on.

On May 5, when the Duke of Wellington's (15th Brigade) were again holding the hill, another gas attack was launched. On this occasion, the gas was released on a favourable wind along the British lines. This attack affected a great length of the line and the advancing Germans were able to get a foothold on the lower slope. Before reinforcements could arrive, a second gas attack was mounted, this time on the Bedfordshire and 6th Bn. King's Liverpool Regiments. In the evening, after a further gas attack, the 13th Brigade were ordered in to counter-attack and regain the hill but, although some KOSB did reach the top, they were pushed back by fire from the Caterpillar.

Another attempt to regain the hill was made by the KOYLI on May 7 but it was a failure, all the men taking part being either killed or taken prisoner. The Germans were in full possession of the hill; they fortified it and retained it until June 1917. In the two periods of fighting, and the comparative lull between them, the 5th Division suffered casualties of over 100 officers and 3,000 other ranks.

In the months following the great May battles, the main struggle went on underground. Deep mining began in August 1915 by 175th Tunnelling Company from an entrance in the bank of the railway cutting some 220 yards behind the British front line. It was to pass 90 feet below the surface. In April 1916 the 3rd Canadian Tunnelling Company took over and mines were commenced on the Caterpillar as well. After a long underground struggle between the miners of both sides, the Hill 60 gallery was finished in July 1916 and charged with 53,500lbs of high explosive. In October, the gallery under the Caterpillar was also completed and 70,000lbs of explosive was placed there. In order to achieve this, the German main gallery had to be destroyed by a camouflet.

In November 1916 the 1st Australian Tunnelling Company took over the maintenance of these mines. This entailed fighting above and below ground to keep the enemy from discovering the galleries and charges.

The two mines were to be the most northerly in the long chain of 24 mines which were being prepared for the attack on the Messines Ridge. In the event only 19 were blown. It was at 3.10 a.m. precisely on June 7, 1917 that these exploded with a tremendous shock, similar to that of an earthquake. It was felt even in London and other places in England.

Immediately after the mines had been fired, and almost before the earth ceased to heave, the entire artillery force of the Second Army opened a three-pronged barrage on the German lines. Fifteen minutes later, at Hill 60, the men of the 69th and 70th Brigades, Yorkshire Bns. attacked the hill and gained the feature with few casualties and no trouble.

The craters which were left after the eruption can still be seen today all along the line of the Messines-Wytschaete Ridge — most of these are small ponds now used by farmers. In 1917, the Hill 60 crater was 60 feet deep and 260 feet wide at the rim, and the Caterpillar disappeared into a hole 90 feet deep and 334 feet wide at the brim. The 204th German Division, which held the two positions, lost 10 officers and 677 men killed by the explosions.

Hill 60 can be visited today as it is in the care of the Commonwealth War Graves Commission. The **Memorial to the Queen Victoria's Rifles**, although badly damaged in

Queen Victoria's Rifles Memorial, Hill 60.

the Second World War, has been re-created on its old site despite the loss of the original stone mounting. One concrete bunker showing British as well as the basic German work remains on another high point whilst the remains of other dugouts can still be discerned. There are vestiges of five of the small craters and, although the walls have crumbled and the base filled in, the high crater, usually dry, still dominates the scene.

The following Victoria Crosses were among the many awards for gallantry in the

This bunker on Hill 60 built during the First War also saw service in the Second.

The Memorial to the Australian Tunnelling Company (with bullet marks from the Second World War) and that to the 14th Light Division on the right.

Hill 60 railway cutting with a modern 'Ypres Express' passing the Dump.

Hill 60 operations: Lieutenant G. R. P. Roupell, 1st Bn. East Surrey Regiment, for his magnificent example of courage and devotion on April 20. Private E. Dwyer, 1st Bn. East Surrey Regiment, for gallantry in bombing and assistance under fire to wounded comrades. Second Lieutenant G. H. Woolley. 9th Bn. London Regiment (Queen Victoria's Rifles). He was the first Territorial officer to receive the VC which was awarded for defence on the night of April 20-21 when, for a time, he was the only officer on the hill. Second Lieutenant B. H. Geary, 4th Bn., attached 1st Bn. East Surrey Regiment, for conspicuous bravery and determination on April 20-21.

Immediately over the railway bridge, beside which a small monument recalls the death of two members of the French Resistance here in World War Two, is a small car park. Overlooking this is the **14th Light Division Memorial**, which in September 1978 was moved here from Railway Wood where it had suffered from subsidence and as local needs required the land for development. Alongside is the **1st Australian Tunnelling Company Memorial**. The entrance to the hill, which bears no resemblance to its original shape, is just beyond the enclosure of this shrapnel-pocked memorial. Here too

is a simple stone carved with an eloquent account of the horrific happenings of this historic place.

Paths lead through the shell-pocked ground to the bunker on the crest between the line of small craters and the large one on the right. Remnants of other strong points are scattered over the hillside. Vestiges of dugouts and trenches can be seen in the far bank of the railway, below the Caterpillar and to the west of **the Dump**.

Supplies to the Dump were manhandled to the line from Ypres and 'Ypres Express' was the name given to the trucks on their return journey as the gradient was just sufficient to travel at a greater speed with less effort.

Trench museums, which existed until just after the Second World War, were situated on the left-hand side of the road opposite the Queen Victoria Rifles Memorial. They no longer exist. Over the years their owners changed, as did the layout of the trenches! However, in 1985 the **Menin Road War Museum** moved to the café across the road from the hill. The rooms off the café and upstairs contain some most interesting items, weapons, badges, equipment and battlefield debris; the larger examples are outside by the café parking area, and much came from the old museum at Sanctuary Wood.

Continuing straight on, in ½ km we reach the road junction in **Zwarteleen**. Turn right towards **Kleine Zillebeke**. In ½ km, take a left turn through the woods. **Shrewsbury Forest** contains several bunkers reminiscent of actions fought here in 1917. It is possible the area will become another leisure park, enabling visitors to wander along the glades off which some trenches are visible. **Mount Sorrel, Observatory Ridge** and **Hill 62** rise to the left. Emerging from the trees the road crosses open ground sloping up the Menin Road. This is **Green Jacket Ride**.

A small road is passed on the left and soon after the woods of Mount Sorrel are seen beyond the fields on the same side. In the nearest copse is one of the mine craters. On the right is **Clonmel Copse**. This road was criss-crossed with trenches and was the scene of many actions, particularly those in June 1916, when the Canadian Corps captured Mount Sorrel and Hill 62. Again in the summer of 1917 this area was the focal point of much action. Since the removal of the circlet of tall maples around the Canadian Memorial on Hill 62, a fine view of it can be seen.

Four kms from Kleine Zillebeke and the Menin Road is regained at Clapham junction. Turn left to return to Ypres (6 kms).

A German bunker, one of several in Shrewsbury Forest.

Queen Victoria's Rifles' Hill 60 Museum.

SCALE 1:100 000 1cm—1km

ROUTE IV

Leave Ypres by the Maarschalk Haiglaan, the N8. After 1 km cross the railway. On the right, immediately after this, is **Reigersburg Château**. This Victorian mansion was used as a base right from the early days of the war. The Royal Field Artillery were in occupation in October 1914 and there are still notices on the walls relating to their presence.

Brielen is 2½ kms further on. A small village, it was totally destroyed in the war, mainly by artillery fire as it was a forward base for the troops in action around the Yser Canal. A short way out of the village the long straight drive to **Château de Trois Tours** bears off to the left. This château was utilised as an HQ by the 1st Canadian Division in 1915 and thereafter many divisions and brigades occupied it. By some amazing chance, although the village was destroyed, this house bore a charmed life and was hardly damaged. After the war it became an hotel whose proprietors specialized in Salient tours. The Ypres League and the Anglo-Belgian Union had their headquarters here.

After 1 km **Dawsons Corner** — the name given to the camp here by the Canadian Corps in 1915. Turn right and after 1 km we reach **Solferino Cemetery** on the right. The

An inscription at Reigersburg Château 'RFA', can still be seen at the side of the door to the stables.

French had a dressing station and camp here, later taken over by the BEF. In ½ km crossroads, turn left, then after another 1¾ km crossroad, turn left again. Just before the cross on the right is a **British concrete shelter**. **Bluet Farm Cemetery** is ½ km further on the right. Bluet Farm was a dressing station during the 1917 battles.

In 1½ kms we reach **Elverdinge**. This large village was the centre of many camps, training areas, stores, hospitals and facilities for leisure. It was almost entirely destroyed by artillery fire being a known British base and road junction. The **château** constantly used as an HQ was also damaged and was acciden-

The Reigersburg Château was an early billet of the BEF, and inscriptions can still be seen on the walls relating to its occupation by the Royal Horse Artillery.

tally burnt on one occasion when a cook let some fat catch fire. Later it was rebuilt. A light railway ran from Poperinge carrying casualties and supplies. Near the church is a Belgian Krupp 95mm gun, recently reinstated after conservation.

Leave the village by the Vlamertinge road, leaving the church on the right and drive past the château grounds. An entrance on the right gives a good view of the house set far

52

Above: **The fairy-tale Château de Trois Tours — haven to many divisions.** *Right:* **A bunker crumbles in the grounds.**

back. In 1 km take the right fork crossing the stream and through the meadows and beet fields which once echoed to the noise of camp life.

Another 1 km to road junction, take the right-hand road. The farm at the junction is **Hospital Farm** — the **cemetery** of this name is a little way to the left. It was a dressing station. The next ½ km goes through the site of **Dirty Bucket Camp**, so named after a farm which was near the small road on the left.

After 1 km crossroads, go straight over. **Canada Farm Cemetery** is about 1 km along on the right. There was a dressing station here between June and September 1917.

In ¾ km **Wip crossroads**. Turn left. A **British concrete shelter** is on the right. Another is some way up on the north side of the hamlet. Then 1½ kms across the Poperongevaart and take the right-hand road in the direction of Eikhok.

After a further 3 kms, road junction, turn left. 1½ kms to **International Corner**, a junction of the British and Belgian lines. The name is to be found on the walls of a barn in the farm here. Turn right. At the next road junction — about 1 km — turn right and in a short distance take the left fork; the right passes **Abdij St Sixtus**. This monastery, with its modern brewery producing the famous Trappist beer and its own very special mead, cultivates much of the area around here which was a very large camp. A dressing station and local headquarters were situated in the abbey buildings. (During the Second World War for a short while in 1940 it was the base of General Montgomery.) The Cistercian monks aided the care of casualties brought here in 1915. It was said that a deserter was brought here and tried after the gas attack and shot *(see page 10)*.

In ½ km turn left, still in this very flat low-lying country of meadows, arable land and small woods. Almost immediately turn right to enter **Proven** in 2 kms. This was a large village which was damaged by bombing and long-range artillery fire. It was the centre of many British activities and camps. There was an aerodrome here and a large supply depot which had light railway connections with Dunkerque and Poperinge.

In the centre of the village turn left onto the N308 and in 2 kms turn left for **La Lovie**. Here, in a beautiful park, is the large **château** which from May 1915 was a British HQ of importance. As it was the centre of the training and stores region, the house was well placed. VI Corps were here until February 1916, followed by XIV and VII Corps. Then in February 1916 the Fifth Army arrived and had their HQ in the house until

November 1917. In July 1917 King George V used the house as one of his bases during his visit to the front that month. During 1918 various divisions and corps used its facilities, among them the 41st, 49th and 34th Divisions. August 30 saw II Corps in possession until the end of the operations to clear the Salient commenced when they moved up.

Above: **Elverdinge Château used as a headquarters building.** *Right:* **The 95mm Krupp gun now on display.**

The château was hardly damaged. Today, the house and its surrounding buildings are used as a school and training centre. In the vicinity is the site of **Lovie aerodrome**, used by the scout squadrons in 1918. Return from the park to the right and the back road into Poperinge. In 2 kms Poperinge, and thence 12 kms to Ypres.

Although over 60 years old, this famous painted sign still remains to be seen.

SCALE 1:100 000 1cm–1km

ROUTE V

Depart from Ypres by Rijselstraat and the Lille Gate (Rijselpoort), the N365, perhaps the most frequented route of the war. Due to the exposed position of the Menin Gate exit, most departures for the front were this way.

After ½ km **Shrapnel Corner**, a most unhealthy spot as it was constantly shelled by the German artillery and then by long-range guns in 1918. Before the railway crossing turn to the left.

Then 1 km to **Transport Farm** and **Railway Dugouts Cemetery** on the right. In the embankment behind the cemetery there are still vestiges of the shelters and dugouts. On the left is the drive leading to **Zillebeke Lake** and restaurant. A promenade encircles this artificial lake so well known to the BEF as a prairie of mud and blasted trees. It is the older of the two great ponds (the other is Dikkebus) formed in medieval times to provide for Ypres. In 1295 there was already a fish pond in existence. From 1914 onwards, there were positions all along the banks and many an artillery unit was bogged down in the mud. It was often a target for the German guns and one English gunnery officer found a unique method to keep his men from being hit: take them out into the lake in an old punt he had found and sit there somewhat damp but in moderate safety. Only a few remnants of the shelters which were in the vicinity of the lake now remain on the north banks.

The eastern end of the lake is almost in Zillebeke village and the woods and fields in that area were the scenes of many terrible battles. In October 1914 the Irish Guards fought a lengthy action in holding Zillebeke Wood. Then, in 1915, the Cavalry Corps were in action and in July the 18th Division held the sector whilst the artillery were always there. In April 1918 the British withdrew from Zillebeke, returning in September. **Hellblast Corner** is at the eastern-most end of the lake.

Retrace the way to the road and turn left, crossing the railway. At the next road

junction note the **British Demarcation Stone** on the right. In a short distance the road on the right leads in 2 kms to **Chester Farm** and **Spoilbank Cemeteries** and the western entrance to **Palingbeek Park**. However, by continuing for ½ km or so **Verbrandenmolen** is reached and a very narrow road between the houses on the right leads down to a group of cemeteries on the fringe of **Ravine Wood**. These are **Woods Cemetery**, made originally by the 1st Bn. Dorsetshire Regiment and 1st Bn. East Surrey Regiment in April 1915; then, amid the fields, **1st DCLI (The Bluff) Cemetery**, dating from the same period; and lastly, up a track on the edge of The Bluff, **Hedge Row Trench Cemetery**. Soon afterwards, the road swings round sharply to the right and rejoins the Spoilbank road. Almost beside Spoilbank Cemetery is the section of the old canal known as **Kingsway** to the BEF. Along it are two ruined locks and dugouts. Our road bends slightly round following the 1917 front line.

Another ½ km and we join the N365, turning left for the **St Eloi (St Eloois)** crossroads. Many actions were fought in this

Shrapnel Corner road junction was a regular target for German artillery.

Zillebeke Lake was the scene of bitter fighting. This is Hellblast Corner at the eastern end.

BUS HOUSE CEMETERY

TO YPRES

TO MESSINES

GERMAN DUGOUT

BRITISH DUGOUT

MINE BLOWN 7.6.17

MINE BLOWN 27.3.16

MINE BLOWN 27.3.16

MINE BLOWN 27.3.16

WARNETON

TO HOLLEBEKE

The St Eloi Craters still straddle the old German lines of 1916-17. More than thirty British and German mines were fired in the area, six of the British, totalling 73,000 lbs, being fired together. The largest single mine of 95,600 lbs was blown here on June 7, 1917.

neighbourhood but it is chiefly remembered for the protracted mine warfare which began when the Germans fired their first mine in March 1915. This was part of their counter-attack to earlier British attacks for this position. In the ensuing twelve months, the British fired 13 mines and 29 camouflets and the Germans 20 mines and 2 camouflets. Six of the British mines were fired on March 27, 1916 and consisted of a total of 73,000lbs of charges but, due to the artillery barrages, it was impossible for our troops to consolidate the position and it was retained by the Germans. During the mine explosions heralding the Messines Ridge attack, the largest single charge was 95,600lbs of ammonal blown at St Eloi and this time the position was captured by the 41st Division.

Two of the largest of these craters, now ponds, lie on the left of the Hollebeke road which forks left off the Warneton road; both are private and used for fishing or swimming. The one nearest the road is surrounded by reeds and the other by tall trees and hedges. In the apex of the Messines and Warneton roads is the third crater, but it is not easily visible from the road. On the higher ground behind it is an excellent example of a **British shelter** with a **German concrete dugout** in front of it. The British concrete retains the elephant iron (large corrugated iron) lining to its roof. It can be seen easily from the Messines road.

Above: **A German bunker near the large crater formed on June 7, 1917, and,** *below,* **a British concrete shelter, still retaining the iron lining, built nearby.**

The Dammstrasse — the drive to the Bayershof German HQ on the horizon.

The Oosttaverne crossroads — scene of two 19th Division actions.

Take the N336, the Warneton road. The country now undulates along gentle ridges and the road passes through pleasant meadows. A short distance, about 1 km along on the left, the ridge of the **Damm-strasse** can be discerned. In the field before it is another good British dugout. The Damm-strasse is the old drive to the White Château occupied by the Germans and known to them as the **Bayershof**.

In 2 kms **Oosttaverne crossroads**. Memorial cross of the **19th 'Butterfly' Division** on the left. This marks the site of the division's attack during the Messines battles of July 7, 1917 and later their great fight during the Battle of the Lys in April 1918. **Oostaverne Wood Cemetery** is on the right as the road runs through rolling country to descend into the Lys valley in 2 kms.

After 4 kms cross the new Lys ring-road before entering **Warneton** (Waasten), dominated by its huge church, the cathedral of the Lys. The opening thrusts of the First Battle of Ypres were made here when the 1st and 2nd Cavalry Divisions were driven back towards Messines, attempting to gain the Lys on October 20, 1914. Warneton remained in German hands until September 1918 and was one of their most important forward bases. The Belgian frontier station is on the north end of the bridge. Turn right in the centre of the town for Ploegsteert and, in about 3 kms at Basseville, take the right fork and cross the railway and the ring-road.

In 4 kms we then reach **Le Gheer**, a hamlet on the eastern edge of Ploegsteert Wood. A kilometre up the road on the right at the crossroad of Le Pelegrin, one of the mines laid in 1917 exploded in July 1955 when a willow tree was hit by lightning during a severe thunderstorm. Fortunately there were no casualties. Le Gheer was the scene of much activity in 1914 when the 4th Division carried out a brilliant counter-attack before withdrawing.

Ploegsteert Wood — **Plugstreet Wood** to the British Army — Ploegsteertbos in Flemish, and now Bois de la Hutte et du Gheer, is again a pleasant forest and game reserve to which access can be had in a number of locations denoted by large notice boards bearing a map of the woods and the tracks to which access is permitted. The main entry used to be from Prowse Point Farm Cemetery in the north and Hunters Avenue in the south about 1 km from Le Gheer. Here is the verderer's house but the avenue is no longer a right of way or marked on the map. The nearest official entry is from a new road about ½ km further west. As the wood is a game reserve there are times when access is forbidden, particularly in the spring when the birds are nesting; and in the autumn, when the guns are out. It would be highly dangerous to venture into the woods without the gamekeeper's knowledge.

For the greater part of the war the wood was a relatively quiet area which every now and then burst into violence. In October 1914 the British Cavalry Division captured it, but later it was partially retaken by the Germans who were not finally dislodged until mid-1917. Although the lines had been fortified on April 10-11, 1918, in the big advance the Germans captured it completely. The British recaptured it in their advance in September. For four years it provided comparative shelter to some one million men in its labyrinth of glades and connecting trenches. Among those who squelched in the mud here was Bruce Bairnsfather, who at one time had a billet in a cottage in St Yvon.

Hunters Avenue was one of the main arteries and almost at the edge of the woods there, hidden in the undergrowth, is the first of a line of eight concrete machine gun shelters which are visible through the trees. Nowadays they provide excellent cover for the breeding birds. The most famous bunker in the wood, **Blighty Hall**, or Hole, is not easily reached, being on a muddy footpath which runs off the glade some hundreds of metres along it. A first aid post shelter, it retains the bench for stretchers but is nearly always flooded or very damp and muddy. If permission has been given, it is possible to get to two of the British cemeteries from Hunters Avenue — **Rifle House** and **Ploeg-steert Wood**. They are two of the most beautiful in the Salient (strictly speaking they are beyond the southern limit of it). The former takes its name from the small fortified building whose remains are nearby. Some of the trees here are those which survived the holocaust.

Continuing westward towards Ploegsteert village along the southern flank of the wood, to the left, amid the fields, clusters of farm buildings can be seen. One of these is **Lawrence Farm**, painted by Winston Churchill when serving with the 6th Bn. Royal Scots Fusiliers. **Lancashire Farm Cemetery** is on the left near the site of **East Lancashire Cottage**, one of 29th Division's positions when they cleared Ploegsteert of the Germans in September 1918. **Hampshire Farm** is in the fields to the right before the ever growing outskirts of the village are reached and the road to the parking area for the wood.

Ploegsteert was badly damaged during the war, being so close to the front line for so long. Behind the church in the village grave-yard are a few early graves, several being Hampshire Regiment casualties of 1914. Turn right at the crossroads and travel along the long straight road to **Hyde Park Corner**. On the right is **Strand Cemetery**, named after a glade which emerges from the wood beside it. Between two houses near the cemetery three British bunkers can be found in good repair.

The site of the mine explosion near Le Pelegrin. Laid in 1917, it exploded in 1955!

Left: **Hunters Avenue as it was in 1917. (IWM)** *Above:* **Seventy-five years of growth have transformed the scene entirely — this is Hunters Avenue today.**

Ploegstreet Wood, which was quickly dubbed 'Plugstreet Wood' by the Tommies, still displays the relics of both sides.

Above left: **A British bunker, and** *above right*, **a German machine gun post mouldering in Plugstreet Wood today.**

Blighty Hall (some say Blighty Hole) — a British first aid post in Plugstreet Wood — still retains the bench for the stretchers.

Deep in the wood is Rifle House Cemetery which took its name from a small building, the ruins of which still stand nearby.

After 1½ kms, Hyde Park Corner is reached. On the left stands the **Ploegsteert Memorial to the Missing** and **Berks Corner Cemetery Extension**. On the right is the original cemetery. The memorial, unique in the Salient, is a circular temple with pillars guarded by two lions, one snarling in defiance whilst the other gazes serenely into the distance. The memorial was designed by H. Charlton Bradshaw, and the sculptor was Sir Gilbert Ledward. The missing from the battles of Armentières, Aubers Ridge 1914, Loos, Fromelles 1915, Estaires 1916, Hazebrouck, Scherpenberg, and Outtersteene Ridge 1918, in all 11,447 men, are listed on the panels within the colonnade. Seventy feet in diameter and 38½ feet high, it was unveiled on June 7, 1931 by the Duke of Brabant. Over 380 men lie in the cemetery beneath the flowering cherries.

The N365 begins to climb up towards **Château de la Hutte** and the highpoint, **Hill 63**, on which was a vital 'O-Pip' defended by the 25th Division in April 1918. The château, now only a few crumbling ruins which lessen as the years pass, is in the fields on the left. Often the road surface is subject to subsidence due to the presence below of crumbling subways running into the hillside.

On the crest of the hill the right turn at the crossroads leads to St Yvon and **Prowse Point Cemetery**. This is some 400 metres from the road junction and is the only one in the area to be named after an individual, and marks the site of a gallant stand by the Hampshire Regiment and the Somerset Light Infantry in the actions for St Yvon in October 1914 at which Major, later Brigadier-General, C. B. Prowse, DSO, was the hero. Later, in the Wieltje sector near St Jean, his brigade was in violent action again and the farm was called **Prowse Farm**. It was in the field behind the **50th Northumbrian Division Memorial**, but today only a portion of the cellars remain and a large water-filled shellhole *(see page 39)*.

In November 1914, the northern edge of the wood was in the sector of the 2nd Bn. Dublin Fusiliers and the 1st Bn. Warwickshire Regiment, many of whose casualties lie in the cemetery. Beside the Cross of Sacrifice the hollow, often a pool, is part of the old front line. Nearby the roof of a concrete shelter can be seen in the grass.

The official access to the Ploegsteert Wood group of cemeteries is down the often very muddy lane beside the cemetery. The first is **Mud Corner**, then in the wood lies **Toronto Farm Cemetery**, which, despite the name, contains only Australians, whilst the former is mostly of New Zealanders. Rifle House and Ploegsteert Wood Cemeteries are found by following the main track through the wood for some 500 metres or more.

By continuing along the road, turning right at the junction, in 1½ kms a circuit of the wood can be made. This is one of the sectors involved in the 'Christmas Truce' of 1914.

British Lions guard the Ploegsteert Memorial to the Missing and Berks Corner Cemetery Extension at Hyde Park Corner.

A comparison between the original and current CWGC signposts.

Peaceful reflections at Prowse Point Cemetery, named after Brigadier-General C. B. Prowse. Ploegsteert Wood is in the background.

The Messines Ridge from Kruistraat road with a British bunker in the foreground.

Return to the N365 and continue northward, with the panorama of the **Messines Ridge** ahead. The road descends into the valley of the River Douve before climbing up the ridge.

Messines (Mesen) was taken by the Wurttemburgers from the exhausted Cavalry Corps on November 1, 1914, the latter having held them at bay for over 48 hours after weeks of continuous fighting. The London Scottish made a gallant but fruitless charge in their support only a matter of hours after arriving in the Salient, being the first TA infantry unit to go into action. Their memorial marks the site on the northern slope before the town. From its ruins the Germans dominated the British lines until June 1917.

As early as August 1915, the first plans for the mining of the Messines-Wytschaete Ridge were made, and for 18 months work was under way in the tunnelling and laying of charges in a number of sites on an arc from Hill 60 to east of Ploegsteert Wood. During this time, the enemy blew a number of mines and camouflets, thereby interrupting the work of the British companies, but all the difficulties were overcome and finally all was ready for the big 'blow'. This was to precede the artillery barrage by a fraction and then the main attack by General Plumer's II Corps was to follow. The Inspector of Mines watched the explosion from a dugout at Kemmel and he described the scene in his diary as the 19 mines, containing nearly 1,000,000 lbs of high explosive, erupted on June 7, 1917:

'3.10 a.m. A violent earth tremor, then a gorgeous sheet of flame from Spanbroekmolen, and at the same moment every gun opened fire. At short intervals

of seconds the mines continued to explode; period which elapsed between first and last mine, about 30 seconds. I found it difficult to concentrate on looking for the mines, there was so much going on, and the scene, which baffles description, developed so quickly that my attention was distracted. . . . The earth shake was remarkable, and was felt as far as Cassel.'

The New Zealand Division captured Messines and the 16th and 36th Irish Divisions captured Wytschaete. By June 10 the German salient west of Messines and Wytschaete had been straightened south from the east of Hill 60.

In 1918 Messines changed hands several times before it was finally captured on September 29 by the 30th, 31st and 34th Divisions clearing the entire ridge.

Messines Church can be seen from far and wide and from it there is an expansive panorama to the south. The only church in the area with a crypt, this was all that was left of the building and in it today can be seen vestiges of the battle. The church was also the subject of a number of water-colour drawings by a German infantryman, one Adolf Hitler.

As our road runs into the village there is a sharp left-hand turning, along which is the **New Zealand Memorial Park**. In the park a white **monument** (similar in design to that at s'Graventafel) rises between the evergreen trees and shrubs. At the edge of the park, overlooking the Douve valley and the hills of Flanders, are **two German pillboxes** — part of the Messines line of defence. It is normally possible to enter one of them, but often the other is full of water.

Messines church, showing the windows of the crypt which was at one time a billet for Corporal Adolf Hitler.

The **Hôtel de Ville of Messines** is in a red brick house overlooking the wide square with its English-looking bandstand on the right of the main road to Ypres. In the Hôtel de Ville is a small but excellent **war museum** which commemorates the actions of the New Zealanders in particular, but also those of the Australians and London Scottish. It was

Left: **The New Zealand Battle Memorial for 1917 on the Messines Ridge which was captured on September 29, 1918,** by the 30th, 31st and 34th Divisions. *Right:* **One of a pair of German bunkers in the New Zealand Memorial Park.**

The London Scottish Memorial, Wytschaete Road, Messines.

Four Huns Dugout on 'Whitesheet' Road.

the work of the then-Mayor, the late Dr. Lambelin, OBE, the Town Clerk and the local schoolmaster, M. Constandt. It is usually open during office hours in the summer. A short distance north on the Ypres road, on the right-hand side, is a **Memorial to the London Scottish** and a little further on **Four Huns Dugout** bunker on the left.

Take the Wulvergem road to the left on leaving Messines and, just before the road drops down into the valley, the **Messines Ridge British Cemetery** and the **New Zealand Memorial to the Missing** is on the left. The New Zealand memorial is a Cross of Sacrifice and around the base the panels bear the names of all those with no known grave from every regiment and corps of the New Zealand Expeditionary Force. In the cemetery is a pavilion similar to the New Zealand memorial at Polygon Wood.

After 4 kms, **Wulvergem** is reached after sweeping down the valley and over the **Kraaienberg** and then down again. The village was close to the front line in 1914 and was on the receiving end of a gas attack in 1916. In 1918 it was taken in the German spring advance but recaptured in September.

The Dranoutre road rises out of the Douve valley and along the undulating slopes of the **Monts des Flandres**, crossing the road direct to Kemmel (2 kms from Wulvergem). After another 2 kms, turn right on to a smaller road to begin the climb up to the western slope of **Mount Kemmel**.

In 1 km crossroad, continue straight ahead when in 1 km the road forks. Take the right fork and then, almost immediately at the crossroad, take the right-hand turn to climb steeply up to the summit of Kemmel, passing the **French Ossuary** on the right just prior to the final steep 50 metres. The mass grave, with the Gallic cock crowing above, is the last resting place of 5,294 unknown French soldiers.

At the summit of Mount Kemmel is the **French Memorial**. This site, 159 metres high, was chosen for the monument to the Frenchmen who died in Belgium, particularly on the Mount in 1918.

The column is 18 metres high and was originally capped with a stone representation of a poilu's helmet crowned with laurel. In the front of the column is a Winged Victory. The memorial was unveiled in September 1932 by Général Petin. During a thunderstorm a few years ago, the pillar was hit by lightning and damaged. When it was re-erected the helmet was not replaced. The memorial stands in a clearing on the thickly wooded summit. As we drive on we pass the entrance to the **Belvedere Hôtel**, the Hostellerie Mont Kemmel, from where there is a magnificent view across to Neuve Eglise and the Douve valley.

Emerging from the trees into the open, the **Café Belvedere** is found on the right. This has been rebuilt on the site of the original one

The New Zealand Memorial to the Missing and the Messines Ridge British Cemetery.

The French Ossuary on the slopes of Mount Kemmel.

The French Memorial unveiled by Général Petin on the crest of the Mount.

60

which was destroyed in the battles of 1918. On April 25 the French division then holding the line was dislodged by a strong German force using air support. From the **look-out tower**, one can see the same view as was had by Sir John French and other senior officers of the British Army during their long occupation. The hill remained in German hands, a constant and dire threat to Allied communications, until the end of August and the advance of the American 27th Division; on August 31 the British 34th Division finally drove the Germans from it. On the walls of the café are some interesting illustrations of before and after the battles.

The road descends steeply for another 500 metres when it comes to a junction where we turn left. The descent is less steep but goes on for a kilometre into the village of **Kemmel**, passing the entrance to **Warande Château**. On the village green will be seen another **bandstand**. Here the military bands of the British Army, including the Brigade of Guards, played to the troops during lulls in the fighting in this area.

The **Kemmel information office** is on the right just before the road junction where we turn right and continue straight over the next crossroads (a dangerous one).

In 2 kms pass through **Vroilanhoek**. Take the second road on the right to reach the largest of the 1917 mine craters. **Spanbroekmolen**, now the **Pool of Peace**, the property of Toc H. In 1930, Lord Wakefield purchased this, the **Lone Tree Crater**, at the suggestion of Tubby Clayton who thought that one of the huge craters should be preserved. The pool has a rim some 4 metres deep; it is 27 metres in depth, with a diameter of 129 metres. The charge used was 91,000lbs of ammonal which had been laid through a tunnel 513 metres long. On the northern side of the lip is the remains of one of the German pillboxes and from here one can get a good idea of its importance and wide field of fire.

Continue along by the farm on the right behind which is **Lone Tree Cemetery** where lie the men of the Royal Irish Rifles killed in the mine explosion, having left their trench too early. Groups of tall trees come into view ahead and at **Kruistraat** crossroad it will become evident they border three mine craters. Turn left and left again to pass the lane to **Spanbroekmolen Cemetery**. Just out

Belvedere Café , Mount Kemmel, is on the site of the original building destroyed in 1918. It provided a perfect observation post for Sir John French.

Kemmel village green was the location of many British Army band concerts.

Kruistraat's two craters provide excellent fishing today.

Spanbroekmolen, the Pool of Peace. This was the Lone Tree Crater of June 1917 purchased in 1930 for preservation by Toc H.

61

Peckham Crater, Wytschaete Ridge — from here King George V viewed the battlefront in July 1917. (IWM)

As near as can be ascertained, this is the same spot today. The late Dr Caenepeel stood in for King George in 1975.

of view as the road regains the main road for Wytschaete, the smaller crater of the **Peckham mine crater** is on the right. This is the one visited by King George V in July 1917.

Turn right for Wytschaete and after ½ km, on the left is the site of **Maedelstede Farm** and another large crater.

Wytschaete (Wijtschate) is entered 1 km further on with the **16th Irish Division Memorial Cross** on the left just before the cemetery. 'Whitesheet' to the Tommies is on a high ridge, even higher than that of Messines in places. In 1914 the village changed hands at least three times before the Germans captured it and began to convert it into a formidable fortress. In the II Corps attack of June 1917, the 16th and 36th Divisions captured the ruins. Among the casualties was Major William Redmond who was mortally wounded and taken to the divisional dressing station at Dranoutre and then to 36th Division Dressing Station nearby, where he died. His body was then taken to the hospice, which was the base of 16th Irish Division, and he was buried in the garden. Now his grave is beyond the walls of the convent, just outside the Locre military cemetery. Wytschaete was lost again in the spring advance of 1918, being recaptured on September 28.

Turn left in the centre of the village, leaving the church on the right, and in 1½ kms across the ridge at the fork in the road; take the right-hand route to pass beside **Grand Bois** and then on the right is **Bois 40** or **Croonart Wood** to the Germans. Once behind the café here was a trench museum including two of the German bunkers of this vital position, renovated trenches and narrow-gauge railway. Since the death of the proprietor it has become derelict and overgrown. Adolf Hitler reportedly served here in 1917 and revisited it on his tour of Flanders in 1940.

Crossing the Bollartbeek at the bottom of the slope, and keeping to the right at the next fork, in about 3 kms **Voormezele** is reached. This village was just behind the British line at St Eloi and was captured after very heavy fighting in April 1918. The ruins were recaptured by the American 30th Division on August 31.

At the road junction turn right, and after 1 km **Bus House Cemetery** is passed on the right. It was named after an estaminet, originally on the same side of the road, but which was later moved to the north side. The café had got its name from an old London omnibus of the 'B' type which had broken down in no man's land after bringing troops to the front in 1914. Legend has it that it was one of those used by the London Scottish.

In 250 metres we reach **St Eloi** (St Eloois). Turn left and after 1 km cross the **old canal** at

The edge of one of the Maedelstede Farm craters.

The 16th Irish Division Memorial above Wytschaete village — 'Whitesheet' to the Tommies.

The grave of Major W. Redmond just outside Locre Hospice Cemetery. He died in the convent nearby.

A group of British concrete shelters on the site of Langhof Château.

The ruins of Rosendal Château in the grounds of Bedford House Cemetery.

the western end of **Kingsway**. A **Demarcation Stone**, with a British tin hat capstone will be seen on the left.

A few metres further up on the right is **Langhof Farm** with its fine cluster of British dugouts on the island site of the old château.

Access to these dugouts is only with the farmer's permission as they are used for his cattle.

Two hundred metres further on is **Bedford House Cemetery**. It is one of the largest in the Salient and has plots of 1939-45 graves as

well as 1914-18. The ruins of the old **Rosendal Château** and its moats remain as integral parts of the cemetery. The drive is, in fact, in the same place.

Ypres is another 3 kms; we enter by the Lille Gate.

The road south

From Ypres to the French frontier at Le Bizet. The direct route is via the N365 and Messines, a distance of 19 kms. Via Neuve Eglise it is 21 kms.

Depart Ypres via Lille Gate; at **Shrapnel Corner** take the right fork immediately before the level crossing. Another level crossing is found directly after turning. **Ypres military barracks** are on the left — note the artillery pieces in grounds. Cross the dry canal in whose banks are remnants of trenchworks. The road travels through pretty country, at first quite flat but gradually, as Kemmel is approached, the landscape becomes more hilly as the Monts de Flandres are traversed.

Elzenwalle Château, an HQ in both wars.

After the crossroads of Kruistraathoek (4 kms), on the right **Elzenwalle Château**, an unusual construction of reinforced concrete with an open-ribbed dome. The lodge house is in the form of a concrete bunker, not unlike that of the Krönprinz in the Verdun area. Behind the château is **Scottish Wood** and beyond that lies **Dickebush Lake** (Dikkebus). As the road rises to Vierstraat crossroads, another well-known copse comes into view, again on the right — **Ridge Wood**.

Shortly, on the left, is the **American Memorial to the 27th and 30th Divisions** who fought with the British Army in this region in 1918. The memorial was erected in 1930. There are fine views of the Wytschaete Ridge and the wooded slopes. This section of the road was known as **York Road** and was much used for bringing up supplies. Another

Wytschaete church crowns the ridge as seen from the American Memorial.

ROUTE CONTINUED ON MAP ON PAGE 68

SCALE 1:200 000 1cm=2km

The Memorial to the US 27th and 30th Divisions near Wytschaete. Both fought with the British Army in this area in 1918.

lie buried with the names of 1,299 Australians recorded on the **Memorial to the Missing** on the panels between the shelters. This is one of the very few **British mass burial plots**.

Continue along the narrow road bearing left at the fork to reach **Fromelles** across the flat low-lying fields. Join D141 and turn right; in 2½ kms **Aubers** is passed through with its **ridge** away to the left. Go right on D41 for **Fauquissart**; the **Bois de Biez** is on the right. Thus the southern boundary of the battle area is crossed. Rejoin D171 and turn left. South of Petillon the road follows closely the 1914-1915 front line and nearby some of the incidents of the 1914 Christmas Truce took place. The area was strongly contested but there is little remaining today to indicate the destruction and devastation which the countryside suffered other than the scattered fragments of bunkers. **Mauquissart**, yet another front line village, is to the east of the road as we approach **Neuve Chapelle** in 3 kms. This was the scene of the first major operation involving the Indian Corps when on October 27, 1914 this formation was responsible for retaking the village

6 km further on the edge of Kemmel is reached; we continue straight on up to reach the next crossroad, **Lindenhoek**.

In 4 kms we reach **Neuve Eglise (Nieuwkerke)**. This village, a junction of many roads, was the scene of fierce fighting in April 1918 when it changed hands several times being defended by an exhausted 25th Division who were finally driven out on April 14. The British recaptured it on September 1.

Turn right into the village and, in the centre, left by the church and small **British cemetery**. The road soon begins to drop down into the Armentières-Bailleul plain with views of the Rodeberg, Mont Noir and Mont de Cats over to the right. Straight over the next crossroad. At the road junction 3 kms further on turn left for **Ploegsteert** which is 2 kms down the road. At the main crossroad in Ploegsteert turn right. The frontier station at **Le Bizet** is 2½ kms away.

Proceed into **Armentières** by the new road, D22a, sweeping behind the old road and through new residential areas. At the junction with D33, turn left into **Place Général de Gaulle** with the gothic-style town hall and **war memorial** on the left.

Armentières was, and is now again, a flourishing industrial town whose industries

are centered around both brewing and linen manufacture. In 1914, the town was briefly occupied by the Germans before being recaptured by General Pulteney's III Corps on October 17. For the next three and a half years, being just behind the lines, it became closely connected with the British Army for whom it was a forward base and recreation centre. Although it was intermittently bombed and shelled during these years, it was barely damaged. In the Battle of the Lys in April 1918, the German Fourth Army attacked and seized the town on the 10th after severe fighting. General Plumer's Second Army liberated the town on October 2. By then it was a heap of ruins for the Germans had mined or destroyed all the main buildings and wrecked the factories before leaving. During the British occupation, the main square was called **Eleven O'clock Square**, as the hands of the Hôtel de Ville clock had stopped at this time during an early bombardment.

Leave Armentières via the rue de Lille and then the rue de Béthune, the D22, crossing the railway by the level crossing west of the station. Shortly afterwards the motorway is crossed by a bridge. Continue on the D22 bis 5 kms to **Fleurbaix**. The road passes through rather nondescript country — the scene of bitter fighting in 1916 and 1918. Continue on the D171 for 3 kms to **Petillon** crossroads passing **Rue de Bois Cemetery**. Here a diversion along the road to the left D175/22c leads in 1 km to **VC Corner Australian Memorial and Cemetery, Fromelles**. This is a very unusual graveyard as it has no headstones. The dead were brought here after the Armistice from the surrounding battle zone. On July 19, 1916, the 5th Australian Division with the 61st South Midland Division attacked the Fromelles positions. Over 400

The graceful Indian Memorial at La Bombe crossroads, Neuve Chapelle.

which had been captured earlier in the German advance. Later the Allies withdrew and, on March 10, 1915, the Battle of Neuve Chapelle commenced with the Indian Meerut Division taking a major rôle in the attack and capture of the village by the 8th Division. Due to the inadequate preliminary bombardment, much of the barbed wire entanglements in front of the German positions remained uncut and caused heavy casualties, especially to the Middlesex Regiment and the Cameronians. By March 14 the

Neuve Eglise from the Kemmel road.

Armentières Grand Place. Today the Belfry clock keeps good time!

VC Corner, Fromelles. Individuality is a cornerstone of British and Commonwealth principles in honouring war dead and this mass grave situated in the Australian Memorial Cemetery is very unusual. The names of each are inscribed in stone.

front had moved forward just over 2 kms before it stabilised. In the Lys battles of 1918, the Portuguese Division held the ruins of the village.

Another 1 km and we reach the crossroads of **La Bombe**, the **site of the Port Arthur Salient** of the Indian Corps in 1915, commemorated in the **café sign** on the right. On the opposite corner is the fine **Indian Memorial to the Missing**. Designed by Sir Herbert Baker in completely oriental style, 4,843 names are inscribed on the walls. A few yards down the D947 is the **Portuguese Military Cemetery** with its fine Manueline gateway.

This road is the direct approach to **La Bassée** 6 kms away. Completely destroyed in the Allied bombardments, it had been taken by the Germans in 1914 and, heavily fortified, it formed an extremely strong bastion in their lines for over four years. It was taken by Fifth Army under Lord Birdwood on October 2, 1918. The town is once again a thriving industrial area and it sprawls far outside its old boundaries. New roads have replaced the narrow busy ones of yore and recently a new ring-road has been instituted.

From Neuve Chapelle we remain on the D17I to **Richehourg l'Avoué**. As the **Indian Memorial** is passed a **private memorial** will be seen outside the wall. This is to the memory of 2nd Lieutenant Cyril A. W. Crichton who died on these crossroads in March 1915 and now lies buried in **Le Touret British Cemetery**, reached after 3½ kms of rather uninteresting angular road. It was just

behind the front of the Indian Corps in May 1915 in the battles of Festubert and Aubers Ridge. The cemetery dates from 1914 and the **Memorial to the Missing** is for those who fell in the battles of La Bassée, Neuve Chapelle, Aubers Ridge and Festubert in 1914-15. The memorial was dedicated at the

same time and day as those at Cambrai, Pozières and Vis-en-Artois in August 1930.

Just beyond the cemetery a small road to the right leads to Richebourg village outskirts and a left turn at the junction with the D170 brings one to **La Couture**. In front of the church is the **Portuguese Memorial**.

Portugal in France. *Left:* The beautiful entrance to the Portuguese Cemetery near La Bombe and *right* the unusual monument at La Couture.

Above: **La Bombe crossroads, Neuve Chapelle, where 2nd Lieutenant Cyril Crichton was originally buried.** *Right:* **The memorial records his death on March 10, 1915.**

The Le Touret Memorial to the Missing is for those who died at La Bassée, Neuve Chapelle, Aubers Ridge and Festubert in 1914-15.

The almost-forgotten cavalry memorial at Vielle Chapelle. Once standing in the village, the 1st King Edward's Horse obelisk is now in the cemetery.

In the cemetery of the next village, **Vielle Chapelle**, near the D182-D172 crossroad, is a **memorial** for which I searched for many hours. It is that of the **1st King Edward's Horse** (The King's Overseas Dominions Regiment), a cavalry unit of the Special Reserve whose squadrons were used as divisional cavalry from early 1915 until in June 1916 they became a corps cavalry regiment. They served throughout the war in France and Flanders and were, I have always heard, a wild, hard-riding bunch. Their memorial was erected in the village after the war but with the changes in the road network and the widening that has occurred, it was moved for safety into the village cemetery . . . and almost forgotten.

Return to **Le Touret** via the D169, noting the **house on the corner** at the junction. The sculpture surmounting it is one of a previous resident's works. Bas reliefs of French and Belgian leaders decorate the walls.

Turn left and at **l'Epinette** take the D166 on the right for **Festubert** 2 kms away. Festubert figured conspicuously in the October 1914 battles, in which the Indian Corps participated with Smith Dorien's II Corps, and later in the attacks on the Aubers Ridge

on May 9-26, 1915. In 1918 the magnificent defence of **Festubert** and **Givenchy** in April checked the German advance in the Battle of the Lys, leaving them and all their neighbours merely heaps of rubble. On the left of the D166 after passing Festubert church is a **British bunker**. It has two chambers and an outside shelter and was a ration point and officers' dugout at the end of a light railway spur. From January 1919 until her death in the early seventies it was the home of a Frenchwoman.

The 2 kms to Givenchy were among the most stalwartly defended positions by 55th Division in the German attacks of April 9-10 and, despite all the enemy could do, the Lancashire units held out. The crossroads before the village is the famous **Windy Corner** with the **Guards Cemetery**. A left turn leads to the village centre on D167 and on a corner beyond the church stands the **55th Divisional Memorial**. On the cross is the Division's formation sign bearing their motto: 'They win or die who wear the Rose of Lancashire'. Here they did both.

Return to the D166 and cross the La Bassée canal for **Cuinchy**, another front line village devastated in 1915 and 1918. Heavy fighting here in January 1915 centred around the brickstacks, where there is a **Guards Memorial**. Here and there, craters can still be discerned in the now peaceful area.

'To the memory of the 55th West Lancashire Division' who held this position against three German divisions from April 9-16, 1918.

At Festubert this British blockhouse, once a ration point and officers' shelter, provided a comfortable home for a local resident from 1919 until her recent death.

FROM MAP PAGE 64

SCALE 1:200 000 1cm—2km

ALTERNATIVE ROUTE •••••

Reproduced from Michelin Sheet No. 51 29th Edition 1989

took place in 1915-1916. Many of the graves in the cemetery are those of the dismounted cavalry who were engaged. Return to the N41 and turn left for Béthune.

A distant view is possible on the unnumbered road from Auchy to Vermelles, from which the scene is laid out with just the gate and the roof of the cemetery pavilion visible over the fields. From Vermelles it is possible to join the N41 at either Auchy by the D75 or via the D166 to Annequin. On the Vermelles-Hulloch road (D39), just beyond the Vermelles railway crossing, is the **46th Division Memorial Cross**.

Béthune. The ancient seat of the Counts of Flanders was fortified by Vauban in the 17th Century. The graceful Belfry, now standing in the centre of the Grand Place, was built in 1346. Most of the houses around the square have been rebuilt in the style of Flanders but those which originally clustered around three sides of the Belfry have not been replaced. As the centre of the mining villages and market gardens which abound in the locality, Béthune was a thriving town in 1914. For the next four years it was an important British headquarters town subjected to intermittent bombardment between 1915 and 1918.

From 1914 to 1915 the Indian Corps held the town which became an important railhead and billeting area for the rear lines, and a corps and divisional headquarters. In the German offensive of April 1918 a particularly heavy bombardment almost destroyed

Further on is **Cambrin** (1 km), a straggling industrial village. At the junction with the main road, N41, a right turn takes you to Béthune, 8 kms distant. To visit the delightful **Quarry Cemetery**, from the vicinity of which an excellent view of the region of the **Höhenzollern Redoubt** can be had, turn left on N41 and head for **Auchy** 1½ kms away. In Auchy turn right into the town centre and after about a km of straight, busy street. which is fairly narrow, it widens slightly near the Mairie. Turn right and then take the left fork and drive out of the built-up area along a straight, narrow road with small houses on the left and scrappy fields on the right for 1 km. At a road junction on the left the

cemetery is signposted along a muddy cart track. I advise walking then along the 300 metres to the cemetery gate. This is on the local land level and steps lead down to the graves. Looking out from the gate the area of the Höhenzollern Redoubt and Fosse 8 (mine pithead) lies before you: a flat plain criss-crossed now with electric pylons and in the distance the slag heap. Sometimes it is possible to discern the trenches in the beetfields around here, where such bitter fighting

The Hohenzollern Redoubt today as seen from the fields between Vermelles and Haisnes. This formidable German strongpoint had underground galleries, dugouts and trenches protected by thick belts of barbed wire. Quarry Cemetery lies in the middle distance. In recent years the slag heap has lost its crown for road foundations.

The Loos battlefield photographed from Dud Corner in 1975. British troops first used poison gas here in 1915.

The houses surrounding the Belfry in Béthune were all destroyed.

the town. The great church of **St Waast** was a mere pile of ruins but the **Belfry** bore a charmed existence as only the top was dislodged, even the well-known gargoyles surviving intact. The top has been replaced in almost identical form but the great doors on the ground floor have been replaced with glass. In 1918, the 3rd, 51st and 55th Divisions successfully held the town which only partially fell to the Germans. The town was damaged again in 1939-45. The **town museum**, currently housed in temporary quarters near the Gendarmerie, is hoping to open a section relating to 1914-1918, in particular, the long occupation by the BEF.

Leave via N4l which joins the N43 in 3 kms. The road crosses the plain dotted with mines and slag heaps, traversing the southern sector of the **Loos battlefield** which lies between the N43 and D947 (the old main road from La Bassée) and the new N47. The D947 can be reached from Loos by the D165 just on the north of **Hill 70**. Now there is a civil airfield and an enormous hypermarket on this part of the old battlefield whilst vestiges of the mine craters and trenches can still be discerned to the west of the hill.

In 10 kms, we reach **Dud Corner Cemetery** and **Loos Memorial to the Missing** who fell in the Battle of Loos in September/October 1915, and on the Lys, Estaires and Béthune fronts in April 1918. The names are recorded of 20,589 officers and men who fell during these actions, amongst whom is the son of Rudyard Kipling (Irish Guards panel).

The Battle of Loos, September 25 to October 13, 1915, was fought by the British I and IV Corps in support of Joffre's offensive in Champagne. It is remembered today as the battle in which very heavy casualties were suffered by only partially trained troops and for the first use of poison gas by the British.

From the roofs of the two pavilions of the memorial entrance, a good view of the battlefield can be gained. It is also possible on a fine day to glimpse in the distance, north of Hulloch (on the D947), the site of the Höhenzollern Redoubt, one of the strongly defended German positions taken by British divisions.

Continue for 4½ kms to **Lens**. This was the chief coal-mining town in France before the war almost entirely destroyed it. Now once more it is a thriving town and industrial area. Many of the mines are still working although the famous pit-head winding towers, so well known to the Tommy, are fast disappearing.

The Germans occupied Lens in October 1914 and, thereafter, set about fortifying it very strongly. It became the centre of a war fought from the warren of tunnels at many levels beneath the shell-torn ground. In August 1917 an Allied attack was launched from the north-west suburbs and Hill 70. The Canadian Corps forced their way through on a 2,000 yard front but the central part of the town held out. In spite of further attacks in September 1917 and January 1918, it was not until October 2 that the ruins were captured.

The Loos Memorial to the Missing at the Dud Corner Cemetery, commemorating over 20,000 British officers and men.

The Spirit of Canada weeps for her fallen countrymen. From Vimy Ridge the view extends over the Douai plain towards Messines. The twin pillars of the Memorial stand on the summit of Hill 145.

Lens is a very busy industrial town with complicated road systems so it is easier to join the C26 autoroute and proceed to the south-east following the signs for Arras and so bypass the traffic-choked streets.

After 6 kms, at **Noyelles**, the Arras road becomes the N17 but for the first 3 kms it is of motorway style. Soon after the complex of the Union Chimique et Minière at Avion, the road swings in a curve before the old road converges with it again below **Vimy Ridge**, thus providing a panoramic view of the twin pillars of the **Canadian Memorial** rising high above the wooded slopes of **Hill 145**.

In 7 kms, at the Vimy—Givenchy-en-Gohelle crossroad, turn right onto D51 to the latter. This straight road crosses the cornfields beneath the escarpment giving more fine vistas. The road now climbs up through **Givenchy** passing a **concrete dugout** — a German tunnel entrance to the subways tunnelled out by the men of both armies and by others in more ancient times. The largest of all, the **Vimy Cavern** was, in fact, mined out by Huguenots and chalk-burners many centuries ago. It was used for defensive purposes in the 18th and 19th Centuries and by refugees from various factions fighting to gain the supremacy of Arras.

The view from the **Canadian Memorial** is extensive — the Scarpe valley, the Lens minefields to the north and to the west, Notre Dame de Lorette and Souchez. On a clear day the Messines Ridge can be discerned over the slag heaps.

In October 1916 the Royal Engineers commenced the construction of the tunnels which were sufficient to house large concentrations of troops on the Allied slopes of the

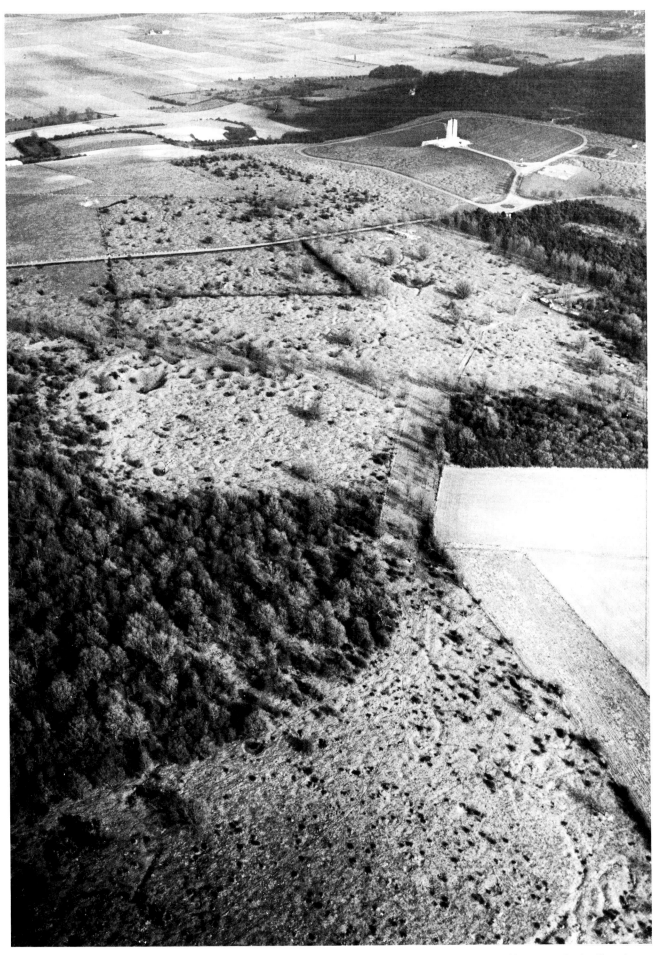

The shell-pocked Memorial Park photographed in March 1976 — a battlefield preserved and owned in perpetuity by Canada.

Canadian trenches lead to Grange Tunnel subway.

The old German front line, surrounded by mine craters.

ridge. Later, Australian and Canadian tunnelling companies completed the work which finally amounted to more than 22 miles of subways on four distinct levels. The top level is some 20 to 25 feet underground, the next 75 feet and the other two at various levels beneath that. On the lowest floor is a narrow-gauge railway still, it is believed, carrying the small trucks used for moving ammunition. Fairly steep gradients bring the line up to higher levels in a few places. The Germans on their side were equally busy.

Mining operations had begun in 1915 by the French, being continued by the Germans and later the British. There are still relics of their work and many craters are to be seen in the 240-acre park owned by Canada. This was a gift from the French Government and is under the management of the Canadian Battlefield Memorials Commission (for whom the CWGC undertake the maintenance and gardening work).

Twelve infantry subways, each averaging half-a-mile with several more than a mile in length, were constructed by the 172nd, 176th, 182nd and 185th Tunnelling Companies, RE, under the command of Lieutenant-Colonel G. C. Williams, Controller of Mines, First Army. In the period October 1916 to March 1917, over six miles of tunnels were dug, 6ft 6ins high and 3ft wide, lit throughout by electric light. Small lighting plants were installed in each subway and operated by the Australian Electrical and Mechanical Mining and Boring Company. Canadian tunnelling companies continued operations in the spring of 1917.

In the labyrinth were constructed assembly chambers, brigade and battalion headquarters, dressing stations, accommodation for men, trench mortar and bomb stores, signal offices, etc. Water supplies were laid on, signal cables connected up throughout and narrow-gauge railways laid. Numerous entrances and exits were provided, some for the railways (which linked up with the exterior tramways) for bringing up supplies

and for evacuating wounded. Ventilation shafts provided excellent air conditioning, the only difficulty being the risk of gas attacks when this good air flow increased the danger.

The tunnel system proved most useful and almost bomb-proof. Here and there large shells did penetrate to the first level, and one remains in situ today. Only the entrances required continuous attention and a repair gang was kept in each main subway for this purpose by the tunnelling companies.

Long before the great memorial was unveiled by King Edward VIII on July 26, 1936, work began on the preservation of the battlefield under the eye of Colonel A. F. Duguid, DSO, RCA. The front line trenches were preserved with concrete sandbags and duck-boards which today look very artificial because of their very neatness. However the sectors do follow the right lines and do provide the visitor with an inkling of the horrors which they held. At the rear of the German part of the line is a pillbox and entrance. A large German trench mortar, found within the park, has been set up and other weapons are scattered around. On the Canadian side, a short length of supporting trench has been left in its natural state. The closeness between the two front lines is clearly indicated across the mine craters.

From the concrete trenches it is only a short distance to the entrance of the tunnel which is open for public inspection during the summer months. The guides are usually Canadian students. This tunnel is **Grange Tunnel** and was re-opened for visitors in 1926 by Captain Unwin Simson, Royal Canadian Engineers. Originally it was nearly 800 yards in length, with many offshoots and three exits near the 'jumping off' trenches. Grange Tunnel was completed and occupied by the 7th Canadian Infantry Brigade. The visitor can see the guard rooms, the cook house, the hospital and ammunition dumps, the general's quarters with many items of equipment lying about, including the disintegrating bed

said to have been used by the general himself. The lower levels are indicated but only two of the upper levels are visited during the tour. Some of the damage done by the occupying forces in the Second World War can be seen and more recent construction to reinforce the original work of the tunnellers. At present no part of the German complex is open as much of it has flooded.

As one arrives from Givenchy, the **French Memorial** commemorating the Moroccan troops who fought here with distinction in 1915 is seen on the right at the roundabout. Swing round to the left, the road being a one-way system as it cleaves across the shell-pocked park. A large car park is provided on the right. Here on the wall flanking the toilets is a bronze map of the battlefield. Access to the memorial is via the footpaths commencing beneath the two tall flagpoles from which the Canadian and French national flags fly. Take a look at the enchanting beavers at the bases of the poles. Beyond the car park is the Superintendent's house and office.

The circuit of the hill provides more excellent views over the **Douai Plain**. There are more car parks at the lower level to which we make our way, passing the memorial and back to the roundabout having passed a German bunker on the right. Proceed southward to take the second road to the left (a detour along the narrow road to the right will take you to two of the cemeteries in the park through acres of shell-holes and wooded enclosure) to visit the trenches and Grange Tunnel. The approach road runs below part of the line of mine craters, many blown in 1915-16, and it too is set off with trees. Driving or walking through the park, the visitor will see many wired off enclosures with small notices attached to the wires. Almost all are planted with fir trees and are definitely *not* for exploration, the signs make it obvious that danger lurks amid the pines and often rusting shells and grenades come to light as the land has not been

GRANGE TUNNEL ENTRANCE

GERMAN FRONT LINE

CANADIAN FRONT LINE

From the air the opposing front lines — Canadian on the left and German on the right — are seen to be separated only by a line of mine craters. Below the surface lies a network of underground workings of which Grange Tunnel can be visited.

Grange Tunnel. Debris in a connecting gallery with upper floors.

A rather dangerous disused entrance to the tunnel.

A first aid post gallery full of battlefield debris.

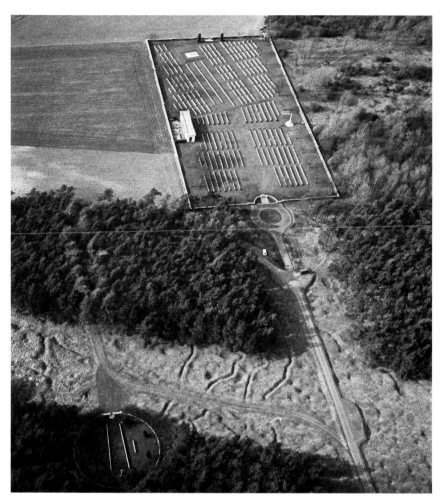

Trenches and craters surround the 'battlefield' cemeteries of Canadian No. 2 (top), and Givenchy Road (lower left) on Vimy Ridge.

The village memorial at La Targette to those Frenchmen who died in 1916.

cleared. The areas of the park which can be explored are clearly defined and indicated by other notices and well-worn paths. Frequently, a flock of sheep can be observed in the beautiful close-clipped cratered areas, doing their bit to aid the Commission gardeners.

Beside the entrance to Grange Tunnel and the preserved trench system is a small building housing the Guides' office (and toilets). Here it is possible to purchase postcards and pamphlets on the Canadian memorials. *Canada on Vimy Ridge* is a reprint from the Canada Yearbook of 1936

giving a useful description by Colonel Duguid of the 1917 operations and after, with an excellent map. The visitor should be wary of walking in the trenches as the concrete duck-boards are lethal to anyone wearing high heels.

The narrowness of no man's land at this point is demonstrated as on either side of **Winnipeg Crater** stands a sign indicating the front line. The long swerve of the craters can be observed from this point in both directions. To the left they arc up towards Hill 145, to the right they swing down to **Folie Farm**. The site of the farm is marked by a

cross. Visitors are asked to remember that the whole park is a memorial; picnics are not allowed among the shell-holes and neither are games.

One way to leave the park is by the road above the trench sector; this skirts the southern limits of the park and joins the N17 1 km north of Thélus crossroads. The other road away from the park is the D55 to Neuville St Vaast. In recent years the aspect of the countryside around Vimy Memorial Park has changed considerably due to the advent of the Calais autoroute which cuts across north of Arras. This is now crossed before entering **Neuville St Vaast**. A side road to the left leads to **Lichfield Crater**, one of two cemeteries where there are no separate graves as all fell together in the explosions. The men were all killed on April 9 or 10, 1917. The other is **Zivy Crater** which is just below the bridge which crosses the A26. Access to it is from the D49 to the east, a spur off the old road being maintained for it. The names of 48 Canadian soldiers who perished here with 5 unknown comrades are engraved below the Cross of Sacrifice.

Neuville St Vaast was totally destroyed in 1915-16. In the centre of the village take the D49 to the right to reach the D937 in 1 km at **La Targette. A large memorial** of unusual

A neat patchwork of graves in the huge French Cemetery at Neuville St Vaast with the British Cemetery at the top left-hand corner.

Zivy Crater Cemetery — here lie those who died in the act of blowing the mine.

The Notre Dame de Lorette French National Memorial and Cemetery. Apart from 20,000 individual graves, another 20,000 unknown lie in the Ossuary.

design and dimensions stands in a small park at the crossroads. The huge hand bearing aloft a torch according to the inscription to the **Cité des Mutilés**. It commemorates the destruction of the village in the mining operations by the French on May 9, 1916. Beneath the whole region are caverns and subways and, for many years until they became unsafe, there was a famous complex which formed part of the **Maison Blanche sector** which was reached from an entrance at the crossroad. Entombed in these caverns are many fine carvings made by the Canadians and others who were billeted in them from 1916 onwards. A short distance up the road is a farm which stands above another of these caverns. Opposite is the huge **German Cemetery** of Neuville St Vaast containing 36,792 graves. There are also large French and British cemeteries in the village.

Turn right on to the D937 and travel 4 kms to **Souchez**. The French fought a fierce action here in June 1915. On the left, before descending the hill, lies **Caberet Rouge Cemetery** and the **Indian Memorial**.

Continue up the hill and take the left turn, the D58e, to **Notre Dame de Lorette** 3 kms further on. At the corner by the junction is a **private museum** which is open in the spring and summer and certain weekends before and after the main season. It records mainly the French operations of 1915. An old legend declares the victor in any war in Flanders and Picardy will be the conqueror of the range of hills which culminate in the crest of Notre

Dame de Lorette. A chapel stood on the eastern spur of the ridge which was won by the French after heavy fighting in May 1915. Today the **French National Memorial and Cemetery** crown the ridge, the site of the old chapel being marked by a simple stone. The cemetery covers 26 acres. A lighthouse tower, 52 metres high, and a chapel are the dominant features. In the top of the tower is a searchlight which shines all night rotating 360 degrees. From the tower magnificent views of all the surrounding countryside can be had. There is a museum within the lower floors of the tower which contains some interesting items. Between the tower and the chapel is a perpetual flame. The chapel is famous for its stained glass windows, some of which were presented by the British Commonwealth. In the crypt below are the remains of tens of thousands of dead.

Return to the D937 and Souchez. 4 kms along the D937 to the left is **Aix Noulette**, where at the roadside on the right are two **French memorials**; down the lane beside them under the shadow of the motorway another stands on a **blockhouse**. All commemorate the fighting here in 1915. The direct route to Arras is 13 kms. A detour (7 kms) to include a visit to **Mont St Eloi** can be made by taking the D58 to **Clarency** and then, after passing through this village, taking the left fork onto an unclassified road.

This French monument stands on top of a former blockhouse at Aix Noulette.

Mont St Eloi was the site of an Augustinian abbey in the 7th Century but the ruined towers are from the 17th Century. They were all but destroyed by German artillery fire in 1914 and used by Foch's army in 1915 as an

'To the glory of the Regiment of Lorette' — the 158th Regiment d'Infanterie. The memorial on the right was erected by the comrades of those soldiers of France who still lie buried in various places on the battlefield. On the left the marker to one such grave: that of Sous Lieutenant Jean Leon killed in May 1915.

The still-ruined towers of the abbey at Mont St Eloi overlook the site of the old Royal Flying Corps aerodrome.

observation post. It is possible, but not advised, to climb the ancient stairs to see the view. In the valley below the village was the **RFC aerodrome of St Eloi.**

Continue via the D49 to La Targette (4 kms), and thence via the D937 to Arras (8 kms). A quieter road than this highway can be taken from Neuville St Vaast. It is the D49e and goes down the slopes of the back of Vimy ridge to **Ecurie**, once a Canadian base. All roads into Arras have changed radically lately and converge into a ring road around the northern approaches.

Leaving Vimy via the N17, going south to Thélus, turn left when you reach the crossroads onto the D49. The **Canadian Artillery Memorial** here was built and unveiled a year to the day after the capture of Vimy Ridge. General Byng performed the ceremony on April 9, 1918. The South African Heavy Artillery Battery, who also participated, are remembered on the plaque. The memorial stands directly over a dugout, the entrance for which was under the steps in front. **Thélus** village is about ½ km from here. It was of course involved in the 1917-18 operations being captured by the 1st Canadian Division on April 9, 1917. A little to the east along our road is the **British Cemetery** and nearby vestiges of trenches can be seen. In the fields beyond stands a lone cross on a stone cairn — the **1st Canadian Division's Memorial** — which they erected at Christmas in 1917 in memory of their several engagements between March and July 1917. Later

there was further fighting over and under these fields as the Germans tried to force Arras in March 1918, but the sector held.

After 5 kms we reach **Bailleul Sir Berthoult** — a German front line position stormed and captured by 51st Highland and 34th Divisions on April 13, 1917 after much heavy fighting. At the far side of the village take an unnumbered road to the left for **Oppy**, 3 kms.

The notorious **Oppy Wood** is on the right as the village is neared. In the years the German Army were in occupation of this village, they transformed it into one of the strongest forts on the Western Front and defied any attack to dislodge them. It was eventually captured by 8th Division with heavy losses on both sides as they evicted the enemy, trench by trench, in September 1918. Fighting in the vicinity had gone on for months and months. It was a sea of mud and destruction from bombardments, and many British battalions had endured periods in the line here — men of the Royal Fusiliers, several Home Counties regiments and the East Yorkshires to mention just a few. Often the trenches changed hands for brief periods and soon there was little of the old wood left. It is approached by various tracks but all are private. On the right is rather an unusual **memorial** with the wood as backdrop. Here the men of **Kingston upon Hull** are remembered with their comrades from the local area, including the son of the donor of the land who died on the Somme in August 1918.

All is quiet now at Fampoux where so many men from the Seaforth Highland Battalion were cut down in the battles of 1917 and 1918. Their memorial stands to record their sacrifice.

The Canadian Artillery Memorial at Thélus crossroads to the men who fell in the Vimy operations of April 1917.

At Christmas in 1917, men of the 1st Canadian Division erected this memorial to their comrades.

The Kingston upon Hull Memorial at Oppy Wood.

Continue across the 1917 battlefield on the D33 to **Gavrelle**. Here was the scene of the attack by 63rd Royal Naval Division on April 23, 1917 and their magnificent defence for many days thereafter through innumerable counter-attacks. It was held until 56th London Division, which stubbornly defended it in March 1918, were overwhelmed on the 28th. The 51st Highland Division recaptured it on August 27 and it was occupied by 8th Division.

Under the bypass turn right and then left onto D33, taking the right fork onto D42e. Traversing the 1917 battlefields and the motorway, descend into **Fampoux** in the Scarpe valley in 3½ kms. Yet another place of evil memory to both cavalry and infantry, as was its neighbour **Roeux**, being the scene of extensive fighting above and below ground. The deep subways were to play a similar rôle in 1940.

As the road drops into the village it joins another on the immediate right. It is a very tight turn but it leads up **York Road** of 1917 towards the **Seaforth Highlanders' Celtic Cross** and 4th Division's **Sunken Road Cemetery** on the crest of the ridge. The Scottish battalion was almost annihilated on these open plains in April 1917 in the operations between Roclincourt and Monchy, on which the Vimy Ridge attack depended upon for being a success. To get there it is still possible to join the N50 by our little road, but it deteriorates considerably as it approaches the dual carriageway. It is better to return to Fampoux and turn right to **Athies** (1 km) and then right up the D37 which reaches the N50 just east of **Pont du Jour British Cemetery**, and just along the main road is the **9th Scottish Division Memorial** on the Pont du Jour. The site is now beautifully landscaped in an oasis between the dual carriageways. The only casualty has been the crumbling dugout used as part of the Divisional Headquarters in 1917. The memorial, still set amid a border of rough-hewn granite boulders, each bearing the name of a unit in the division, provides an excellent place to view the terrain. The boundary markers carry the thistle badge of the division and newly planted trees edge the ample car parking.

Arras is a mere 5 kms away, but a detour can be made up the first road to the right as the descent into the city suburbs begins. This passes the large **German Cemetery of St**

Laurent Blangy where over 30,000 men are commemorated on the grassy slopes and under sombre trees, many in a mass grave. At the junction with the D919 is **Bailleul Road East British Cemetery** with many Scottish graves. Turn left for Arras with the smaller **Bailleul Road West British Cemetery** on the right before rejoining the N50 to go right and enter Arras through **St Laurent Blangy**.

'Remember with honour the 9th Scottish Division who on the fields of France, and Flanders 1915-1918 served well.'

North-west of Arras beside the N39, a trench runs like a phantom image across the fields after 65 years of ploughing.

ARRAS

The focal point of many wars in this region, the various occupying powers have each left their mark on this ancient city. Long before the Romans came and established a Legion here, there was a thriving Atrebates community here. By 863 it was part of Flanders, then the Normans came and sacked it. In the centuries thereafter the English, the French, the Austrians and the Spanish held sway for varying periods. In 1431 it was the era of Joan of Arc and she was imprisoned here for a while. Then, in 1541, the English and the Spaniards fought the French for the city. Between 1633 and 1707 the great Citadel was built on designs by Vauban. Marlborough was here in 1708, and Arras was also Robespierre's birthplace; his house can still be seen.

From September 18, 1914 Arras was occupied by the Germans but they were forced to retire by General Maud'huy and many fierce battles were fought with the French army holding on to the town against von Bulow. In the years which followed the 'boves', or **underground caves**, became an underground city. Above them the town was badly damaged and in ruins after the attacks of 1915. Arras suffered also from aerial bombardment, the heaviest raid being possibly that of November 10, 1916 when forty German machines raided the town. In the aerial battle which took place, six enemy machines were shot down.

Despite all, the French and British garrisons held on to the somewhat small salient which the city formed. The Battle of Arras began on April 9, 1917 with a British attack on a 12-mile front from Givenchy-en-Gohelle in the north to Croissilles in the south. Four Canadian divisions advanced against the Vimy Ridge with notable success and many prisoners and guns were captured in the first few days of the offensive as the Germans retreated towards Lens. Then followed a period of indecisive engagements, very costly to both sides with few gains or losses with a return to static warfare, until the German advance of March 1918. Von

The 'Boves' of Arras. This is the corner of a large hall on the second level.

The entrance to one of the underground caves beneath the Grand Place.

British telephone wiring and terminals still remain in one tunnel.

78

Arras. Place d'Heros and Hôtel de Ville.

Bulow's army attacked toward Vimy but the British Third Army, after falling back to Feuchy and Neuville St Vaast, held the line.

In 1940 the city was once more under seige when the British Army was involved in a rearguard action. Among the last to leave were the Welsh Guards; at the end of August 1944, this regiment was one of the first to re-enter.

Today the city has been completely rebuilt. Among the notable buildings are the **Palais Saint Vaast**, a former Benedictine abbey, rebuilt in the 18th Century and again after its destruction in the war; **the cathedral**, a 17th Century edifice which was almost destroyed in the 1915 artillery bombardment, and the **Hôtel de Ville**. This beautiful building was entirely demolished by fire and bombardment but has been rebuilt in the original style of the 15th and 16th Centuries with more modern 19th Century wings. The Belfry, which was first completed in 1553 and which collapsed in October 1914, is now one of the most beautiful. There are various memorial plaques in the foyer and, on the first floor and, on the exterior near the main entrance, is the modern **1939-44 Resistance Memorial**.

On the Faubourg d'Amiens in the **British Military Cemetery** and the **Arras Memorial to the Missing**, is a beautiful colonnade with the **RFC, RNAS and Royal Air Force Memorial** as a central monument. The memorial records the 35,928 missing in the battles of Arras, Vimy Ridge, the Scarfe, and those of Arleux, Bullecourt and Hill 70 of 1917. The **Air Services Memorial** records all those missing on the Western Front. High up at the head of the panels are the names of Major Lanoe Hawker, VC, and Major E. Mannock, VC. The globe which surmounts the pillar is decorated with a flight of doves on the exact path of the sun on November 11, 1918. In the cemetery are over 2,600 graves.

By the side of the memorial is a narrow road which leads to the moat of the Citadel and the extremely sombre **Mur des Fusilées** with its 200 plaques forming the memorial to the French patriots who were shot in this dismal place between July 1941 and July 1944. A solitary stone post stands where the execution post was sited. Remembrance services held here are extremely moving and simple. Other sections of the massive ramparts are incorporated into public parks.

From the basement of the Hôtel de Ville, in which is a **museum** of the history of Arras, guided tours take visitors through some of the 'boves' beneath the Place d'Heros. These subways, many of great antiquity, were occupied by harassed citizens and defenders throughout the centuries. At other times they provided excellent cellars. Tens of thousands of British soldiers lived and worked in the complicated maze of tunnels. Visits to the Belfry and the magnificent salons on the first floor of the Hôtel de Ville can commence here as well.

The combined Memorial to the Missing to those of the Royal Flying Corps, Royal Naval Air Service and Royal Air Force forms the centrepiece to the British Cemetery and Memorial to the Missing at Arras.

The grimmest place in Arras — the Mur des Fusilées with its execution post and memorial plaques for those who died there during the Second World War.

The story and legend of Captain Albert Ball, VC, DSO**, MC, is probably so well known that it is unnecessary to go into details here but it may be of interest to visit the scene of his fatal crash and final resting place whilst in this part of France. Perhaps the simplest route is to use the A1 autoroute between Arras and

Lille, leaving it at the Carvin-Libercourt turn-off, and proceed westward on to the D954 to Carvin. In the centre of this busy town, turn right on D925 for a short distance and then left on the D163 reaching Annoeullin in 4 kms. Turn right soon after the road becomes D41b to join the D41 on the edge of Carnin, crossing the flat farmland on which the Germans had a small airfield. Turn left on D41c driving for ½ km. There is a solitary house on the left-hand side of the road and immediately after it a grass track is seen in the field. It is not suitable for cars and it is only a short walk to the place where the grey stone marker stands some 30 metres in front of a small copse. This appears to be a composite of the original erected by his father made from two of the original stones which indicated the place where the aircraft fell — the third has disappeared. Today it is watched over by those who have inherited the traditions he and his fellows built so many years ago in No. 60 Squadron — still alive and well in the modern RAF.

Although Annoeullin and the other towns and villages hereabouts have grown, the immediate area around here can have changed little over the years. Maybe the lanes have deteriorated into paths and tracks but there has been hardly any development between these small fields and copse and the German Cemetery. When the German airmen carried his body from the broken plane to lay him to rest, they traversed tracks which still cross the dull land to arrive at the cemetery entrance from the opposite end of the road used by cars.

From the crash-site follow the D41c into Allennes lès Marais (1 km), and turn

left for Annoeullin. After 1 km at the crossroad (traffic lights), turn left and in 400 metres left again at the T-junction and follow the signs for the German Cemetery and the Communal Cemetery, bearing left off D41 onto a cul-de-sac. This is the road which 200 metres beyond the cemeteries peters out into the track.

FROM ARRAS

The Battles of the Somme

wood and reached the outskirts of the village which did not completely come within our line until February 27, 1917. Not far from the village is the triangular-shaped **Bois de Riez** — a landmark used by the RFC on patrol.

Taking the small road on the right, in less than a kilometre we reach **Hébuterne**, a British fortress village immediately behind the front line from which the 56th (London) Division attacked Gommecourt on July 1, 1916.

Now take the D27, the left-hand road to **Puisieux** (4 kms). This is an example of the many villages in this undulating country which were completely destroyed by artillery fire. It did not fall to the Allies until the spring of 1917 when it was merely a ruin.

Rejoin the D919 turning right for **Serre**, 2 kms. A little way out of the village is the **Memorial to the 12th Battalion York and Lancaster Regiment** on the right hand. The road drops down through a group of British and French cemeteries marking this area of very severe fighting on July 1, 1916. Here the 31st Division fought their way across the hilly country in a vain attempt to reach their objectives. They were mown down by hidden and well-placed machine gun nests or impaled on the barbed wire entanglements, supposedly cut up by the tremendous artillery bombardment preceding the attack. Beside the farm on the right at the bottom of the hill a track leads up to a scattered group of small cemeteries, **Serre Road No. 3, Queens, Railway Hollow** and **Luke Copse**. This last was one of several hotly contested positions of which four were named after the Evangelists. **Sheffield Memorial Park** is a small enclosure on the reverse slope up which the British had to fight. A length of the front line trench and shell-cratered rear line is preserved around the shelter of the **Sheffield Memorial**. Away to the back of the crest of the hill, **La Signy Farm** can just be seen. In between, a clump of trees marks the site of **Basin Wood**, the casualty clearing station.

Back on the D919 **Serre Road No. 1 Cemetery** is just beyond the farm with the French one beside it and, further along on the left, the largest of the group — **Serre Road No. 2 Cemetery** with over 3,300 graves. On the roadside a **private memorial** is set on a grassy mound — the original wooden cross of the same design is preserved in the crypt of Winchester Cathedral.

In 1½ kms the crossroads at the top of the hill was once the site of the **sucrerie**, an important position in the British lines. Turn right for the direct route for Auchonvillers,

The graceful entrance to the Indian and Chinese cemetery at Ayette, 16 kilometres south of Arras. Ayette was the scene of fierce battles in 1918.

Leave Arras by the D919. It is 12 kms to **Boiry** and another 4 kms to **Ayette**, scene of fierce fighting by 31st and 32nd Divisions in March and April 1918. It has a rather unusual **Indian and Chinese Cemetery**. We then reach **Bucquoy** 4 kms. This village was behind the German lines, providing a base and billeting area until it came within the range of British artillery. The village was captured in March 1917 and for a year was well known to the BEF. In the German spring advance, it was desperately defended by the 62nd Division after the first battle on March 26 by British Whippet light tanks.

Turn right in the centre of the village onto the D8 for **Hannescamps** (6 kms) — always behind the lines but heavily bombarded. Then turn left onto the D3 for 2½ kms to **Foncquevillers**, in the lines from 1915-16 and badly damaged by artillery.

We then take the D6 road past **Gommecourt Wood**, 4 km to **Gommecourt** which was the Third Army front of July 1, 1916. The 46th North Midland Division attacked the

Above and below: Gommecourt Wood with vestiges of the trench lines which straddled the shattered treescape in 1916. After the desperate fighting of that July, Gommecourt fell almost peaceably during the German retreat in February 1917.

The church at Mailly-Maillet with its medieval doorway still intact. Its preservation during two particularly fierce bombard-ments in 1916 and 1918 owes much to its face being protected . . . and no doubt to the fact that the door faced west and the German shells came in from the east.

From the shelter of the Sheffield Memorial the view is down across the undulating ground of the former battlefield to Railway Hollow Cemetery, the Accrington Pals' Valhalla.

Above: Serre, scene of the 12th Bn. York and Lancaster Regiment's attack on July 1, 1916. *Below:* The price paid in human lives — Serre No. 1 British Cemetery.

Sheffield Park with a sad memorial to Private A. E. Bull of the 12th Yorks and Lancs. Killed on this spot on July 1, 1916, his remains were not discovered until April 13, 1928, when they were buried in Serre No. 2 Cemetery.

but it is worth continuing on 2½ kms to **Mailly-Maillet**, observing the fine views of the **Thiepval Ridge** to the east across the Ancre valley, to visit the village church to see the unexpected sight of a medieval west doorway preserved through the forethought of the curé who had it protected during the war. This village, as with all the others just behind the British lines, was a very busy place before July 1 and also, like its neighbours, had many underground tunnels in the quarries below it from which the material for building the houses was taken. These subways provided vital cover for the troops and, although no longer open to view, still retain carvings and graffiti on their walls.

Take the D73 for **Auchonvillers** 1 km beyond which is the **Newfoundland Memorial Park** entrance. Just before it a lane is signposted for **Hawthorn Ridge No. 1 Cemetery** near the clump of trees marking the site of the crater.

The D161 from Auchonvillers to Beaumont Hamel village passes through the valley behind the ridge. After 1 km, on the left a lane runs up onto **Redan Ridge** and back to Serre. At one side is the **Memorial of the Argyll and Sutherland Highlanders** tucked under the slope and in the fields; on the other the small **Beaumont Cemetery**. Up the steep field on the right of the road, a pathway has been made up to the rim of **Hawthorn Ridge crater**, indicated by a multi-language signpost at the roadside. Although the crater is now filled with trees and bushes, the farmers having over the years tried to fill it in, a swathe has been cut down its precipitous side to show the depth. The crater was 150 yards in length, 100 yards wide and 80ft deep, 40,000lbs of ammonal being used to create it. The eruption was caught on film as it was prematurely exploded and is one of the best known and frequently screened examples of the 1914-18 cameraman's art.

Newfoundland Memorial Park covers more than 80 acres of which some 40 are in the sector held on July 1 by the Royal Newfoundland Regiment of the 29th Division. The regiment was annihilated in the initial attack following the explosion which, being ten minutes too early, enabled the ground to be occupied by the enemy.

At the entrance to the park is the **29th Division Memorial** and all around are the grass covered trenches of the battlefield. All have been preserved as they were left in 1918 and, due to the fact that later battles did not alter them very much, it is possible to study and appreciate the actions fought here. Even on a fine, sunny summer's day, the park seems to have a definitely foreboding atmosphere and, after a thunderstorm, I have smelt the awful stench of battle in the still, deep, trenches. Nowhere else in my travels

The battlefield of the Somme — at peace. The attack on July 1, 1916 began at this spot at 7.20 a.m. when the 252nd Company of the Royal Engineers blew up the German trenches held by the 119th Infanterieregiment. The explosion formed what came to be known as Hawthorn Ridge Crater. *Above:* The view from the lip of the crater down towards Beaumont Cemetery. *Below:* Looking from Beaumont village across Redan Ridge. The crater, now tree-filled, is in the centre.

on the Western Front has the horror of war come nearer to me than here on one very hot evening following a clear day. It was late July and, as I wandered across the shell-torn slopes towards the German lines, the sound of thunder was heard in the distance, getting gradually nearer as might an artillery barrage. The light grew dim and black clouds gathered overhead. Lightning streaked across the sky — a veritable reincarnation of what a barrage must have been like.

As the rain drops began to fall, I dived into one of the trenches for cover and tripped and stumbled along until I found better shelter close to the great **Caribou monument** which stands guard over the park from a raised mound above a dugout. All the light I had was a tiny torch and this gave little help in avoiding the occasional shell-case or jagged pieces of iron which litter the trenches. After the hot day, the usual smell of rain-soaked grass began to permeate my nostrils

The 29th Division's simple monument at Beaumont Hamel — all around are the grass-covered trenches of the battlefield.

Beaumont Hamel Newfoundland Memorial Park is one of the best preserved of the trench memorials on the Western Front to be seen today. St John's Road and the Caribou Memorial above a dugout at Beaumont Hamel.

. . . but with a difference . . . I realised that this was the smell of battle. It was a never-to-be-forgotten experience, and one which I have found on return visits when the conditions have been similar.

Before the visitor to the park reaches the Caribou, along the gravel path between the trenches a memorial plaque bearing a verse by John Oxenham bids the beholder to tread softly over the hallowed ground. At the base of the Caribou is the **Memorial to the Newfoundland Missing** on land and sea and the names of over 800 men from this small country are listed on the bronze panels. Around the foot of the plinth of stone on which the monument stands is an orientation table. From this level a good view can be had of all the park and beyond to Beaumont and Thiepval. Across the expanse of the park the various lines are indicated by signboards, the British and German front lines being clearly marked amid the rough shell holes.

The modern house of the Superintendent can be seen across towards Thiepval and, over the small ridge where the skeleton of the **Danger Tree** rises in front of the German trenches, is the ridge where the **kilted Scotsman of the 51st Highland Division** gazes out across the countryside. Tall fir trees, planted many years ago when this area became the Newfoundland National Memorial, grow around the statue. The sweep of these trees is interrupted down in the hollow by the **Y Ravine Cemetery**. Hidden over to the left is **Hawthorn Ridge Cemetery No. 2**. Between it

Y Ravine Cemetery contains the headstones of men known or believed to be buried there, their graves being lost in later battles.

A relic of 1916 — the petrified Danger Tree in no man's land. Y Ravine is in the background.

Overleaf: A trench map in reality; Beaumont Hamel Memorial Park, seen in April 1976.

HAWTHORN RIDGE

HAWTHORN RIDGE CEMETERY No. 2

BRITISH FRONT LINE

ST JOHN'S ROAD

ROYAL NEWFOUNDLAND REGIMENT MEMORIAL

MAIN POSITIONS

Y-RAVINE

51st HIGHLAND DIV. MEM.

'S
RY

GERMAN FRONT LINE

Y-RAVINE CEMETERY

DANGER TREE

and the 51st Highland Division Memorial is the smallest of the cemeteries in the park, **Hunter's Cemetery**. A small wall encircles the Cross of Sacrifice around the base of which are the headstones of 46 men, mostly of the Black Watch of the 51st Highland Division, who died here when the area was captured by the division in the autumn of 1916. The division memorial overlooks the infamous **Y Ravine** which was a German position and from which their machine guns wreaked a devastating fire. Entrances to dugouts were cut in the sides of the ravine, but these are now peacefully covered with grass.

As the visitor crosses the battle area, it is noticeable that some of the shell holes contain much battlefield debris: rusting helmets, broken shells, barbed wire and the iron pickets on which the wire was hung. These collections are not there for the taking and it is requested that they should be looked at and not pilfered. Even today many shells and often hand-grenades can be found emerging from the greensward. Should the visitor find a dangerous item, leave it alone and advise the Superintendent or one of the gardeners working in the park.

In 1959, the Canadian Battlefield Monuments Commission took over the park and the CWGC provide the work force to keep it in beautiful condition. To aid them a flock of sheep grazes peacefully. Before the CWGC took over, long lines of pickets and barbed wire were to be seen across the park, since removed to the shell-holes. The Newfoundland Roll of Honour is kept in the Superintendent's house together with other interesting references to the history of the regiment and park.

Leave the park and continue eastward, dropping suddenly down into the Ancre valley at **Hamel**. We then follow a short but interesting circular detour by taking the left fork in the village and joining the D50. Then, after a few hundred metres, take the left fork on the D163e for Beaumont, leaving the railway which runs between the D50 and the Ancre. In **Beaumont** take the right-hand road, the D163, for **Beaucourt**. There are several **monuments** to British units which took part in the Battle of the Somme including the **63rd Royal Naval Division** and very fine views out over the battlefield.

In Beaucourt rejoin the D50 and turn left for **Miraumont** where the Germans had a supply base and a reserve ammunition store near the **old water-mill**, close to the railway line. This was blown up by the British

The Kilted Scotsman of the 51st Highland Division looks out over Y Ravine.

artillery on August 5, 1916, destroying much of the village.

Take the D107 and cross the railway and then take the D151 to the right for **Grandcourt**, which was part of the German entrenchment on the River Ancre. Go straight through the village, taking the D163e to **St Pierre Divion**, travelling along the region where the Germans were securely dug in. At the junction with the D73 will be seen the **ruins of the mill**. Turn left and climb up the steep slopes to Thiepval. At the top of the hill the **Memorial to the 36th Ulster Division** is reached.

Set in a small park on the left of the road, on a site venerated as being the place where the 36th Division won glory on July 1, 1916 in their gallant attempt to reach Thiepval and take the Schwaben Redoubt, is a tall grey memorial. It is a copy of the memorial to Helen, the greatly loved mother of the Marquis of Dufferin, in the family park at Clanboye, County Down, where the division had its training grounds before coming to France. Within the tower are a chapel, visitors' room and an apartment normally occupied by a CWGC official. At present access to the tower can be gained as indicated on a notice by the door.

In the grounds is a flag-pole from which the flag first flew on Armistice Day 1921

when it was hoisted by the Duchess of Abercorn at the unveiling of the memorial. In the spring and autumn, after the ploughing has been done, the fields behind the memorial are criss-crossed with chalk slicks which follow the course of the German trenches leading to the **Schwaben Redoubt** which lies in the fields under **Mill Road Cemetery**, and Thiepval hamlet. In 1966, 1976, and in 1986, gatherings of survivors of 1916 met to celebrate the 50th, 60th and 70th anniversaries of their heroism. The 36th Division held special ceremonies at the Ulster Tower recalling their 5,500 casualties.

A little higher up the road is the cemetery where many of them are buried, **Connaught Road Cemetery**, with part of **Thiepval Wood** as a backdrop. Others lie in Mill Road Cemetery, away in the fields on the left. Here, due to the continual subsidence caused by the movement underground as the many subways and caverns of the Schwaben Redoubt crumble, the headstones in the path of one of the tunnels are laid flat. The cemetery marks one of the main entrances to the underground fortress. It was one of several in the area, the others being Stuff, Zollern and Leipzig. It was from these underground strongholds that the German forces emerged to cause such devastation among the attacking forces.

The tiny Hunter's Cemetery of Highland graves with the 51st Division Memorial in the background.

The 63rd Naval Division Memorial at Beaumont.

Even after nearly sixty years of ploughing, the trenches of the Schwaben Redoubt are still visible from the air.

Insets: The 36th Division Memorial *(top left)* and the Mill Road Cemetery *(bottom right)*, both visible in the aerial photograph.

Continue 1 km to **Thiepval**. This hamlet, once a flourishing village, was totally destroyed by the end of 1916. It was a German fortress, both above and below ground, and was a vital position to be taken by the British. Terrible injuries were suffered on both sides in the attacks which were made on that dreadful first day of the Somme, and it did not fall until September 28, 1916 when the 51st Highland Division captured the ridge. At the crossroads is a small, rather unprepossessing house, once a café, which for many many years was owned by one Isobel. She had been there in 1916 and twice had to be evacuated by the Germans because she obstinately refused to leave voluntarily. Until her death in the early seventies, she still dispensed the beer and coffee and was a great source of stories.

The great **Memorial to the Missing** is along the road behind the church on the right. This colossal arched memorial was designed by Sir Edwin Lutyens and is built of brick with stone facing. The immense central archway is flanked by smaller arches resting on 16 main pillars. On the panels of stone are recorded the names of 73,412 men who died in 1916-17 and have no known graves. Behind the memorial is a **cemetery** where equal numbers of British and French unknown soldiers lie buried.

An inscription at the entrance to the memorial, which stands on the site of the grounds of **Thiepval Château** and on part of the **Leipzig Redoubt**, records that the monument is dedicated to both the British and French. The memorial was unveiled by the Prince of Wales on July 31, 1932 and can be seen from every direction for considerable distances. Beneath is the labyrinth of trenches which formed the vital arteries of this impregnable fortress. **Moquet Farm**, over the valley towards Courcelette, was the forward advance HQ of the defending German army. The majority of the casualties recorded here were lost in the attempts to capture this fortress. The siege dragged on for nearly two months but the most disastrous day was July 1 when the British lost nearly 60,000 men. In September, the 11th and 18th Divisions, following in the footsteps

Thiepval Memorial to over 73,000 men who have no known graves. Built on the site of the old château — scene of commemorations in 1966, 1976 and 1986.

of the 36th, 8th and 25th Divisions, finally took the village. The ridge was retaken by the Germans in their 1918 offensive when it was only lightly defended but on August 24 it was recaptured with ease by V Corps.

Across a wide green lawn from the great edifice is the **18th Division Memorial**. This is passed as the D151 is joined for **Authuille**, 1½ kms away. The road descends to this village which clings to the east bank of the Ancre. Across the river and its bankside marshes is the railway and the road to Albert via **Aveluy Wood**. This wood is still cut by the remains of the trenches of the British lines; 36th Division's HQ was here, and **Lancashire Dump** was on the site of **Aveluy Wood Cemetery**. This road is the D50 and it rolls up and down to Albert, some 3 kms away.

However, before we enter this historic place, take the D104 from Aveluy to visit Ovillers and La Boisselle via Pozières. Shortly after crossing the D151 there is a rise in the road and, on the right, a small road leads to **Ovillers**, passing its large **cemetery** and overlooking the valley called **Mash Valley** by the BEF. Along the ridge of this valley up which the D929 rises there were many mine craters in years gone by. They were part of the almost continuous series blown in the mine warfare of 1915-16. Ovillers was stormed on July 1, 1916, but did not fall until the 16th.

Aveluy Wood Cemetery, where men sleep amid crumbling trenches, was laid out on the site of the Lancashire Dump.

The Australian Memorial at Pozières is located on the site of the mill — then a German observation post on the top of Hill 160.

The Tank Corps Memorial lies on the opposite side of the road.

Passing through the village take the right-hand road to join the D929. Turn left up the slope to **Pozières**. This village, astride the main Albert—Bapaume road, was the focus of much heavy fighting and, by August 1916, had ceased to exist. It was taken on August 23 by the 1st Australian Division and the 48th British Division of General Gough's Fifth Army. Beside the long straight road before the village is reached, the **Pozières Military Cemetery** and the **Memorial to the Missing of the Fifth Army in 1918** are passed. This memorial records the names of 14,690 men of the Fifth Army who died in the battles of the Somme up to April 5, 1918, and all other casualties up to August 7 with no known graves.

Continue up the gradient, which increases until the crest is reached, beside the **Tank Corps Memorial** opposite the site of **Pozières Mill**. The obelisk of the Tank Memorial is set off by four fine scale models of tanks of the 1916-18 period, one of which bears bullet marks from the Second War. It was from this area that the first tanks went into action towards Flers in September 1916. Pozières Mill is now a grassy mound behind a trim lawn with simple stone markers of the **Australian Memorial** recalling the action of the Australians who stood here in July and August 1916, attempting to capture this feature, **Hill 160**. Here in this small sector they suffered their most severe casualties in the battle. The mill was fortified by a German bunker of which there is little left today. By looking around, it is possible to appreciate what a fine 'O-Pip' this was. Over to the westward, the Thiepval Memorial can

The memorial gateway to the Fifth Army Missing at Pozières Cemetery on which 14,690 names are recorded of men who died on the Somme.

be seen. The sites of other prominent actions can also be discerned, even the **sugar refinery** on the ridge. The **Australian 1st Division** and **KRRC memorials** are to the south of Pozières.

Another 1½ km further north and the **Canadian Memorial of Courcelette** is reached

which commemorates their great actions in November 1916 when they took, among other positions, the longest trench built by the Germans on the Western Front, which ran across this ridge — **Regina Trench**.

Turn right on to the D6 for **Martinpuich** (1 km). Martinpuich was battered to pulp long

South of the village is the 1st Australian Division Memorial.

The Canadian Memorial at Courcelette. Here in November 1916 they captured the longest trench constructed by the Germans on the Western Front.

The 19th Division Memorial on the village green at La Boisselle.

The 34th Division Memorial above La Boisselle.

Becort Wood and Albert — the ridge towards Fricourt and upwards to Pozières and back to Ovillers. Nearer to hand are the small craters of the **Glory Hole** blown in 1915, easily visible behind the houses of La Boisselle and along the road which connects with D929 beside the **Tyneside Scottish and Tyneside Irish Memorial** close to their positions when these battalions fought to win this sector in that infamous July. All around there is still evidence in the shell holes of the many months of fighting in this valley. **Y Sap**, another of the large mines, lay on the western side of D929. It was filled in some years ago and built over and today it is merely discernable by a white circular patch in the field behind the bungalows.

Albert is 3 kms down the D929 or, taking the Bécourt-Bécordel road below Lochnager Crater, more of the battle area is traversed. Little now marks the landscape except the chalk slicks in newly-ploughed ground or the occasional artillery position in the embankments. Such a position is very clearly seen behind **Norfolk Cemetery**. The two hamlets were in the British rear lines and were bases from which units moved into action. After Bécordel turn right on to D938 to reach Albert in 3 kms.

before it actually fell to the British 15th Division on September 15, 1916 after the attack on Flers. Some of the tanks first used that day were in action here. After it was recaptured by the Germans in March 1918, they remained here until V Corps troops retook the position in August.

We now take the small unclassified road to the right for **Bazentin-le-Grand**, another village with a similar history. Turn right for **Contalmaison** on the D20 and proceed to **La Boisselle**. Above the village is the **Memorial to the 34th Division** and, on the green before the church, is the **19th Division Memorial**.

Taking the small road on the left and the immediate left fork in a few metres arrive at **Lochnager Crater**. The purchase of it in 1979 by Richard Dunning of London has made its preservation more secure and the erosion of the site by encroaching agriculture halted. The crater, the largest on the Western Front, was one of a group blown on July 1, 1916, the explosion being felt for hundreds of miles. This mine alone comprised 60,000lbs of explosives, all carefully dragged underground along saps emanating from the direction of the **Tara-Usna line** near the main road to Albert, and the crater today is some 300ft across and 90ft deep. From the rim there are extensive views over Chapes Spur — **Sausage Valley** — so called by the British for the German observation balloon which hung over it. In the slopes of the shallow valley can be discerned the positions of some of the machine gun posts which poured forth their deadly fire to cause such devastation among the troops advancing from Tara and Usna —

In April 1976, when the photo *centre* was taken, what was left of the battlefield surrounding Lochnager Crater at La Boisselle was gradually being reclaimed. Although this, the largest crater on the Western front, created on July 1, 1916 by the explosion of 60,000 lbs of guncotton, still remained amid the ruins of the old German front line, other smaller craters near the village were being filled in. The latest to go now has a house built over it. In 1979 Richard Dunning decided that this gradual encroachment of a unique piece of First World War history, and the Somme battles in particular, must be reversed and he purchased Lochnager Crater personally that it might be saved as a permanent memorial, The picture *right* of the area in 1982 shows how the surrounding fields had crept closer in those six years. In 1980 a memorial was erected; in 1986 a wooden cross.

Albert, once called Ancre, is an industrial town which was very much in the front line in the various battles of the Somme and the Ancre. At the end of September 1914 it was almost occupied by the advancing German Second Army but the French Tenth Army stood in its way and, with the support of the British cavalry, pushed them back. For the next two years Albert was only a few kilometres from the front line and was frequently bombarded. On January 15, 1915, the **golden virgin** on the tower of the Basilica was toppled from her plinth when a shell hit the dome on which she stood. The statue did not fall but hung, precariously, head down out over the tower. The sight of the statue hanging almost at right angles was one of the most talked of incidents of Albert and led to the legend that when the 'Leaning Virgin' fell, the war would be over. In due course the base of the statue was secured, first by French and later British engineers.

Being close to the front, Albert was always filled with the military, at first mostly by French forces but in March 1916 the British took over. Until October 1916 the town was well within the range of the German guns and was very badly damaged. On March 26, 1918 the German offensive swept through Albert after bitter fighting, and the town remained in German hands until the British advance in August when, on the 22nd, it was recaptured. As the Basilica tower was being utilised by the Germans as an observation post, orders were issued for its destruction. At 3.30 p.m. on April 16, the 35th British Divisional Artillery shelled the tower extremely accurately and, with the third shot, the tower fell with of course the Virgin. So much for the legend!

None of the buildings in Albert are old, all having been rebuilt, although the Basilica and the imposing Hôtel de Ville were rebuilt in the 1920s very much in their old style. On the front wall of the **Hôtel de Ville** is a memorial plaque to the **Machine Gun Corps**.

To resume the tour of the battlefields, leave Albert via the D938 for **Fricourt** (5 kms). At the beginning of the village, the **Fricourt British Cemetery** and the **7th Battalion, Green Howards Memorial** is on the left. This was another of the villages turned into fortresses by the Germans during their long occupation. Mine warfare was fought for many months around the village which was, in time, utterly ruined. On the left of the D147, on the crest of the rising ground, the cratered ground of the **Tambour Mine** is visible. Above it is **Fricourt New Military Cemetery** out in the fields. Fricourt fell to the 17th Division on July 2, 1916 and this cemetery was one of their burial grounds. On the north-east side of the village is **Fricourt Wood**, again captured by 17th Division.

Left: **The Leaning Virgin on the tower of the Basilica was dislodged in a bombardment in January 1915 and finally toppled on April 16, 1918.** *Right:* **Once again the Golden Virgin gleams over modern Albert.**

The Machine Gun Corps Memorial on the façade at Albert's Hôtel de Ville.

Artillery lines have left their mark behind Norfolk Cemetery just outside Albert.

Beside the Bray road on the outskirts of Fricourt lies the British Cemetery and the 7th Bn. Green Howards Memorial.

Three kilometres up the D147 is **Contalmaison**, captured by the 17th and 38th Divisions on July 9, 1916, after being attacked by the 7th, 17th and 23rd Divisions since the 3rd.

East of the village **Mametz Wood** stretches southward for 1½ kms with **Mametz** itself another ½ km beyond the southern tip. The first right-hand road on entering Contalmaison follows the western boundary. Eastward from Contalmaison, the D20 leads towards **Bazentin-le-Petit** and **Bazentin-le-Grand** with their woods on the left skirting the northern edge of Mametz Wood with **Sabot Copse** and **Flat Iron Copse** and its cemetery down a narrow lane to the right. These features were in German lines, a labyrinth of trenches and deep dugouts. For several days the British divisions fought every inch of the way, enduring bitter fighting in the battles for **Bazentin Ridge**, clearing the villages and woods by July 14, as

The Royal Welsh Fusiliers' Memorial in Danzig Alley Cemetery.

The 82nd Field Company Memorial at Bazentin-le-Petit refurbished in 1989 by the Junior Leaders Regiment, RE.

This striking red Welsh dragon surmounts the 38th Division Memorial commemorating Mametz Wood 1916.

In Mansell Copse is the Devonshire Cemetery where men of the regiment lie in their original wartime graves.

they slowly but steadily pushed on during that dreadful summer. An unclassified road from Bazentin-le-Petit leads to **Montauban-de-Picardie** and the D64 thence to Mametz. In the vicinity are several British cemeteries including **Danzig Alley** where there is a **memorial to the 14th (S) Bn. Royal Welsh Fusiliers**, on the D64 at the edge of Mametz.

A short way along the road from Mametz to Contalmaison there is a narrow lane on the right just before the road dips into the valley. This leads to the **38th Welsh Division Memorial** hidden in the folds of the hills. The lane (which is approached more easily from Mametz) follows the contours of the site of the famous **Queen's Nullah** before there is a fork; the left track peters out as it crosses the fields to the **Willow Stream** over **Cliff Trench** so continue straight on. Even though the surface deteriorates it remains quite passable as it, too, drops downwards towards the cliffs. Suddenly, on a spur overlooking the **Hammerhead** of Mametz Wood, the fantastic **Red Dragon** glowers defiance. It was from here the 38th Division fought through the wood to Bazentin Ridge suffering heavy casualties. Below the memorial is a small car park and turning circle. The lane beyond this point becomes a muddy rutted track (unfit for cars) as it winds its way to **Flat Iron Copse Cemetery**.

Return to Mametz bearing right to join the D938 and then turn left. A short distance along the recently widened and straightened road, a track proceeds up the slope to the right. The little wood here is **Mansell Copse** in whose shelter is **Devonshire Cemetery**. It stands on the old British front line. Here lie 163 men of the 8th and 9th Devons as they were buried by their Padre. A small memorial erected in 1986 records that they held

this position then and they hold it still. Among their number are Captain D. L. Martin of the 9th Devons and the poet W. N. Hodgeson. Many of the casualties were victims of a German machine gun mounted by the crucifix in Mametz Cemetery which can be seen across the valley. Incidentally,

down on the Becordel Road is another Devonshire Cemetery — **Dartmoor Cemetery** — where lies Lieutenant Harry Webber, at 67 the oldest man killed in action on the Somme; Private J. Miller, VC, of the 7th Bn. King's Own (Royal Lancaster) Regiment, and two members of one family.

Today there are over 420,000 marked graves from the Great War in France but of every four men that died, one was unidentified. In the horrific Flanders battlefields in Belgium the proportion is even higher with a third of the graves being those of unknown casualties. Every grave tells its story of tragedy and bereavement; none more so than that of the Lee family whose father and son lie side by side in Dartmoor Cemetery, both killed serving in the same unit on the same day.

A little to the east of Mansell Copse is the small **Gordon Cemetery** created by 2nd Gordon Highlanders in one of the British support trenches which ran along here. Like the Devons, the Gordons were units of the 7th Division whose memorial at Mametz has disappeared.

The next two roads on the left lead to **Carnoy** but continue on to **Maricourt**, 3 kms, passing the road to Bronfay and Bray on the right. It was at Maricourt that the British and French lines merged in 1916. At the edge of the village, on the left facing **Happy Valley**, is the large **Peronne Road Cemetery** made by the concentration of battlefield graves. Turn left either via the unclassified road to the centre of **Montauban-de-Picardie** or the D197 which joins the D64 at the crossroads east of the village near the site of the **brickworks** which were completely destroyed in the battle when captured by the Liverpool Regiment when the 18th and 30th Divisions captured Montauban. During the Allied advance in August 1918, Montauban was once more captured by the 18th Division. These divisions, having withstood various counter-attacks, advanced eastward towards **Bernafay** and **Trones Woods** which will be passed soon after turning right on the D64. The 30th Division occupied Bernafay Wood between July 1 and 3, but the attacks on Trones Wood — the **Bois des Troncs** — did not begin until July 8. Between the woods is an open stretch of ground from which there is an excellent vista over Caterpillar Valley with **High Wood** on the further crest to the west and **Delville Wood** to the east. From July 8 to 13, the 30th Division made several attacks capturing the wood but then being forced to retire by enemy counter-attacks, both sides suffering heavy casualties. On July 13, the 18th Division took over the assault with the 7th, 3rd and 9th Divisions on their left. After further difficult fighting, with German snipers hidden in the undergrowth and up in the trees, the wood was cleared finally on July 14. At the bend in the road

This is the tiny cemetery at Mametz created by the 2nd Bn. Gordon Highlanders. Trenches still remain below the hedges in the middle distance.

of the sucrerie where **Waterlot Farm** once stood still dominating the landscape. Just beyond the modern buildings of the station

site, in the field is a **lone memorial** to 2nd Lieutenant George Futvoye Marsden-Smedley, 3rd Bn. The Rifle Brigade, killed in action in the attack of August 1, 1916. Guillemont fell to the 20th Light Division and a brigade of the 16th Irish Division on August 23, 1916, after bitter fighting which had involved many units since the end of July. Turning down into the village, the **16th Irish Division Memorial** stands by the church. Go straight ahead up the D20 to Longueval.

Before visiting Deville Wood continue into **Longueval** village. In the center is the **Café Calypso** which has behind it a **trench museum**. The owner does not claim it is in any way authentic but is a representation of what this area was like in 1916. Only the many objects which lay scattered over the ground and along the trench and dugout walls are genuine. Beside the short complex of trenches is a small museum of uniforms, badges and ephemera, photographs and other equipment. Entrance fee.

stands **18th Division's Memorial Obelisk** at the edge of the wood. Today the woods are healthy young forests and bear little resemblance to the muddy shattered areas the troops knew.

Guillemont is 2 kms, but just prior to reaching the village we pass on the left **Guillemont Road Cemetery** where Lieutenant Raymond Asquith, the son of the then-Prime Minister is buried. He was killed at Ginchy in September 1916. Over 2,200 others lie with him on the site of a once formidable German entrenchment. Here again the views are panoramic; across the fields can be discerned the route of the old railway, now an agricultural complex, with Longueval and Delville Woods behind the rotting ruins

The enterprising collector and owner of the Café Calypso at Longueval has simulated very effectively a small trench system as it would have appeared in 1916 where genuine artifacts and equipment are realistically displayed.

Memorial Cross to 'Bristol's Own' at Longueval with High Wood in the background.

The New Zealand Battle Memorial lies between High Wood and Delville Wood on the site of Crest Farm.

Further along the road is **London Cemetery**, where the fallen from 1916 were joined in 1946 by men of the 51st Highland Division and others killed in 1940. Opposite on the edge of the wood is a small cairn. This was unveiled in 1972 by Madame Mathon whose family own the wood; it is the **Memorial to the 9th Bn. Highland Light Infantry — The Glasgow Highlanders**, 192 of whom fell in the trench here on July 5, 1916 fighting shoulder to shoulder. They are now commemorated by 192 stones brought from Scotland by the

One of the most poignant of memorials: 192 stones from Scotland erected to remember a similar number of Highlanders who fell in High Wood.

Proceed on D20 turning right onto D107. Here on the corner is the **wooden cross** of the **12th (Bristol) Bn., Gloucestershire Regiment**, recently erected on the site of the original lost some time ago.

Away on the rise between the woods can be seen the **New Zealand Memorial** on the site of **Crest Farm**; it can be reached from the Longueval to Flers road, and behind is a small cratered area.

About 1 km along is **Bois des Fourceaux** or, as it is better known, **High Wood**. On the roadside is the **Memorial to the 47th (London) Division** which fought here and finally cleared the wood of its German defenders on September 15, 1916 after fierce fighting. One of their trenches ran along the edge of the wood about where the right-hand ditch is now. The British cavalry penetrated the wood on July 14 but the Germans were well dug in with concrete dugouts and positions, one of which can be seen from the road among the trees. On the eastern flank of the wood — reached by a muddy track at the edge of the field — is the **Memorial to the Cameron Highlanders and Black Watch** who fought here on September 3, the day when the large mine was blown. The crater, now

filled with water, can be seen on the left beyond the memorial.

The Cameron Highlanders and Black Watch Memorial beyond which lies a water-filled mine crater in High Wood.

Scottish historian Mr Alex Aitken and his wife, and carefully constructed on a slate plinth to a height of 5 feet 7 inches, the minimum height of men of the battalion.

The wood is privately owned and should not be entered without the permission of the owner who lives in the large house near the road. The trenches and some of the strong points remain amid the trees, but the area has not been completely cleared of battle debris and it could be dangerous to trespass. From the edge of the wood overlooking Delville Wood is the area fought over by the London Battalions after taking the wood. It was a pocket of resistance which the capture of Flers had outflanked.

Not far along the D20 from the Gloucester Cross is **Caterpillar Valley Cemetery**, one of the largest in the Somme. Nearly 5,600 are buried here and by the eastern wall is the pavilion of the **New Zealand Memorial to the Missing** on the Somme.

Left: **The South African Memorial in Delville Wood, unveiled in 1926, with the new museum opened in 1986** *(above)* **in the background.**

The new museum has been sited to encompass the Voortrekker Cross — the cross upon a cross — *(left)* which formerly stood isolated as the Cross of Consecration. Now etched plate glass windows tell the story of South Africa's participation in words and pictures. *Centre and right:* **Around the walls massive bronze panels depict the various aspects of the conflict.**

Return through Longueval to visit **Delville Wood** and the **South African National Memorial** and **Museum** on the road to **Ginchy**. As the wood is approached one reaches the large car and coach park, the shop and toilets. The entrance to the memorial and museum is opposite **Delville Wood Cemetery** a little further along the road. This cemetery contains the graves of men of the divisions who contested this sector — the 9th Scottish Division and the 2nd, 14th Light and 17th Divisions.

The **Bois d'Elville**, approximately half-a-mile square in an irregular shape, skirts the eastern flank of Longueval and reaches almost into Ginchy on the east. The battle for the wood, often called **Devil's Wood** by the troops, was the scene of the baptisms of fire of the South African Brigade of the 9th Scottish Division from July 14-20, 1916. Commanded by General H. T. Lukin, the South African Brigade had a strength of 121 officers and 3,032 NCOs and men. On July 14 they had been in reserve at Montauban. Less one battalion (which went to assist in the clearing of Longueval), the brigade went into action on the morning of the 15th. Under heavy bombardment by the defending force, the battalions fought their desperate way into the wood and, despite heavy losses, had taken all the wood except the south-west corner by July 17. The 3rd Battalion was cut

The sole remaining tree to survive the 1916 battles, despite its shrapnel-filled trunk, is carefully tended by the CWGC.

off and had to surrender — three officers and 150 men. The colonel of the 2nd Battalion gathered together 140 of all ranks from the four battalions and fought his way through to rejoin the brigade. At 6.00 am. on the 20th the brigade was withdrawn — 29 officers and 751 other ranks were all that were left.

The graceful memorial is approached across a broad lawn between two double lines of oak trees grown from acorns brought from French Hook, Cape Colony. Hundreds of young trees were planted in the 1920s to form a frame for the memorial which was designed by Sir Herbert Baker, ARA. A triumphal archway, surmounted by a bronze group, is flanked by a curved wall of flint and stone with a pavilion at either end. The bronze group of two figures either side of a great horse by Alfred Turner represents Castor and Pollux clasping hands in friendship, and was originally entitled 'Union'. The memorial itself was unveiled by General Botha's widow in the presence of General Herzog, Field-Marshal Haig and other dignitaries on October 10, 1926. The altar Stone of Remembrance, placed in front of the arch, was added after the Second World War to commemorate South Africa's 1939-1945 war dead. This was unveiled by Mrs O. M. Swales, mother of Captain W. Swales, VC, on June 5, 1952.

On November 11, 1986, the Hon. P. W. Botha, President of the Republic of South Africa, inaugurated the **Commemorative Museum** which is situated behind the memorial crescent. In the shape of the Castle of the Cape of Good Hope which is depicted in the South African Defence Force insignia and the Cape of Good Hope Star, the five bastions enclose the beautiful **Cross of Consecration** (the **Voortrekker Cross**) in a central patio. The story of South Africa's participation in both World Wars and in Korea is told on massive bronze panels, delicately engraved windows, and in photographs, paintings, documents and relics. The central entrance is flanked by artillery pieces. Pride of place in the gallery is taken by the **Memorial Books of Honour**. To the west of the museum is the **sole surviving original tree** — a hornbeam — carefully tended by the Commonwealth War Graves Commission and, despite being full of shrapnel, it is remarkably healthy.

In the rehabilitation of the wood the original glades, which were named after

streets in London, Edinburgh and Cape-town, have been maintained and make a walk through the wood a very pleasant experience. It is difficult to realise the terrible past until a trench is noticed in the undergrowth where rusty pieces of shell-case, water bottles and odd rounds of small arms ammunition are frequently found. All the glades have stone signposts at their junctions so it is quite easy to follow the course of the battles which raged in all for sixteen days before the 2nd Division finally cleared the wood on July 28, 1916. In 1918 heavy fighting again took place during the Allied advance when the 17th and 38th Divisions were engaged. On **Buchanan Street**, just north of the cross with **Rotten Row**, is a monument marking the site of the **South African Brigade HQ dugout**. From it several trenches can be followed away into the wood.

Close by this memorial are the trenches leading to the South African Brigade HQ dugout.

The 20th Light Division Memorial on the D20 between Ginchy and Combles.

From Delville Wood continue eastwards to **Ginchy** — a forward position in the German defence line standing high on the plain above Combles. It was first captured by the 7th Division on July 3 but lost in a counter-attack only to be recaptured on July 9 by the 16th Irish Division. Turn right in the centre of the village to join the D20 in ½ km at the **20th Light Division Memorial** and turn left for Combles. In 1 km **Leuze (Lousy) Wood** appears on the right. Through land reclamation its twin, **Bouleaux Wood**, on the left, is barely discernable. Only a fragment remains up a muddy track. These woods were the scene of heavy fighting by the 56th London Division in September 1916. Amid the remaining scrubby trees and bushes of Bouleaux Wood, right at the far end, stands a wooden cross erected to commemorate the death on September 9, 1916 in Leuze Wood of a grandson of the novelist Charles Dickens. Major Cedric Charles Dickens served with the 1/13th Bn. (Kensington) London Regiment. Across the fields to the northwest lies the site of the formidable **Quadrilateral**, a fortified position captured by 6th Division on September 18, 1916.

In 1 km **Combles**, a small town built on a hill, was the last German redoubt to fall in September 1916. Just opposite was the junction between the BEF and the French lines. Protected by its surrounding hills, Combles did not suffer to the same degree as neighbouring villages. During their occupation of it, the German Army strongly fortified the town, which eventually fell to a joint Anglo-French attack on September 26. In the rock beneath **Lamotte Château**, tunnels and shelters had been cut before the war which the Germans extended, making a complete subterranean headquarters.

Two kms along the D74/DIIe is **Morval** which was captured on September 25, 1916. It was re-entered again by the advancing Germans in March 1918 as it lay in the gap between the Third and Fifth Armies.

A kilometre further on is **Lesboeufs** captured by the 6th and Guards Divisions on September 25. In March 1918 the 63rd Division was in action here, delaying the German advance. Machine-gunners fired 250,000 rounds whilst covering the division, creating havoc among the oncoming German forces. Keep to the left and return to Ginchy by the road which crosses the heights. A stop at the **Guards' Memorial** provides excellent views of the area of the September conflict and the March 1918 advance.

Continue to Ginchy (3 kms) and take the right turn for Flers, crossing the wide open country over which the tanks rolled for the first time on September 15, 1916.

We reach **Flers** 3 km further on. At the end of the main street is the **41st Division Memorial** (*see front cover*) a 'New Army' division with units from many parts of England, their badges decorate the enclosing pillars. The rifle of the infantryman points in the direction that the tanks came from Pozières. Flers was the target of three corps of the Fourth Army on September 15, 1916 when, in the early morning, the tanks first took to the fields.

Proceed northward and at the next crossroads turn right on D11, passing **A.I.F. Burial Ground Cemetery** away to the right and reach **Gueudecourt** in 2 kms. The hub of many actions in September 1916, little remained of the village when it was captured. About ½ km on D74e/D11, the Beaulencourt road, is the **Newfoundland Memorial** in a small fir-lined enclosure amid the expanse of cornfields, The memorial is a Caribou similar to the one at Beaumont Hamel. This one stands above a strong point within a curve of trenches and a machine gun post

Here died Major Cedric Charles Dickens. A simple wooden cross to commemorate the death of a grandson of Charles Dickens in Bouleaux Wood.

which were the site of a regimental position in September 1916.

Leave Gueudecourt by the D11 for **Le Sars** crossing the **Warlencourt Ridge**. The hamlet of Le Sars is astride the D929 on the crest of one of the rises of the hills overlooking Bapaume, and marks the limit of the British advance on this sector in the 1916 Somme battles.

Turn right on to the D929. As we descend the hill, over to the right ahead, in the fold of one of the slopes of the hills, is a wooded mound. In 1916 this was the chalk-covered eminence known as the **Butte de Warlencourt**. At that time it was higher than it is today and it stood out above the rest of the battlefield. The Butte was an artificial mound which had played a prominent part in the war of 1871, and was honeycombed with many tunnels even before the Germans took it and fortified it so strongly that it was

The Guards' Cemetery is laid out on the slopes beyond Combles. This town, just opposite the junction of the British and French lines, was heavily fortified by the Germans. It was captured on September 26, 1916.

The Guards' Memorial on the Lesboeufs road — a windswept viewpoint of the field of battle.

Beneath the streets of Bapaume, these bottles recall the German occupation of the Bastion de la Reyne.

almost impossible to capture. Several times it was overrun by British units but the defenders from below counter-attacked and driving off the attacking forces until, on February 25, 1917, success was achieved and the Butte fell into British hands. During the following year, five of the attacking units erected memorials on the shell-torn crest including the **Durham Light Infantry**, the **South Africans** and other territorial units. None of these survive here today. In March 1918 the Germans retook the mound and they erected a cross on the summit. It was not until August 1918 that the Butte was again overrun.

The remains of some of the fortified entrances can be traced in the undergrowth beneath the trees and the **base of the German memorial** can be found on the crest. In 1944, the German infantry battalion in the region erected a replacement cross on the old base and this survives, hidden in the brush.

The D929 continues across the undulating country to Bapaume, 5 kms away. Vestiges of the old trench lines remain here and there with the occasional concrete shelter, such as the one on the Thilloy-Grevillers crossroad, and, nearer to Bapaume, the ridges and hedges show evidence of usage as artillery positions. To visit the town, turn right at the road junction.

Bapaume is a quiet market town with a long history dating back to Roman times. Situated at a strategic crossroads, it was frequently the scene of conflict and in the 16th Century was a fortified town. Beneath the quiet streets, many of the cellars are in fact relics of this period.

The town was in the battle-line in late August 1914 and, after the German push to the west, remained in their hands until March 17, 1917 when the Australian 2nd Division captured it. All the old buildings had by then been destroyed. Only one building remains today and that is a **barn** on the very outskirts of the town on the Péronne road. Parts of the old ramparts, stripped of their brick cladding, can be seen on the eastern side of the town in a park. The **town museum** is housed in the Lawrence School, just above the square, and includes relics from 1914-18. The school was the gift of a manufacturer from Sheffield. In the foyer of the Hôtel de Ville are huge reproductions of the Croix de Guerre and the Légion d'Honneur awarded to the town.

During the German occupations of the town in both wars, they made use of one of the underground bastions, which dates from 1551, and on occasions this can be viewed. The galleries of the **Bastion de la Reyne** lie beneath the houses north of Place Faidherbe and are in remarkable condition. The entrance is through one of the houses in rue de la République. The main gallery is some eight metres below the level of the pavement and consists of two large halls connected by narrow vaulted passages.

In many of the old gun ports there are piles of debris from the German occupations, including hundreds of bottles, proclaiming it as the site of an old mess. On the walls are earlier relics; on one brick is inscribed the palindrome '1551' which legend has it was scratched by Charles V. On another is a representation of the arms of Austria, Spain and Burgundy, the three major contestants for the town in the 16th Century. The wiring for telephone and electricity dates from 1916. Enquiries for further details should be made to the Société Archéologique de Bapaume.

When the Germans evacuated Bapaume in March 1917, they left many of the buildings booby-trapped or mined. The Hôtel de Ville was one of these and it blew up some days after the Australians had entered the town. The Germans re-entered the ruins of Bapaume on March 24, 1918 but were dislodged by the New Zealand Division on August 29.

Leave Bapaume for Arras by the N17. This road swings up and down through several small villages and hamlets well known to the BEF. In its day, this agricultural plain was a scene of utter devastation and sometimes, usually in the evening light, the tracks of a tortuous trench line can be discerned.

Some 4 kms further on **Sapignies**, and a little further **Behagnies**, were both in the front line in March 1918 when they fell in the face of the German advance. Both were recaptured in August by the 2nd Division.

We then pass through **Ervillers** in 2 kms, a German garrison village until March 1917 and then in March 1918 the scene of heavy fighting with the 42nd Division trying to delay the advance. It was recaptured on August 23. **Gomiécourt**, a short way to the south-west, was where the 3rd Division had a fierce fight in August 1918 when they took the village with many prisoners.

It is 6 kms to **Boiry-Becquerelle** (the modern road goes over the old highway by a bridge as the villages are entered) and 3 kms to **Mercatel**. This village was the junction of the **Hindenburg Line** with the old German line of 1914. We then reach **Beaurains**, a suburb of Arras through which the front line ran in 1917 and where the CWGC now have their offices.

Trenches occupied by the Royal Newfoundland Regiment whose Caribou Memorial surveys the German lines at Gueudecourt.

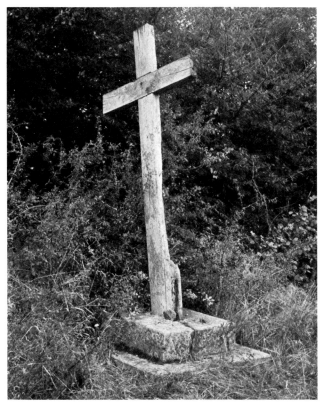

German memorial on the Butte de Warlencourt which was purchased by the Western Front Association early in 1990.

Arras to Cambrai
ROUTE 1

The direct route via the D939 is 30 kms, an absolutely straight road of Roman Origin.

Tilloy-lès-Mofflaines (4 kms). North of this Arras suburb is the famous **Observatory Ridge** with the **Harp position** from which the Hindenburg Line swung southwards to Croisilles and Quéant. There were many actions fought around here in 1917 during the battle for Arras but few signs remain evident today. The construction of autoroutes A1 and A26 has removed most of the prominent ones but here and there a steep-sided ditch or a long earthwork may be a remnant of the old trench lines.

La Chapelle de Feuchy (2 kms). Access point for the Lille-Paris motorway. This was the furthest extent of the first day's advance in the April 1917 battle and the village where the 15th Scottish Division stood in the defence of Arras in 1918. Here, too, in April 1917 the **12th Division** fought an action and their **memorial** stands on the south side of the road near the spot. This cross is one of two memorials, the other being at Malassie Farm near Epehy, south of Cambrai, a position held by the division in the capture of that town in September 1918. Both crosses are copies of a cross in York Minster. Opposite is a Demarcation Stone.

Leave the D939 by turning to the left on the D33 for **Monchy-le-Preux** (1 km). This village, built on high ground, provided the Germans with a commanding view of the Allied lines. It was captured by the 37th British Division, on April 11, 1917 during a blizzard. It was protected by wide bands of barbed wire, such as those which covered the Hindenburg Line, making an attack a very costly affair. However, Monchy, despite many counter-attacks, was retained until the March 1918 advance. East from Monchy rises **Infantry Hill** which was in the 29th Division line held by the Royal Newfoundland Regiment. On a bunker in the village, in the front garden of a house, stands the Caribou of the **Newfoundland Regimental Memorial**. Monchy was recaptured on August 26, 1918 by the Canadian Corps. Return to the D939 via D34.

Vis-en-Artois (4 kms) is reached after crossing the River Cojeul. On the upward slope is the **Vis-en-Artois Cemetery and Memorial to the Missing** who fell in the 1918 advance in Picardy where 9,903 names are remembered. In the cemetery lie over 1,700 British and 573 Canadians who died in the capture of this sector on August 27, 1918.

The Memorial to the 12th Division on the HQ dugout site at La Chapelle de Feuchy.

The 37th Division's soldier trio which stands at Monchy le Preux.

Vis-en-Artois Cemetery and the Memorial to the Missing.

Dury Crossroad (3½ kms) with the **Canadian Memorial** almost directly after it on the left.

About 8 kms of undulating road stretch across the expansive plain before the Canal du Nord and **Marquion** are reached. To assist the 4th, 63rd and 1st Canadian Divisions to take this small town in September 1918, the Royal Engineers built several bridges over the canal during the nights beforehand.

An interesting detour can be made by turning right onto the D15 at the end of the village and in 2½ kms reaching the edge of **Sains-les-Marquoin** with the **British Cemetery** at the crossroads with the D16. Go straight ahead to the fork and take the right D22 for **Inchy-en-Artois** and then the D19 in the village for **Moeuvres** (2 kms). Both villages were German strongholds which did not fall in the 1917 battles despite all attempts, but in 1918 the former was captured by the 63rd (Royal Naval) Division on September 3, and the latter by the 52nd (Lowland) Division on the 19th. The **Canal du Nord**, crossed as Inchy is entered, was still under construction and formed a deep and vital barrier for both attacker and defender.

As Moeuvres is reached, on the right is **Moeuvres Communal Cemetery Extension**. Near the entrance is a mass German grave of 94 officers and men named on the surrounding plinth. Lieutenant C. Pope of 11th Australian Battalion, a posthumous VC recipient, is also buried here. He died on April 15, 1917 at Louverval in the action for which he won the decoration.

In November 1917 the 56th London Division were heavily engaged between the two villages.

In Moeuvres take the D16e left of the church to proceed for **Bourlon** 4 kms further on. Bourlon Wood is to the east of the village on rising ground. The **Canadian Memorial** is on the edge of the wood on the hillside and is reached up a stepped path between ancient chestnut trees planted in Napoleon's honour. In the undergrowth of the wood are remains of a bunker. A path leads into the wood from the entrance to the memorial (up to the left as you face the village). There is also a **memorial to the Free French** of the Second World War here.

From Bourlon take the D16 to gain the D919 in 2½ kms. Turn right and Cambrai is 8 kms further on.

After passing through Raillencourt we enter **Cambrai** via the rue d'Arras and, after crossing the St Quentin Canal, the rue des Feutriers leads into the great Place Aristide Briand, once the Place d'Armes. Cambrai, an historic town, is once more a bustling, prosperous industrial and market city.

In 1815 Wellington took the surrender of the city after the fall of Napoleon. In 1870 the Germans took it and in August 1914 von Kluck recaptured it. The Germans held the town as a large garrison base until October 8, 1918. In 1916, Prince Rupprecht of Bavaria

At Moeuvres, a German mass grave lies alongside the Allied war graves. Here Lieutenant Pope, an Australian VC, is buried.

had his headquarters here. In the autumn of 1917 the city came within the range of the Allied artillery and damage was effected on the ancient buildings. However most of the destruction was caused in 1918 when the retreating Germans mined and fired it as 3rd Canadian Division and the 57th Division converged on the city, from the north and the south respectively, to complete the operation on October 9.

The impressive **Hôtel de Ville** was severely damaged but has been rebuilt in its former design of the 19th Century. In the Belfry, above the central façade, are the oldest inhabitants of Cambrai: 'Martin' and 'Martine', the two mechanical figures of blackamoors which date from 1510 and which appear as the clock strikes the hour. In **le Mail St Martin** is the rebuilt **Belfry**, all that remains of the church of St Martin which dates from the 15th Century. Two of the city gates have survived, the **Porte de Paris** in the south and the **Porte Notre Dame** in the northeast. The **cathedral** in the rue de Paris is a Gothic church built in 1859 which was badly damaged. There is a **Municipal Museum** in the rue de l'Epée which is also a good provincial art gallery.

At the edge of the Jardin Public to the right of Place du Maréchal Leclerc is the **City War Memorial** and a little distance away further right is a **memorial to the Battle of 1917** unveiled in 1977 by the British Ambassador. The Jardin Public covers remnants of the ramparts designed by Charles Quint and Vauban. The crumbling ruins of the old fortress and barracks of Château de Selles lie at the north end of Boulevard Faidherbe.

On the D942, the Solesmes road, about 1 km out of town, is the **Cambrai East Military Cemetery**. This was originally a German graveyard later taken over by the CWGC. As with almost all the German burial grounds, it has green lawns about which are scattered lines of graves and very Teutonic monuments with the central huge black cross within a small walled area.

Originally German, Cambrai East Military Cemetery is now looked after jointly by the CWGC and the Volksbund Deutsche Kriegsgräberfürsorge. Photo *below left* shows the original German memorial and *right*, the British section.

ALTERNATIVE ROUTE ∎∎∎∎∎

Reproduced from Michelin Sheet No. 236 12th Edition 1989

Arras to Cambrai
ROUTE II

Leave Arras by the D939 and, about 1 km after crossing the railway, take the D37e to the right through the centre of **Tilloy** and then out into the country, crossing the area of the April 1917 attacks during the Arras battles.

In 8 kms, after going under the autoroute, enter **Wancourt** and, at the church, turn right on the D33 for **Héninel**, 1½ kms away. Both these villages played important rôles in the attacks by General Allenby's Third Army in 1917 and General Currie's Canadians in August 1918.

Turn left for **Chérisy** (2 kms), a pleasant if narrow road across the rolling countryside which was very cut about in 1917 and 1918. At Chérisy turn right onto D9 for **Fontaine-lès-Croisilles** (1 km). On the outskirts of the village, which lies on the east bank of the River Sensée (and before crossing the river), on the right is a very well preserved **German concrete dugout**.

The D5 leads to **Croisilles** and **Ecoust St Mein**, while the first small road after the church leads to **Hendecourt** and the second one to **Bullecourt**. This is all the area fought over by Australians and several British divisions during the Arras battles, and the breaching of the **Hindenburg Line**, which ran over the open country with wide belts of barbed wire entanglements. Bullecourt was the scene of many gallant deeds by the West Riding Division and has retained long associations with units which took part. Before the church is a **memorial to the British and Australians** erected in 1980, and outside the village **a plaque** recalls the Australian effort.

Either take the D5 to **Noreuil** from Ecoust or the D38 from Bullecourt via Riencourt to

German bunker near Fontaine les Croisilles.

Memorial at Bullecourt to the British and Australian dead of April and May 1917.

Bas reliefs carved by C. S. Jagger on the Cambrai Memorial at Louverval. This remembers those who fell in the Battle of Cambrai and have no known graves.

Flesquières was strongly defended by the Germans when, on November 20, 1917, the Battle of Cambrai began with the advance of 400 tanks from Havrincourt Wood to attack across the open fields on a 15 km front. From artillery emplacements in and around the village, the Germans hit hard at the Allied tanks. Although several divisions of General Byng's Third Army carried their targets, Flesquières proved to be a difficult proposition and a fierce battle ensued before the 51st Highland Division successfully captured the village.

Marcoing, 3 kms to the east, was captured by the 29th Division. The West Riding Division then went forward to take Graincourt and Anneux with many prisoners. The 6th Division took Ribécourt, whilst the 36th Division took Moeuvres in the north and 12th Division, Bonavis Ridge and Lateau

Quéant (thence by the D14 to Lagnicourt-Marcel) to go over the sites of the **Hindenburg Line** or the **Quéant Switch** which stretched to Drocourt in the north. This region was eventually captured by the 63rd Royal Naval Division.

From **Lagnicourt** take the D5 through **Louverval** to the crossroads on the N30 where stands the **Cambrai Memorial** to those who fell in the Battle of Cambrai and have no known graves and the **Louverval Military Cemetery**. On the walls of the memorial are some fine bas reliefs by Jagger relating to the Cambrai battles. Whichever route from Chérisy is taken, it is about 20 kms.

Turn right onto N30 for a short way and, at **Doignies**, turn left for **Hermies** on D34, 3 kms away. This is a pleasant village of which the green was once a **large mine crater** in 1917 when the I Anzac Corps were here.

After 3 kms the D5 crosses the Canal du Nord and the autoroute to enter **Havrincourt**. The **chateau**, which dominates this village, was for a long time in German hands as an HQ and here, on occasion, the Kaiser stayed. Before the end of the 1917 campaign, the village and château were in ruins, either through constant artillery bombardment or demolition. In 1917 British divisions could

not dislodge the enemy from the village or the wood which was fortified with concrete bunkers when the main attack on the Hindenburg Line began. Havrincourt was also on the edge of the Battle of Cambrai in November to December 1917. The 62nd Division fought here in 1917 and they captured the village in 1918. The New Zealand Corps took **Havrincourt Wood** on the edge of which is the **62nd Division Memorial**.

As with other villages in the area, Havrincourt has retained close relationships with its liberators and, each year, the Bradford Pals Pilgrimage used to pause here to meet the Maire and other personalities to drink a 'Vin d'Honneur' before visiting the château. This large, red brick house has been destroyed three times by fire or battle this century and, after each tragedy, has been rebuilt exactly as it was. In the meadows behind the château, and in the wood beyond, are remains of concrete shelters and bunkers.

A pleasant detour through the woods, and **Trescault** with the **42nd Division Memorial**, is via the D15 and then the D17/29 to **Ribécourt-la-Tour** rather than the direct road. Then take the D89 from Ribécourt, or the D15 from Havrincourt to Flesquières and the area of the Cambrai battle.

At Havrincourt a detour can be made (see map on opposite page) to take in the 42nd Division Memorial in the village of Trescault.

Above: **Havrincourt Château served as a German headquarters and was visited by the Kaiser. The 62nd West Yorkshire Division, whose memorial** *(right)* **is to be found on the edge of the village, captured the château ruins.**

Wood. Meanwhile the 20th Light Division had taken, and then after a heavy counter-attack lost, Les Rues des Vignes in the south. The 51st Division went forward to capture Fontaine-Notre-Dame and, as the 40th Division were attacking Bourlon Wood, the German Second Army counter-attacked. The 40th Division took the wood following a period of severe fighting with gas attacks but, by the end of November, the British divisions had taken nearly 11,000 prisoners and 140 guns. However, by the end of the first week in December, the reinforced German army had driven back the Allies to the Flesquières Ridge.

During the Allied advance in September 1918, the area was captured by the 2nd, 3rd, 5th, 42nd and Guards Divisions with the Canadians taking Bourlon Wood. The 57th and 63rd took Anneux and Graincourt and then Marcoing before reaching Cambrai.

From Flesquières go over the autoroute to **Graincourt-les-Havrincourt** (2 kms) and turn right in the village for **Anneux** and there turn left on the D15 to reach the N30. Near the crossroads, where we turn right (and the D16 continues ahead to follow the south-western slopes of Bourlon Wood), is **Anneux British Cemetery** where many of those killed in November 1917 and in September 1918 are buried. In 2 kms **Fontaine-Notre-Dame**, captured on November 21, 1917 by the 51st Highland Division, is passed through and in 4 kms Cambrai is entered.

After leaving Cambrai there is not a bend in this old Roman road over its total length. It sweeps up and down through open country and few towns or villages lie directly in its path. In recent years it has been greatly widened and is now a very fast road indeed, with narrow stretches only through the outlying parts of Beauvois, Caudry and Inchy.

ROUTE IV

For the more circular route via Le Catelet, leave Cambrai through the Porte de Paris on the N44, 7½ kms to **Masnières.** Here the **St Quentin Canal** is crossed not far from the **site of the bridge** which, after being mined by the Germans but not completely blown, was used by the British in their attacks in the Battle of Cambrai. However, when a tank attempted to drive across it, the much weakened structure gave way and the accident was to cause a considerable hold up to the advancing forces. On the crest of the hill going down into the town on the right is the **Newfoundland Regiment's Caribou Memorial**; the 29th Division fought here. Another 4 kms is **Bonavis**, the southern end of the line for the battle. Take the left-hand fork, the N44 for Le Catelet, travelling up and down across the plain (10 kms). Join the D912 about 7 kms south of the town.

ROUTE V

For those wanting to travel direct from Ypres (Ieper), our route follows the most picturesque and historic roads. However, soon it will be possible to make the journey entirely by autoroute.

Take the N8 from Ypres to **Menin** (Menen), 18 kms. This industrial town (with its twin Halluin on the southern French bank of the Lys), was the major German base and supply depot for the battles of Ypres. In 1914 it was overrun before Sir John French could seize it and for the next four years the

Five routes to Mons

ROUTE I

Cambrai is 65 kms from Mons on the A2-E19 autoroute.

ROUTE II

Alternatively, we can use the N30 to Valenciennes (30 kms) through some varied countryside, increasingly industrial, as the coalfields are reached between Bouchain and Douchy-les-Mines and into **Valenciennes**. This former lace-making city was occupied by the Germans in August 1914 and suffered considerably during the next four years. Factories and other establishments were taken over for use by the invading army, converting the area into a large base. By the time the Germans were driven out of the city in November 1918, by the Canadian Corps and the 4th, 49th and 61st Divisions, much had been destroyed. Damage was also caused by artillery during the Allied advance.

Some 12 kms out of Valenciennes on the N30 is the frontier post at **Quiévrechain**, from where the long straight road continues 22 kms to Mons. In its latter stages, the road passes through the region, south of the **Condé Canal**, which figured greatly in the 1914 BEF defence of Mons. General Allenby's Cavalry Corps were defending the bridges along the canal with the 19th Brigade in support from Valenciennes. The 5th Division was in action along the canal and, after the retreat had been ordered, the four bridges were blown. Today, however, there is nothing left to recall the brave acts of 1914.

ROUTE III

The D932 route to Mons can be joined from Cambrai either at Le Cateau or Le Catelet. Using the N43, Le Cateau is 22 kms.

Below: **A modern bridge now spans the canal at Masnières, replacing the original one** *(above)* **sited a few yards to the side of it, which collapsed under the weight of a British tank, causing a hold-up in the Allied advance in 1917.**

Save for a month, Menin remained in German hands throughout the war. This is their war cemetery where over 48,000 are buried.

Tour Henri VIII provides a medieval setting for the Musée des Armes at Tournai. A relic of Bluff King Hal's fortifications of the 1513-19 era.

Germans retained it. On October 16, 1918, the 34th Division took the town in the great Allied advance. On the northern outskirts of the town (beside the road to Moorsele) is the **Menin German Cemetery** where 48,049 are buried.

Another 10 kms out of town on the N8 is **Courtrai** (Kortrijk), also used by the German Army as a large base. It fell to the 9th Division on October 17, 1918. The town was damaged during the Second World War by a number of air raids. One of its older fortifications, the **Broelen Toren**, survived. This is a bridge over the Lys with two huge towers, in one of which is a **small museum**.

A little way out of the town on the Ghent road (the N43), on the left-hand side just before **Harelbeke**, is the **Royal Newfoundland Regiment Memorial**, the Caribou marking their exploits here in 1918.

Our route is now the N50 to Tournai (Doornik), 29 kms away. A pleasant road through varying country which for the last 10 kms follows closely the course of the Scheldt. At **Esquelmes**, 7 kms from Tournai, in the little churchyard on the river bank, are a group of **British war graves** from late 1918. Away in the fields, a kilometre or so along the narrow road running parallel with the canal, is a **1939-45 cemetery**, where lie men killed in May 1940. Among these many Guardsmen is the 8th Duke of Newcastle.

The ancient city of **Tournai** is entered through a long avenue of magnificent trees. The centre of the city is dominated by the enormous cathedral with its five towers. At the eastern end of the **Grand Place** is the **Belfroi**, the oldest in Belgium, and a magnificent view is gained from the gallery near the top.

Until the foundation of the modern Belgium in 1830, Tournai held allegiance to France. Many sieges have been withstood, including that by Edward III in 1340, and from 1513 to 1519 the city was in the hands of Henry VIII. He improved the old fortifications of the city and today one of these remains, the **Tour Henri VIII**. A solid two-storey building, it now houses the small but most interesting **Musée des Armes** including ancient and modern weapons. At the entrance is a 'Tallboy' and other smaller bombs from the Second World War.

To the German Army, Tournai was a very important centre with routes connecting with their forward bases. They finally retreated in the face of the Fifth Army in the last Allied advance. The British Army entered the city on November 8, 1918 to find many wrecked buildings and the bridges destroyed.

In **Tournai South Communal Cemetery**, approached by a left fork off the Avenue Montgomery (N508), in the Allied Extension, lie two officers of the Royal Flying Corps who are presumed to be the first killed in action in 1914. They are Lieutenant Vincent Waterfall and 2nd Lieutenant

Our RFC heroes: George Bayley and Vincent Waterfall, the first to fall on August 22, 1914.

George Gordon Bayley of No. 5 Squadron. On August 22, 1914, they set out at 10.16 a.m. in an Avro from their base at Maubeuge on a reconnaissance flight and flew over Mons and Soignies and were brought down by enemy action near Enghien. It was from this success that the Germans received their first confirmation that British forces had arrived in Belgium. A fragment of the observer's report was picked up by Belgian peasants near the wreckage of their plane and eventually was sent to London. A photo of this tattered document is in the first volume of the official history *The War in the Air*. The two men were buried originally in the communal cemetery of Labliau Marcq, before their bodies were later transferred to the Tournai cemetery, where they lie in Plot III, Row 9, Grave No. 3 (Bayley) and 4 (Waterfall). For many years there has been a pair of rusting iron plaques beside the Villers St Ghislain—Harmignies road which intimated they marked the position of the crash, but investigations by Mr André Englebert have proved this false. I wonder how the error came about. Lieutenant Bayley was an officer in the 56th Field Company, RE, and 2nd Lieutenant Waterfall was in the East Yorkshire Regiment. Both were attached to the RFC and were 23 years of age.

The Tournai South Communal Cemetery was used extensively by the Germans during the occupation as it was close to a major hospital, the Hôpital Notre Dame, where British and Allied casualties were cared for. German casualties were sent to another

hospital not far distant. The German graves were later moved and those of the British and Allied, mainly Russian and French, were concentrated into national plots. There are over 700 British Commonwealth graves and very many Russian.

Leave Tournai by N7 and at Warchin join the A16-E42 autoroute. In 28½ kms, join the Paris-Bruxelles autoroute (A7-E19). It is constructed partly on the old Condé Canal and some of the buildings between which it passes were originally factories and warehouses with quays. The first exit (25) after the merging of the autoroutes is for Saint Ghislain and Tertre. Some of the earliest fighting took place in this area and indeed in **Saint Ghislain** is a **memorial** to the casualties of an artillery battery which occupied a factory site near the canal. On one of the pillars of the ancient **Hôtel de Ville** in the

main square is a **bronze plaque** to the memory of Major Holland, RA, and 120th Battery, 27th Brigade, who was killed in action on August 23, 1914. At first he was buried beneath the factory wall but later his body was moved to **Hautrage Military Cemetery** (on the southern side of the Tertre-Hautrage road) where British and German dead lie side by side. Major C. Holland is in Plot I, Row B, Grave 2. It is believed that the Saint Ghislain plaque may be the earliest memorial to be erected in the Mons region; it was dedicated on November 9, 1919.

Leave the autoroute at either junction 24a or 24 to enter Mons (Bergen). From Saint Ghislain take the N51 through the busy industrial areas of Quaregnon and Jemappes with their sudden and unexpected areas of wild country. Exit 23 of the autoroute is for SHAPE and Nimy and joins the old Mons to Brussels road at Maisières.

MONS

Mons, as the run in will have shown, is a modern industrial town with a coalfield on two sides. Along the modernized Condé Canal, factories stand with loading bays on the banks. In the distance, on either side, rise the hills, Mons itself being built on one.

Of the famous Battle of Mons of August 1914, or that of November 1918, no sign remains, for neither action lasted long enough to leave any lasting physical marks. There are, however, a number of memorials set at points which recall the actions of the corps to which they belong and, in spite of the German bombing of 1940 and fighting of 1944 (when the US VII Corps captured the town), the ancient municipal buildings and private houses look today very much as they did to the Old Contemptibles on August 21, 1914. In recent years, however, there have been many changes on the outskirts with the presence of Supreme Headquarters Allied Powers Europe (SHAPE) and as autoroutes and their link roads have been carved through the region. Encircling the town are wide boulevards which mark the lines of the old ramparts. The large modern railway station overlooks one of these boulevards.

The **Hôtel de Ville** which dates from the 15th and 17th Centuries is on the Grand Place. The **Musées du Centenaire**, in particular the **Musée de Guerre**, through the large gate to the municipal heart of the town and the garden behind it, is one of the main reasons for visiting Mons. Housed in an old pawnshop built in 1625 is one of the finest collections of relics from the First and Second Wars in Belgium. It represents the work of two men, Georges Licope and Léon Pepin. On the ground floor is the Great War collection, and on the third floor exhibits from the Second. In between are fine ceramic, numismatic and archaeological displays.

The Mons Tourist Office has produced a useful guide to the ten salient points in the region. Each is clearly labelled. The earlier guide by the late Georges Licope is also still available. M. Licope was the recognised authority on all matters concerning the four battles of Mons: August 1914, November 1918, May 1940 and September 1944.

At the gateway of the Hôtel de Ville there are several **bronze plaques**, including one for the **5th Royal Irish Lancers**. This regiment took part in both First World War battles

A few hours after the first cavalry patrols entered Mons on August 21, 1914, this photograph was taken of Private Carter of the 4th Middlesex on sentry duty at La Bascule. The picture of the smiling 'young Contemptible' epitomised the spirit of the time.

and an Irish Lancer was the last British soldier to be killed on Armistice Day, November 11, 1918. Another plaque is the **Canadian Memorial** commemorating the liberation by the Canadian 3rd Division. In the collegiate **church of Sainte Waudru**, on the wall of the south transept, will be seen a **British Memorial Plaque** similar to the one in Ypres. Unlike those erected in France, the inscriptions are in English and Latin.

The highest part of the old city is the site of the Citadel and the old château. Rising here today is the baroque **Belfry**, the only one of its type in Belgium, built in 1662. A carillon of 47 bells is housed within and a lift goes to the upper chamber. Until the current restoration began, visitors could enter the onion dome above via some rickety, precariously-balanced ladders to view the panoramic explanation of the battles of Mons seen through the windows. Subsidence forced the closure of the **Parc** and Belfry, and I understand that when this work has been completed an explanatory exhibition will be installed in the upper floor. From October

1952 until 1984 a memorial unveiled by Field-Marshal Earl Alexander stood on the high point of the park, commemorating the two Battles of Mons of 1914 and 1918.

In 1935 the Belgians presented a silver model of the Belfry of Mons to HM King George V to mark his Silver Jubilee, and at the same ceremony was buried on the left-hand side of the entrance to the Belfry, the **Special Symbol of the Battle of Mons** in another casket. This contains earth from the grave of every British soldier killed at Mons. Among these, of course, are Canadians, including George Price, their last casualty. The place where this man lost his life, killed by a sniper, was in **Ville-sur-Haine**. In 1968 a plaque was placed on the wall of the house he was in, No. 71 rue de Mons, not many yards from the canal. In the modernization of the canal, the house has been demolished. Today the **plaque** is to be found on the wall of the Ville-sur-Haine **Hôtel de Ville** and school, located on the corner of the rue du Coron at the crossroads with the rue de Mons, some 400 metres higher up the Roeulx road than No. 71.

The plaque recording the death of the last Canadian at 10.58 a.m. on November 11, 1918.

Left: Memorial tablet in Sainte Waudru church. Above: In the Mons Hôtel de Ville, the Musée de Guerre includes a comprehensive collection of weapons and uniforms. This display of drums covers every regiment which fought at Mons in 1914.

Mons Battlefield Tour

A railway bridge still spans the canal where Lieutenant Dease and Private Godley of the 4th Battalion, Royal Fusiliers, won their VCs. On the far 'German' side stands Nimy station. This is Stand 2 of the official Mons Battlefield Tour.

In the last ten years, the outskirts of Mons have been drastically altered with new road systems and many new buildings changing the landscape. The advent of SHAPE at Casteau is a major cause but the change of emphasis in the industrial life of the city, modern factories replacing the old smaller establishments, and the revival in the canal traffic, has all played its part. The road systems are not yet complete as work on the ring-road from Ghlin and Jemappes to Frameries, Spiennes, Havré and Obourg is still in progress. New bridges, flyovers and the autoroute now dominate the region.

Leaving Mons by the Chaussée de Bruxelles (N6), in 1 km reach **Nimy**, an old industrial suburb through which the main railway passes. Soon the first of the battlefield tour signboards will be seen as the road swings past the town square to the foot of the new road bridge on which it is placed. Take the small road on the right to go under the bridge and along the narrow road by the canal bank. The modern bridge spans the canal over the **site of the old swing bridge** which was so gallantly defended by 4th Bn. Royal Fusiliers. Further along the canal is the **modern railway bridge** which replaced that defended so well by another company of

4th Bn. Royal Fusiliers. **Nimy station** is on the far side of the canal. A **plaque** on the wall supporting the bridge commemorates the actions of Lieutenant M. J. Dease and Private S. F. Godley of the machine gun section. Every man in the section was either killed or wounded as they held up the German advance, permitting the battalions of their division to retire to new positions. Lieutenant Dease continued to keep the last gun firing until so badly wounded that he was unable to carry on. Private Godley then volunteered to man it until his wounds also forbade further action. He destroyed the gun and flung it into the canal before being taken prisoner. It is said that he was the inspiration for Bruce Bairnsfather's 'Old Bill'. The artist, away over in the Plugstreet Wood area, saw a photo of British prisoners from Mons entraining; in the foreground was the stocky, bushy-moustached Godley. Dease died from his wounds and both he and Godley were awarded the Victoria Cross — the first of the Great War.

The bridge can be approached via the narrow road running along the canal bank to the artificial lake and marina, either by turning left at the traffic lights in Nimy and then taking the small entry between the

houses or by using the slip road on the right at the foot of the new bridge and turning left beneath it. A fine panorama of Mons opens out beyond the railway bridge. Return to Nimy and turn left over the bridge, bearing right to the next traffic lights and go straight on under the autoroute. This is **Maisières**, a front line position on that August day in 1914. The village straggles on either side of the modern highway to the capital and forms one of the dormitories of the huge SHAPE complex but retains still many of its older buildings. To the right of the traffic lights in the centre of the village is the church where a **plaque** commemorates the units of the BEF who were in the line in the Maisières region. Further up the hill, as the houses peter out, a slip road to the right signposted 'Cimitière' gives access across the highway to the communal cemetery on the left. At its entrance stands the village **war memorial** surrounded by evergreens. This is unusual for on its panels are the names not only of the village dead but also those of Captain J. Knowles and other British casualties who died here in 1914. They were buried in a small cemetery nearby but, when the autoroute was built, they were moved and now lie in the peace of Cement House Cemetery *(see page 38)*.

The Belgian war memorial at Maisières unusually includes the names of seven British casualties from the Middlesex Regiment.

Supreme Headquarters Allied Powers Europe now dominates the whole countryside to the left, the woods and copses which lined most of the road now replaced on the left-hand side by military blocks. One impact on Mons of the presence of the organisation has been the substantial growth of residential building and another one has of finding hotel accommodation in the district.

At 5 kms from Mons, having passed the main gates of SHAPE and the crossroads above, lies the village of **Casteau**. Almost on the crest of the rise on the left is a **stone memorial to the first contact between the BEF and the First German Army** at 7.00 a.m. on August 22, 1914. 'C' Squadron of the 4th Royal Irish Dragoon Guards, commanded by Major Tom Bridges, were on patrol on the road and in the woods following reports of German cavalry between Casteau and Soignies. Captain C. Hornby, the second in command, was in the van of the first two troops when a group of German 4th Kuirassiers were sighted. Corporal E. Thomas fired the first shots of a British Expeditionary Force on the Continent for nearly 100 years and Captain Hornby, sword raised, led the first charge. Across the road on the wall of the Hôtel Medicis is a **bronze plaque**. This

The first shots of the First World War rang out near this monument on the Casteau road at 7.00 a.m. on August 22, 1914.

Left: **Almost directly opposite, a hotel now stands on the site of the 116th Canadian Infantry Battalion advance outpost at the** cease-fire on November 11, 1918. *Right:* **The plaque, moved from the hotel car park, is now on the wall.**

memorial records that outposts of the **116th Canadian Infantry Battalion** were on this spot on November 11, 1918 when the cease-fire rang out at 11.00 a.m. 'Here beginneth and endeth the lesson . . .'

Return to the main crossroad and take the left-hand road to St Denis for 1 km and then turn right over the autoroute to reach **Obourg**, taking the road and bridge over the canal signed for Mons. At the south end of

the bridge a hairpin turning leads to **Obourg station**. A foot-bridge takes one over the railway line and, on the canal bank where once stood the station building, now stands a **red brick memorial**. This was fashioned in 1981 from bricks of the old station then being demolished. It was on the exterior wall of the old waiting room that the stand by the **4th Bn. Middlesex Regiment** was remembered. They held the most easterly, and exposed,

sector of the Salient around the north-east of Mons and had opened up on the oncoming Germans from every vantage point with fantastic rifle fire, ably displaying their skill with the Lee Enfield, typical of the regular British infantryman. All the units involved in Mons were capable of firing 16 aimed rounds per minute, some even more, thus giving the enemy the notion that every battalion was equipped with many machine guns instead of

Obourg is a name synonymous with the first demonstration in action of the skills of the British rifleman equipped with the Rifle No. 1, Short, Magazine, Lee Enfield Mk III — the SMLE which had been adopted in January 1907. *Above:* This was where the station stood until it was demolished in 1981. The plaque recording the events of August 23, formerly to be seen on the wall of the waiting room, has since been remounted on a memorial *(right)* built from bricks salvaged from the old building. The author with the late M. René Langouche, Burgomaster (left) and a survivor of the Middlesex Regiment, ex-Fusilier H. J. Hart, in August 1985.

the pitiful few they actually had. Some of the company were sited on the roof of the station and the **plaque**, now on the memorial, records the events at about 8.00 a.m. on August 23. Each year a ceremony is held here on that day.

Another position of the 4th Bn. Middlesex Regiment — 'A' Company (Major W. H. Abell) — was above the canal and railway, beyond the woods, around a farm now on the fringe of the modern residential estate. To get there, leave the station and drive up the hill towards Mons, taking the second turning on the right, passing through a wooded area. In 1 km the road, now in more open country, bears to the left with a smaller, older road straight ahead. This is, in fact, the original road, the Vieille Route de Binche. Take it and drive past several of the old houses on the right, set much as they were on that morning so long ago. In about 300 metres one of the new estate roads comes in on the left. It is **Avenue du 4th Middlesex** (so named since 1965) and, as our road becomes a lane, over to the right ahead the **L'Hermite Farm** comes into view. The Middlesex men had set up their outpost line in the farm and its field and orchard behind it on August 21-22.

The 23rd dawned misty and wet but blossomed out into a hot, dry, summer's day. Early in the morning, as the enemy began shelling, the men took up their positions and soon grey-clad figures began to emerge from the trees bordering the fields. Major Abell's bugler said he recognised them as Germans — he'd seen their like in the Legation Guard at Shanghai years previously. Now the peaceful fields resounded to the heated exchange of rifle fire as the enemy advanced. Major Abell was shot through the head, the **first British officer to be killed** in action in the Great War and soon his second in command, Captain J. Knowles, was mortally wounded, as was the subaltern, 2nd Lieutenant Hancock. During the day, the 4th Middlesex suffered heavy casualties as they strategically retreated south-west, but they had inflicted considerable devastation on the overwhelming numbers of the enemy.

Major Abell and some 40 of his men were originally buried in the orchard but 26 months later were moved to St Symphorien Cemetery. Today they lie there surrounding the memorial erected by the German Army in 1916 by the order of Prince Ruprecht of Bavaria in honour of their gallant foe. Captain Knowles and a few others were buried near Maisières in a little cemetery there, but when the complex road system and the autoroute were built they, too, had to be moved and are now in Cement House Cemetery near Ypres. After being badly burned the farm was rebuilt but I understand from survivors that I have met there that the

The farm at Obourg occupied by the 4th Battalion. The road has been renamed 'Avenue du 4th Middlesex' in memory of their stand and the death of the first officer killed in the Great War in a nearby orchard.

fields look much as they did — even the stone trough which gave support to the wounded is still there.

Return to Obourg and cross the bridge, turning left under it, and drive along by the canal to **Ville-sur-Haine** for 4 kms. The road is for the most part a new wide highway running parallel to the now enlarged canal with its modern locks at intervals, but soon after the access road to the motorway joins it on the left, it narrows radically to enter the village. Now it turns and twists to become the rue du Coron up to the crossroads with the Roeulx-Havre-Mons road. There, beside the village War Memorial is the **plaque**, erected by his surviving comrades in 1968, to the **last Canadian to be killed**.

Turn right down rue de Mons (N538). With the new canal and road works the site of the houses including No. 71 has disappeared; it was at the bottom of the hill about 200 metres before the bridge over the canal. The road now climbs up through the cobbled streets of Havre, a mining and industrial town, and passes the ruined château. which itself is receiving restoration and conservation.

Turn left near it for **Villers St Ghislain**. In 4½ kms at the N90 junction turn right and then first left up through the village. After a sharp left-hand corner the road comes out onto the plateau, offering a magnificent panoramic view of the whole battle area. For many years two rusty plaques could be found near the crest of the road. It was thought these commemorated the site where Lieutenants Bayley and Waterfall of No. 5 Squadron, RFC, had crashed on August 22, 1914. Now it has been established that this was not the case — they were erected in the

memory of horsemen who died nearby! The road now drops into **Harmignies** through the quarries which played a vital part in the battle. The hill to the right sheltered the Royal Horse Artillery who were based at Harmignies and, with other battalions, fought around it and the railway here.

At the major crossroads turn left onto N40 and drive 3½ kms through pleasant undulating country to **Givry**. Here it was that I Corps held the line immediately prior to the retreat. The commander, Sir Douglas Haig, had his headquarters on the road to Bavay. Their line was along Givry—Harmignies—Nouvelles, and General Allenby's cavalry were in support behind them in the Waudruz—Binche region.

Turn right onto N563 at the next crossroad, follow the very straight road and the 10 kms to **Waudrez** are soon accomplished. Turn left on to the N90 and take first right on to N27 which rises over the ridge prior to dropping down into **Péronnes**. About 200 metres along on the left is a water tower opposite a factory. This is an excellent vantage point to view the countryside littered with slag heaps and belching factory chimneys. In the near foreground is one large slag heap with a cluster of houses nearby. In the fields here, 'E' Battery, RHA, fired the **first artillery round of the war** on August 22. On the right side of the road, about three metres from the pavement outside the factory boundary fence, is a small stone which commemorates this event. From these positions on August 22, 1964 the same gun fired again in the presence of many of those who had participated 50 years previously. The artillery piece can be seen today in the Imperial War Museum.

From the field beside the slag heap, the guns of 'E' Battery fired on August 23, 1914.

General Allenby had his quarters in this red brick house belonging to the school mistress at Villers St Ghislain.

Retrace the road to the N90 and turn right for **Villers St Ghislain** (5 kms). Here General Allenby was billeted in the **house of the school mistress**. This house on the left has changed little over the years.

Continue another 2 kms to **St Symphorien**. Turn left (signpost) to visit the **British War Cemetery**. The road runs through a new estate and then deteriorates somewhat as it follows a brick wall and worsens as the lane comes to a junction at the cemetery gates.

This is possibly the most beautiful of all the British cemeteries in the Western Front area. It is also very different in layout, typifying a traditional English garden. There are shady paths and glades and many varieties of trees and shrubs in addition to the flowers on the actual graves and borders. The land was originally given to the Germans for use as a cemetery by a local landowner and here they buried both their own and the British casualties of August 1914, erecting a number of **special memorials**. One of these, set in a small circular glade surrounded by the graves, is in memory of the **'Royal' Middlesex Regiment** — the German personnel could not believe that any regiment which had discipline and courage of the kind displayed by the Middlesex was not a 'Royal' regiment. This part of the cemetery is reached by taking the path to the right as you enter and is on the left, a little way up.

Nearby is buried L/14196 Private J. Parr, Middlesex Regiment. It is very probable that he was the **first man to be killed in the BEF** in the Great War. His death on August 21, in the evening when he did not return from a scout mission with his bicycle, has now been confirmed and the date on the headstone has been corrected. Opposite is the headstone of the **last man to die** on November 11, 1918 — Private G. E. Ellison of the 5th Royal Irish Lancers. Beyond is the **German plot** where the original headstones have been retained. In contrast to the plain white British stones, these grey granite markers differ with officers often having more flamboyant styles than those of the NCO or private soldier.

Up to the left, a group of British graves can be seen. Here lies Lieutenant Dease, VC, who died on August 23, 1914. In the row behind him is the grave of Private Price of the 28th North West Bn. Canadian Infantry, who was killed at Ville-sur-Haine at 10.58 a.m. on November 11, 1918.

On the same level as the Cross of Sacrifice, which is placed at the highest part of the garden on the other side of the path, is a

If one had to choose to visit just one cemetery from the First World War, that at St Symphorien would be high on the list where both British and German casualties lie side by side together with some of the most notable of the Allied dead. Here two old Contemptibles stand at the grave of Lieutenant Dease, VC.

General Sir John Akehurst, Deputy SACEUR, and ex-Fusilier Harry Hart pay tribute at the German Fusiliers Memorial at St Symphorien on August 23, 1989.

Left: **Another memorial erected by the German Army to their gallant foe, the 'Royal' Middlesex Regiment.** *Right:* **The German obelisk to the dead of both armies.**

Left: **Originally Private Parr's headstone was 'dated' August 23, 1914 but detailed research by the author established that he went missing on the evening of August 21; thus most probably** the very first man to be killed. *Centre:* **Here also lies Private Price, the last Canadian to die (page 106) and also Private G. E. Ellison** *(right)* **the very last man to be killed.**

small rectangular lawn with a curved stone seat at the far end. In front is **another of the German memorials** to their British foes, this time to 53 members of the **Royal Fusiliers**. All about are a varied selection of shrubs and trees providing colour throughout the year.

Leaving the cemetery, the path goes through a fringe of fir trees in the centre of which is the **German memorial to the men of both armies who died on August 23-24, 1914**. From this memorial a flight of steps leads back to the entrance.

Return to the road junction and turn left. In ¾ km, turn right onto the N40. On the left rises the **Hill of Panisel**, through the woods and fields of which run paths making very pleasant walking areas. Many fierce actions were fought in the orchards and fields on the lower slopes; this was the scene of the stand of the 3rd Infantry Division.

In 3 kms our road arrives on the northern slope of Mont Panisel and converges at the wide crossroads with Beaumont and Obourg roads. This is **La Bascule** where on August 21-22 the 3rd Division's 8th Brigade was centred. This was the formation to which the 4th Bn. Middlesex belonged, together with the 2nd Bn. Royal Scots, 2nd Bn. Royal Irish Regiment and 1st Bn. Gordon Highlanders.

Here was taken one of the best-known photographs of the Mons period, a cheerful young sentry of the 4th Middlesex in the late afternoon sunshine *(see page 106)*.

On August 23, 1986, the **BEF Memorial,** which stood in the Château Park under the Belfry, was unveiled on the spur of ground between the two major roads. On the far side of the Charleroi road, on the corner of the smaller road from Obourg, the Celtic cross of the **Memorial of the 2nd Bn. Royal Irish Regiment** has stood for 60 years to record their gallant stand here for many hours that August day, delaying the enemy's advance and suffering very heavy casualties. The brigade's Scottish battalions were in between the Beaumont and Charleroi roads, and their positions can be viewed along the Beaumont road not far from La Bascule. From around here the brigade fell back on Mont Hyon and Mont Erebus on the road south towards Ciply.

The centre of Mons is now only 1 km away down the hill, passing the place where the **stables** of the **Château Gendebien** once stood. These were used as a Field Dressing Station in August 1914 and were set on fire by the advancing Germans' artillery fire. The château has in more recent times been the official residence of the Supreme Commander Allied Powers Europe. We enter Mons along the attractive Avenue Reine Astrid.

The Royal Irish Regiment Memorial on the corner of La Bascule crossroads.

The BEF Memorial at Mons was moved in 1986 to La Bascule, and now stands appropriately near the spot where Private Carter had his picture taken in 1914.

Mons to Le Cateau

The route south from Mons is basically that of the retreat but the final advance followed much the same route.

Leave Mons by the N6 and in 3½ kms at **Ciply** take right fork N543. Pass straight through **Noirchain** (3½ kms), and reach **Blaregnies** 9 kms further on.

The area just passed was in the II Corps lines, the commander of which, General Sir Horace Smith-Dorrien, had his headquarters in a small château at **Sars-la-Bruyère**. The village and the château can be reached by taking the right-hand road at the crossroads in the centre of Blaregnies. In about 1 km, near the church of Sars-le-Bruyère, go right and in a short distance the drive to the château is found on the right.

Château de la Haie (also called Château de la Roche), a quiet white house set in delightful surroundings, was the scene of a momentous meeting at 5.00 a.m. on August 23, 1914. Present were Field-Marshal French and his corps commanders, Lieutenant-General Sir Douglas Haig, I Corps, Major-General Edmund Allenby, Cavalry Corps, and of course Sir Horace. Also present were Major-General Sir W. R. Robertson, the Quartermaster-General, and Major-General Sir A. J. Murray, Chief-of-Staff. The confer-

ROUTE CONTINUED
ON MAP ON PAGE 116

SCALE 1:200 000 1cm—2km

Reproduced from Michelin Sheet No. 236 12th Edition 1989

Château de la Haie, the scene of the momentous meeting on August 23, 1914, which decided the retreat from Mons.

A plaque in the hall reminds visitors of the historic meeting between Field-Marshal French and his corps commanders.

ence covered all eventualities including that of retreat. A **plaque in the hall** commemorates this momentous meeting which took place in the large room to the left of the front doors. On the morning of August 24 the headquarters was moved back to Hon.

The château was owned by the Comte d'Hendécourt, who was later killed in action. His son now lives in the house which remained unoccupied for many years. In 1940 the invading Germans attempted to remove the artillery pieces flanking the front doors but left them on discovering they were mounted in concrete.

Return to Blaregnies and right onto the N543 and within 1 km arrive at the frontier. Between the two stations is the **battlefield of Malplaquet** and a **monument** on the left commemorates Marlborough's victory on September 11, 1709. On November 8, 1918 there was a sharp action here as the Allies advanced. Here the N543 becomes D932.

Another 8 kms and we reach **Bavay**. This little town is situated on a hill close to which are **Riez de l'Erelle** and **Hon** where Haig and Smith-Dorrien had their respective headquarters at the beginning of the retreat. French had his advance headquarters in the **Mairie of Bavay** during the Battle of Mons, General Headquarters being then at Le Cateau. By August 25, all the British corps in the vicinity were making their way south on either side of the Forest of Mormal. The Guards Division recaptured the town on November 7, 1918.

Take the D942 for **Le Quesnoy** (14 kms). Le Quesnoy is a charming old town still enclosed with its 17th Century ramparts, another of Vauban's fortresses. On August 25, 1914, the town echoed to the noises of

The 1st Division Memorial at the La Groise crossroads. Here the Division held the German advance on August 26, 1914; in November 1918 it passed back through the same road junction.

At Landrecies, the 25th Division remember their commander, Sir Ronald Charles, who liberated the town with 600 men on November 4, 1918.

The ramparts at Le Quesnoy. Beside the site of the assault, the New Zealand Memorial depicts soldiers climbing these walls just a week before the Armistice was signed.

the retreating BEF and the refugees who hindered the army in their routes south. Thereafter, for four years, it was a German garrison town. On November 5, 1918, the town was attacked by men of the New Zealand Division who scaled the high walls of the outer ramparts and seized the German commander and his garrison of over 1,000 men. On the face of the walls climbed by the New Zealanders is a **memorial** to their effort which details, in bas relief, the use of mediaeval methods which proved so successful.

The D31 leads in 4½ kms to **Jolimetz** on the D932 at the western edge of the **Forest of Mormal**. The D912 was the road taken by II Corps, I Corps being on the eastern flank of the forest. The advancing German army made its way through the forest. This huge woodland of some 22,000 acres, which covers the slopes and high ground between Bavay and Landrecies, gave good cover and the wide glades provided routes for the German transport. In November 1918 the forest again lay in the path of advancing troops, this time the 3rd and 4th British Armies who drove all before them and had cleared the area by November 5.

Turn right on the D932 to **Englefontaine** (5 kms) and travel 8 kms on the D934 to the outskirts of **Landrecies**. On August 25, 1914, the Germans were said to have entered the town with some men dressed in French uniforms whilst the Guards slept, but once roused, the 4th Guards Brigade, 2nd Division, fought briskly in the streets as the rest of I Corps proceeded to retreat. In November 1918 the 25th Division captured the town and forced their way across the River Sambre, which is canalised here. On the bridge into the town is a **memorial to General Sir Ronald Charles**, the GOC, who, with 600 men, was killed in liberating the town on November 4.

Continue on the D934 for 5 kms to **La Groise**. The straight road undulates through attractive country to the crossroads of **Chapeau Rouge**. Here, on August 26, 1914, the 1st Division stood and defied the German advance and, on November 4, 1918, the crossroads were in the centre of the line held by the same division as it advanced. A rather elegant **memorial** on the left of the road recalls these facts. Just 6 kms ahead on D946 is **Etreux**, the scene of the heroic stand of 2nd Bn. Royal Munster Fusiliers. The **memorial and graveyard** mark the site with the headstones ranged in alphabetical order around the walls, the men being buried in three plots. The fields behind the cemetery and the farms close by are little changed

'To the Glory of God and in proud and lasting memory . . . the Royal Munster Fusiliers who laid down their lives . . . in the cause of freedom and justice . . . their name liveth for evermore.' Fine words on a fine memorial at Etreux.

from the dreaded day of August 27, 1914. In **Etreux Communal Cemetery** other British soldiers lie buried. They died in the village in August 1914 but include one man who was concealed for months in the village but, when discovered by the enemy, was shot in April 1915.

Return to Chapeau Rouge and turn left onto the D934 for **Catillon**. Then in 3 kms cross over the Sambre and join the N43 for Le Cateau.

ALTERNATIVE ROUTE

An alternative route from Landrecies is via D959 through **Bois l'Eveque**, scene of battles in 1914 and October 1918. In 4 kms turn left for **Ors**. In the **British Communal Cemetery** by the station lie the poet Wilfred Owen, Lieutenant-Colonel J. N. Marshall, VC, MC, and 2nd Lieutenant J. Kirk, VC, all killed in 1918. At Bazuel join the N43 via the D160a.

Ors Communal Cemetery: 2nd Lieutenant James Kirk, VC, Lieutenant-Colonel James Marshall, VC, and Lieutenant Wilfred Owen.

LE CATEAU

Le Cateau is a name engraved in the memory of all Old Contemptibles, if not as the first location of British General Headquarters, then as the battle honour on so many of their Colours. Here on August 26, 1914 was fought a desperate battle by the 3rd, 4th and 5th Divisions of II Corps against seven of von Kluck's Army's divisions. The Germans held the advantage, not only in infantry but also in artillery. The battle began to the west of the town, just south of the Cambrai road, and on through Caudry where the country is reminiscent of Salisbury Plain.

The site of the battle can be visited from tracks leading off the D932 or the D21. Amid a grove of trees is a **simple cenotaph** on which the actions by the 2nd Battalion of the Suffolk Regiment, the Manchester Regiment, the Argyll and Sutherland Highlanders and the Royal Artillery batteries in their support, are remembered.

As one enters Le Cateau from Landrecies, look right at the crossroads with the Hostellerie du Marche on the corner. In front of the café (on the rue de la Fontaine à Gros Bouillons), is a horse trough now used very charmingly as a flower garden. This is the **Memorial of the British 66th Division** who fought here on August 10, 1918 and who liberated the town. Resistance in the station area lasted a week longer and was finally eliminated by the South African Brigade. After that, Le Cateau was shelled heavily by

the Germans until their guns were forced out of range by the Allied advance.

Many of the narrow streets which climb the hills are still cobbled. In the main street is the **Hôtel de Ville**, where for many years just inside the entrance under the tower stood a **British 3.7 howitzer** flanked by pictures by one of the town's most illustrious sons, Henri Matisse. Now these are displayed in the **Palais Fenelon Musée Matisse** further down the main street on the right. The gun was presented to the town by the 93rd Battery, Royal Field Artillery, to cement the friendship between the unit and the town for which it fought. Most years, gunners return to the

Bravery recalled on a French hillside.

town using the Hôtel du Midi in rue du Maréchal Mortier as their headquarters. Today the howitzer — of 1932 vintage — is proudly displayed in the **town library** in the rue du Marche aux Chevaux in a fine building, once a bank, rebuilt with reparations money. Beside the gun is a wooden bench seat — a most useful comfort to the old soldiers who have walked up the street from their hotel. Festivities and receptions are held in the upper rooms. Both gun and seat are to be seen by going through the entrance foyer to the corridor, off which is the library itself.

The **British Military Cemetery** is just north of the N43 and D932 crossroads and it gives a good overall view of the battlefield. The cemetery was opened originally by the Germans and there are several large memorials erected by them midst the many British and German graves. In one cluster are a group of Russian graves. Recently the German war graves authority have made considerable renovations to their cemetery and many old crumbling memorials have been removed and the graves reset with new markers. There are now separate entrances to the British and German sections. In the British plot men lie together who died in the battle of 1914, as prisoners of war, and in the 1918 actions. Among these is Lance-Corporal John W. Sayer who won the VC on March 21, 1918 and who died of wounds in April 1918.

There is another British cemetery in Le Cateau, the **Communal Cemetery** in the town cemetery. Here some 150 casualties of the battle are buried. There also is a German memorial to them and their German and French comrades.

The 66th Division's practical memorial, a horse drinking trough, is now an integral part of the town's floral decorations. Along the street in the background is the municipal library, the present home of the 3.7in howitzer presented to Le Cateau by the 93rd Battery together with their memorial seat.

Men from Germany, Russia and Great Britain lie together at Le Cateau. This is the Commonwealth War Graves section.

Le Cateau Cemetery was originally opened by the Germans and it contains several German memorials — and a mass grave.

FROM MAP PAGE 112

ALTERNATIVE ROUTE ------

TO AMIENS AND PERONNE

ROUTE CONTINUED ON MAP ON PAGE 119

SCALE 1:200 000 1cm=2km

Reproduced from Michelin Sheet No. 236 12th Edition 1989

Le Cateau to Amiens

In nearby **Caudry** is rather a unique **town war memorial**. On the plinth are commemorated four incidents in the war; the defence of the town in 1914; the trials of the occupation; the battle of 1918 and the final liberation on October 10, 1918, in which the figures carved in bas relief actually represent the personalities concerned — the officers and NCOs of the 17th Division.

Proceed from Le Cateau along the D932. This long straight highway cleaves its way across the plains of Picardy to the St Quentin canal at Riqueval, but we leave it in 18½ kms at **Poncheux**, taking the D28 (on the right) for **Beaurevoir** and Le Catelet (5½ kms). This wide country was the terrain of the Australians under Sir John Monash in their advance in October 1918.

Le Catelet is a straggling village across the N44 Cambrai-St Quentin road, and is the northern entrance of the **tunnel** of the **St Quentin Canal**. About ½ km along the D57 to **Vendhuile**, under a group of chestnut trees on the right of the road, footpaths lead down on either side of the early 19th Century canal to the tunnel entrance. This tunnel, over

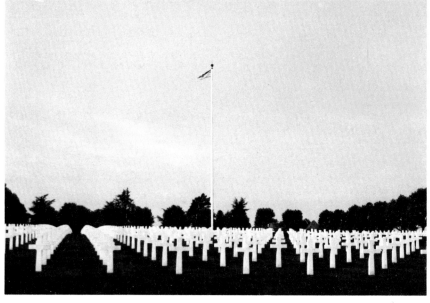

One kilometre south of Le Catelet lies the Somme American Cemetery at Bony.

7 kms in length, was built in the time of Napoleon in 1802-10. During the German occupation of the area, they incorporated this tunnel, and the shorter one between Le Tronquoy and Haucourt, into the defences forming the Hindenburg Line.

On an average, the tunnels are 16 metres below the surface and therefore almost impregnable. They were connected to the main works of the Hindenburg Line by shafts and were fully equipped with offices, stores, stables and hospitals. Barges were used as billets and the whole system was electrically lit.

At this northern end of the tunnel all is now peaceful and few marks recall its use as a fortress. Neither do the banks of the sleepy canal carry many reminders that they were once part of an intricate trench system. The northern end of the tunnel figured in the heavy fighting in September and October 1918, when the American 27th and 30th Division and the British 50th Division fought successfully to breach the Line.

The canal re-emerges into daylight south of **Bellicourt** village, which is 5 kms from Le Catelet. On the heights before the village, and directly above the tunnel, is the impressive **American Memorial**, the Bellicourt Monument of the American Battle Monuments Commission. On the west face of the monument is an interesting map of the operations of the two divisions of 90,000 men who served with the British in the battles in the region. On the terrace overlooking the battlefield is an orientation table.

About 2½ km south (via N44) of Bellicourt village at **Riqueval**, a small road (to the right) leads over the gorge at this end of the canal and eventually back to Bellicourt. Not far along this road is the actual **southern entrance** of the tunnel which is easily reached through the trees. A **memorial to the soldiers from Tennessee** who were killed in the canal battles stands near this entrance.

Right: **High above the canal tunnel, the American Memorial at Bellicourt overlooks the remnants of the old Hindenburg Line.**

Above: **The northern entrance of an unassailable fortress — the St Quentin Canal Tunnel at Le Catelet. This was an integral part of the Hindenburg Line.**

Left: **The southern entrance to the St Quentin Canal tunnel at Riqueval.** *Right:* **The Memorial to the soldiers of the American** State of Tennessee, killed in the battles for the canal, stands near the entrance.

117

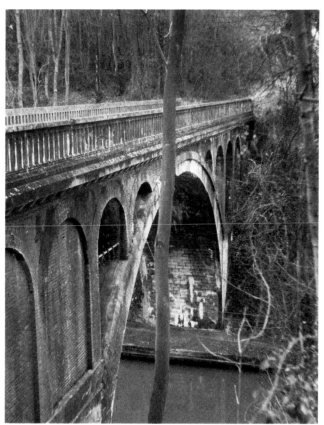

General Campbell, VC, addresses men of the 137th British Brigade on the slopes of the St Quentin Canal from the ruined bridge at Riqueval.

Seventy years have passed. This is the author's comparison photograph taken from the same spot . . . the bridge is virtually unchanged.

Riqueval bridge appears in one of the most impressive photographs in the Imperial War Museum collection. Brigadier-General J. V. Campbell, VC, is shown on the ruined arch addressing his troops of 137th Brigade, 46th Division, who cover the steep banks of the gorge after they had captured this sector of the Hindenburg Line on September 29, 1918 by wading across the canal and scaling the walls here.

In 1½ kms La Baraque crossroads are reached. **Bellenglise** village (also captured by the 46th Division) is to the right, on the left is a small **British Cemetery** and nearby the crumbling remains of part of the German defences were still hidden in the undergrowth in 1986. Shortly, the obelisk of the **46th Division Memorial** can be seen on the left. For a number of years after the road improvements in this region the memorial fell into disrepair, but now it has been renovated. To visit the other **tunnel** at **Le Tronquoy**, take the D31 on the left and in 1 km turn right on D71b to **Le Haucourt**. The entrance is on the right, ½ km out of the village. Another ½ km further on is the other entrance. The D71 follows the canal to **Lesdins** where, by joining the D8 and crossing the **canal**, St Quentin is then entered in 6 kms.

St Quentin is a large industrial town on the River Somme. The British General Headquarters was here on August 25-26, 1914 before moving to Noyon and Compiègne. Units of II Corps arrived from Le Cateau exhausted and demoralised by the continuous march. The knowledge that the advance troops of the German Army were hard on their heels ceased to have any urgency for them and they fell where they stood, tired out, when the order to halt was given. Soon after, some squadrons of the 4th Hussars led by Major T. Bridges came on the scene. Bridges was horrified by the sight which met his eyes and was determined to move the men out of St Quentin. He realised

that the most effective adjunct for making men march was missing — he had no band. Seeing a toy shop he went in and bought a toy whistle and a drum. With his bugler on the whistle and himself on the drum, he succeeded in rousing the men and led them out of the town after the infectious music had induced others to join in with mouth organs.

The Germans held the town from the end of August 1914 until October 1, 1918. In March 1918 they had set forth from St Quentin on their Spring Offensive driving back the British Third and Fifth Armies, taking many prisoners. In the Allied advance, the town was outflanked by the British and was entered by the French army of General Debeney. By then the town was in ruins, **the cathedral** had been burnt and, as the French army arrived, the Germans were completing the laying of charges in the bases of the great pillars in the church to complete its demolition. The swift intervention of the Frenchmen saved the building, but one or two pillars still show the holes that had been drilled.

The 46th Division Memorial at La Baraque near Bellenglise.

The impressive French Memorial at St Quentin with its interesting bas relief.

SCALE 1:200 000 1cm–2km

ALTERNATIVE ROUTE ▪▪▪▪▪

ROUTE CONTINUED
ON MAP ON PAGE 121

FROM MAP
PAGE 116

FROM ST QUENTIN

St Quentin Cathedral. Bore holes drilled for demolition charges still remain.

Down near the station is an impressive **French memorial** depicting many different aspects of the army. The British and French lines joined opposite St Quentin and, after 1914, the British Army did not return again until 1918.

To return to the western sector, take the N29 from St Quentin to **Francilly-Selency**. Today the route of the **Hindenburg Line** here is crossed by the A26-E17 autoroute. Then we reach **Vermand** (5 kms), a small town totally destroyed in the German retreat in March 1917 and again in the front line in 1918 during March and the autumn of that year. A pleasant detour can be made from here by taking the D73 on the right at the entrance to the town and driving along the valley of the River Omignon through the hamlet of Villecholles and close to the Etang de Bihecourt to **Maissemy** (3 kms), a village entirely ruined in 1918 during the stout defence put up by the 24th and 61st Divisions on March 21, 1918.

Cross the river after joining the D735 and turn left in the village. At the next junction turn right onto the D33. In 1 km on the left is the large **German Cemetery** of Maissemy. On the gentle slope the main path is lined with stones bearing the arms and crests of many German cities and regions, and 23,292 men are buried in the beautiful greensward or in the mass graves which stretch across the centre. A gaunt chapel encloses the symbolic bronze tomb as the central feature.

Turn left at the next crossroads onto the D57 and at the fork go left on D31 to reach

Le Verquier in 2 kms. During 1915-16 the German aerodromes in the area were frequent targets of RFC raids. It was captured by the Allies on April 9, 1917, but the village really suffered when it fell in the path of the German Spring Offensive of 1918. The position was stubbornly defended by 24th Division on March 21-22 and was eventually recaptured in September by the Australians. The church tower at Le Verquier is in fact a **memorial to the 24th Division**, given by them and dedicated in October 1926. Just outside is the rather unusual **village memorial** which in addition to bearing the names of its own heroes includes mention of the 24th Division losses in their village.

Take the D577, rue du 24e Division immediately opposite the church, to arrive at **Vendelles** in 4 kms and by the D121 to the left in 5 kms return to **Vermand**. All this region was in the Fifth Army area in March 1918. In 7 kms. at **Estrées-en-Chaussée**, turn right on D44 for Péronne (10 kms).

Péronne is an ancient town located at the confluence of the Somme and Cologne rivers. It fell into German hands in 1914 and remained a most useful base, protected as it

was by the artillery on Mont St Quentin, about 2 kms to the north. This hill was strongly fortified with subways and deep trenches to give support and shelter for the guns. On its forward slopes many observation posts were set up commanding extensive views over a very wide area. This formidable fortress was the cause of the French Army's inability to advance in July and August 1916, although they reached Biaches, 1½ kms to the west of the city. In March 1917 the Germans evacuated Mont St Quentin when they retreated to the Hindenburg Line but, before doing so, destroyed both the fortress and the town. A year later they were back in possession of both, capturing many valuable supplies. During the Allied advance, the 2nd Australian Division took the fortress on August 31, and Péronne itself was captured on September 2, 1918.

Completely ruined, the town has been rebuilt around the large square, the Place du Commandant Daudre. The Renaissance town hall has been rebuilt in its old style. In 1990, a new military museum will be opened in the region of the ruins of the medieval château.

In death all men are equal. France, so often a battleground for warring European nations, provides burial grounds for both friend and foe. This is the vast Soldaten-friedhof at Maissemy, last resting place for the sons of many German cities, towns and villages.

Leave Péronne by N17, climbing up **Mont St Quentin** where proudly stands a bronze Digger — the **Memorial of the 2nd Australian Division**. This statue, mounted on a square

plinth, replaced the one erected here originally but destroyed by the Germans during the Second World War. It was one of the very few which suffered this way, but exception was taken to the symbolism of the Digger stabbing the German eagle with his bayonet. On each face of the plinth, which was not destroyed, bronze plaques depict infantry and artillery in action and the list of battles fought by the division. Behind the statue is a wide view of the valley where so many Aussies fought.

Continue up the slope before dropping down to cross the **Canal du Nord** and climbing up and over another ridge and descending to the village of **Buchavesnes-Bergen**. This was the location of a storming attack by the French Army in September 1916; and in March 1918 there was heavy fighting as the enemy prised apart the Third and Fifth British Armies. In nearby Marières Wood, South African units of the 9th Scottish Division held out until their ammunition was exhausted and only a 100 men remained unhurt. The village was retaken on September 1, 1918 at the end of the first phase of the British advance. On the left of the road is a fine **statue of Maréchal Foch** presented after

the war by Mr Haakon J. Wallem of Bergen, Norway. The addition of the name Bergen to the village is in honour of their Norwegian benefactor. The **Rancourt group of cemeteries** are just over 1 km further up the N17.

The large French one with its chapel is on the right; the small British one on the left; the German being down the D20 Combles road.

Turn round and take the D149 just south of Buchavesnes for **Clery-sur-Somme** 2 kms distant over the rolling country. In the village where the 35th Division tried to stem the flood in March 1918, and which the Australians took in September (the French having captured it in September 1916), take a right turn onto the D938 and in just over 1 km, having crossed the motorway, turn left on the D146 to descend into Hem-Monacu and cross the Somme into Feuillères, where, by using improvised bridges, the 5th Australian Brigade crossed the river en route for Mont St Quentin in August 1918.

In 2 kms **Herbécourt**. Turn right then immediately left onto D71 for **Dompierre-Becquincourt** in 2 kms, going through the village. At the crossroads in 1 km turn right onto D164. Just beyond the junction is a large **sucrerie** and also a **railway museum**, for

here is one of the **only remaining stretches of narrow-gauge track** dating from the First World War, part of which is still in regular use. From the sucrerie it runs across, and then on either side of, the D164 to skirt Cappy and end at **Froissy**. **Cappy**, up to March 1918, had been behind the Allied lines but after the German advance the aerodrome became one of Richthofen's bases. The **airfield** is on the D1, east of the

town, and the **château** used as the Officers' Mess by the Geschwader is on the left, hidden on the old road by an avenue of trees, right at the edge of the town. Today it appears much as it did in April 1918. Cappy was finally captured by the Australians in August 1918. Thus it was a well-known base for all.

Crossing the Somme onto the D1, **Bray** is reached in 2½ kms. This town, built on the northern steep banks of the river, was the junction between Third and Fifth Armies in March 1918 and was recaptured on August 24-25 in a moonlight attack by the Australians. Their memorial is on the D1.

From Bray, the D1 is the direct road to Corbie on the north bank of the river, crossing open country with few villages. It was the route of the retreat in March 1918,

but there are few signs of the battle today. From Bray the D329 goes south back across the river, and its marshes to **Proyart** (5½ kms), notable for the stand made by the 39th Division in the March 1918 retreat, and for its enormous village **war memorial**, a miniature Arc de Triomphe complete with Poilu. The Australians took the village in August 1918.

A small unclassified road leads westward to Morcourt where it joins the D71 in 2 kms. Thence along the pretty river to Chipilly and

Cerisy. On the **Chipilly** side of the river is the **Memorial to the 58th London Division** — an artilleryman with his wounded horse.

In 4 kms **Le Hamel** is reached. Near here, on the roadside, is a **Memorial to No. 57 Squadron**. From Le Hamel to Corbie the road is never far from the river and in 8 kms, crossing the Somme once again, we enter the quiet market town of **Corbie** with its huge church of St Pierre. This old abbey church, with its massive twin towers, was badly damaged in 1918 but the towers survived and the rest of the building was repaired in the original style. Corbie was a very busy forward town during the Battle of the Somme.

On April 21, 1918, on the left of the D1 a few hundred metres north of Corbie, Baron Manfred von Richthofen fell to Allied guns, either those of Captain Roy Brown of No. 209 Squadron or the Australian machine gunner serving with the 53rd MG Company.

Corbie was also a headquarters of the Army Graves Registration Service and, later, the Imperial War Graves Commission which was responsible for the work on the cemeteries. Even during the war, these were in many cases quiet flower gardens where the troops went for a peaceful hour.

In **Corbie Communal Cemetery** lies Major William (Billy) La Touche Congreve, VC, DSO, MC, the son of Captain W. N. Congreve, VC, who died at Longueval in the action which won him the VC on July 20, 1916. In Corbie's magnificent abbey church there is a **memorial** to him.

The D1 recrosses the Somme and follows the south bank into **Aubigny** and then recrosses the river to reach Amiens in 12 kms.

To reach Villers-Bretonneux turn off the Aubigny road at Fouilloy, taking the left, the D23, to the **Australian Memorial**.

ALTERNATIVE ROUTE

If time does not permit the deviation from Estrées-en-Chaussée to include the Péronne-Somme valley, keep straight on along the N29-E44 through **Villers-Carbonnel** (11 kms) and over the front line of 1917. This flat plain with gentle slopes was excellent tank country and, in the 1918 advance, they were used with great effect in the capture of the many positions around here.

Pass through **Warfusée-Abancourt** in 22 kms and 5 kms further on we reach **Villers-Bretonneux**. As the village is entered a **Demarcation Stone** will be seen. Most of this small industrial and agricultural town lies south of the road. Before April 1918 this sleepy town was well behind the British lines with, an RFC aerodrome on its outskirts. Among the squadrons stationed here were Nos. 11, 25 and 27.

As the Germans advanced in April 1918 it is probable that they had visions of repeating their victory of November 1870 when they defeated the Armée du Nord and went on to capture Amiens. However the Australian Corps with the 8th, 18th, and 58th Divisions stood in their way across the main road. The town fell to the Germans on April 24, and the battles that day were notable for the presence of German tanks and, for the first time, some light British Whippet tanks. The Australians and the 18th Division counter-attacked in the night and during the 25th the Australians regained the town. For the next four months a static war existed in this area with both sides digging-in and trenches were constructed in the woods south of the town.

On August 8, the Allied advance commenced with Fourth Army making a surprise attack with the Canadians and Australian III Corps together with over 400 tanks and low-flying aircraft. They advanced eastward over the rolling downs and through the woods completely dislodging the second German Army of General von der Marwitz. Tanks and cavalry played important rôles in the advance on the Somme itself and, within a few days, Villers-Bretonneux was well behind the lines.

High on the hill, north of the village, soars the tower of the **Australian National War Memorial**. The **British Military Cemetery** lies before it. It is reached via the D23 road to Corbie. An orientation table is incorporated in the lantern at the top of the tower, which gives magnificent views of the battle area. In the spring and autumn, the outlines of the old German trenches can be clearly seen as chalk slicks through the brown tilled fields to the east. To the west, on a fine clear day, the view extends to Amiens, with the spire of the cathedral clearly in sight. To the north is Corbie, and to the south Villers-Bretonneux on its ridge. Beyond the slopes, out of sight, is the location of the old aerodrome. Further still are the woods of **Hangard** and **Demuin** — scenes of very heavy fighting.

Each year a special ceremony is held on Anzac Day to recall the April and August battles, services being held at the memorial and celebrations in the town itself.

In 1975, the **Sir William Leggatt Museum** was opened in the school building which had been given to the children of Villers-Bretonneux by the Australian children whose fathers and brothers (1,200 of them) had lost their lives in the defence of the town. This museum is run by the Franco-Australian Welcome Committee and gives a very good record of the part that the

The Australian National War Memorial in the British Military Cemetery at Villers-Bretonneux. The town was captured in the advance which began on August 8, 1918, led by tanks and low-flying aircraft.

A corner in the Sir William Leggatt Museum showing Australian uniforms.

Australians and the villagers played in the battles. Access to the museum is by application to the Hôtel de Ville.

Continuing westward along the N29 the road skirts the **Bois d'Aquenne** where the Whippet tanks made their initial appearance. We then pass the **Bois de l'Abbé** and away to the left is **Bois de Blangy**. Soon after Blangy Cabaret and Petit Blangy — a mere hamlet — are passed, on the right **Glisy Aerodrome** comes into view. Sometime back, a **memorial to von Richthofen** was erected in the airfield precinct. Then, 17 kms from Villers-Bretonneux, Amiens is entered.

Amiens, the capital of Picardy, makes a good centre for visiting the Somme battlefields. Amiens has had a long history of contact with the English since the reign of King Edward III. There in 1550 Edward VI and Henri II of France signed a peace treaty and, in 1597, an English force assisted Henri IV to capture the city from the Spaniards. In 1802, the Treaty of Amiens brought a short respite in the Napoleonic wars.

In August 1914, Amiens was the first base for the troops arriving from the UK but, on the 30th of that month, the rapid advance of the Germans necessitated the evacuation of the city. For 12 days, until September 11, it was occupied by a German force which, after making demands for money, supplies and seizing 12 hostages, withdrew as the French Army under Général d'Amade arrived and drove them back to Fricourt. The French remained in the city until it was taken over by the British in 1916. Thereafter, the town bustled with Allied soldiers. It was a centre for all manner of depots and facilities for the army, hospitals and recreation centres and, of course, for the railway to the coast and Paris. Trains from Le Havre brought in reinforcements and took away the injured. In 1918 it came within range of the German artillery until some of the large guns were captured on the Plain of Santerre, east of Chaulnes.

In the Second World War, Amiens was again badly damaged but today a modern city has been re-born with many new buildings. The **Picardy Museum** includes a large art gallery and collection of material relating to the history of the city. In 1966, the **Maison de la Culture** was opened in an attempt to bring together theatre, conference and exhibition halls. There are several interesting **memorials to the Allies** in the magnificent **cathedral** and also a **plaque** to Lieutenant Raymond Asquith, the son of the Prime Minister, Herbert Asquith, who lies buried at Guillemont.

Tunnel Ferroviaire
en construction

Calais

Wissant

Cap Gris Nez

Marquise

Wimereux

Boulogne

Hardelot

Le Touquet-
Paris-Plage

Étaples

Montreuil

Berck-Plage

Fort-Mahon

Rue

le Crotoy

Cayeux

St Valery

Ault
Mers

Moyenneville

Hallencourt

Airaines

Oisemont

Bourbourg

Audruicq

Guînes

Ardres

St Omer

Arques

Cassel

Haze

Wormhout

Steenvo

Aire

Lumbres

Thérouanne

Fauquembergues

Hucqueliers

Samer

Desvres

Fruges

Heuchin

AGINCOURT

Campagne-lès-H

Hesdin

St Pol-s-T

Frévent

Crécy-en-P

Auxi-le-Ch^au

WAVANS

Nouvion

St Riquier

Abbeville

Bernaville

Doullens

COUIN

Ailly-le-
H^t Clocher

BEAUQUESNE

Flixecourt

NAOURS

BERTANGLES

Villers-
Bocage

Picquigny

Corbie

Acheux

AMIENS

PAS-DE-CAL

DE

DIRECT ROUTE VIA ABBEVILLE	————
ALTERNATIVE ROUTE	············
ROUTE VIA ST POL-SUR-TERNOISE	—·—·—

Reproduced from Michelin Sheet No. 989 17th Edition 1989

SCALE 1:500 000 1cm=5km

Amiens to Calais VIA ABBEVILLE

Take the N235 to **Picquigny**, 13 kms, along the south bank of the Somme. Here the main road crosses the river joining the N1 to reach Abbeville, via **Flixecourt**, in 44 kms. The D3 keeps to the south bank of the river and is probably the more attractive route (49 kms). Both roads travel through the rear areas where training was carried out and concentrations took place before the troops were moved up to the front.

Little of the old **Abbeville**, known to all British soldiers, remains for them or their descendants to visit today, for in May 1940 the town was bombed by Stukas and the entire centre burned out. Not long afterwards, tanks entered the town and the 4th Division de Cuirassée (under the command of a certain Colonel Charles de Gaulle) were in action against German forces which had crossed the river. The defence of Abbeville continued into June with Scottish and other French forces relieving each other until it was finally taken by the Germans on the 4th.

During the First World War Abbeville, the capital of Ponthieu, was a sleepy market town with cloth-weaving as its main industry. In 1914, groups of marauding Germans entered the town in August and September, but, by the end of that month, it was firmly in Allied hands. On October 8, Field-Marshal French set up General Headquarters here. Later it became a most important British base, a centre of communications, supply and transport. There were several hospitals and training areas in the vicinity. The main British base was outside the town and many wooden huts were erected to house the thousands of troops. In 1918 the town and surrounding area was subjected to frequent air raids. Set in very attractive country, and only 20 kms from the sea, it was a much favoured place by the BEF.

The direct route to Montreuil-sur-Mer is via the N1 and skirts the **Forest of Crécy** for a short distance some 15 kms out of Abbeville. The distance to Montreuil is 42 kms. The longer and more interesting route is via the D928 and Hesdin.

Travel north on the D928 for 16 kms to **Fontaine-sur-Maye**. To visit the **battlefield of Crécy** take the left road, D56, at the crossroads. In 2 kms, an old **cross** on a modern plinth marks the **spot where John of Bohemia was killed**. The cross is said to be one of the earliest battle monuments surviving in France as it was set up shortly after the battle in 1326.

It is 2 kms to **Crécy-en-Ponthieu**, a small town amid very pleasant country. In the centre of the town is another old **monument** with an amusing English text relating to **Eleanor of Aquitaine** and her sons. Leave the town by climbing up the D111 and, on the right, a double-decked wooden viewing tower is close to the **site of the windmill** from where Edward III watched his son, the Black Prince, lead his troops in the battle.

Continue 6 kms to **Dompierre** and turn right onto the D224. Then 7 kms to **Le Boisle** and left on to the D928 to Hesdin (17 kms). **Hesdin** was a 'British' town from 1916 onwards. Various branches of the Staff were quartered here and there were also hospitals. It was also the RFC headquarters. This attractive town, set amid the hills, made a pleasant leave centre.

From Hesdin, the N39 leads to Montreuil along the marshy valley of the River Canche for 23 kms. **Montreuil** is an old walled town which once was a seaport. The ramparts encircle the town on its rocky height and within them the streets are narrow, but they lead to the huge market place and the **statue of Field-Marshal Haig** on his charger, 'Miss Ypres'. The original was destroyed during the Second World War and, in the 1950s, another bronze was cast from the plaster model, now housed in the Musée des Trois Guerres at Château Diors in Indre.

From March 1916 to April 1919 Montreuil was the British GHQ. Field-Marshal Haig resided in the **Château de Beaurepaire**, some 4 kms from the town on the D138 near **St Nicholas**. A **plaque on the gateway** records his stay. The **military college buildings**

Left: **Château de Beaurepaire, Haig's residence from 1916-18.** *Above:* **The old barracks were used by GHQ.**

123

The magnificent vista at Etaples Military Cemetery where flag-bedecked cenotaphs flank the Stone of Remembrance.

In Wimereux Communal Cemetery, because of unstable ground, the gravestones lie flat around the Cross of Sacrifice.

housed the administrative staff and it is said that over 5,000 men were attached to GHQ here. In 1918 it was within the range of German bombers and suffered several heavy raids. As a result, at one time the HQ was evacuated at night.

Continue along the N39 beside the River Canche 13 kms to Etaples. **Etaples** was one of the largest centres for reinforcements to the BEF with training depots, hospitals and facilities for 100,000 men. In the sand dunes near the railway was the infamous **'Bullring' training ground**. This is overlooked today by the beautiful **Etaples Military Cemetery** where over 11,000 men from all over the

'If ye break faith with us who die, We shall not sleep, though poppies grow in Flanders fields.' Immortal words composed by Lieutenant-Colonel John McCrae. (See also page 34.)

world, friend and foe, lie buried together. The cemetery is just outside 'Eat-apples' as the Tommy called it, on the D940 to **Boulogne** (27 kms).

On August 14, 1914, the first units of Sir John French's army began to disembark here and from then on Boulogne was on the main route for all troop movements from England. This famous old seaport and holiday centre became a bustling British base with hospitals, supply depots and camps being erected on the Camp de Boulogne, built in 1801 as the base for Napoleon's invasion army for England. All around the town, on the hills and coastal downs, camps were built, some semi-permanent hutted camps, others just masses of bell tents.

Except as prisoners-of-war, the Germans never reached Boulogne; the nearest being in 1914 when a few squadrons of roaming German cavalry came within 40 kms. In 1917-18 the town was heavily attacked from the air and much damage was caused both to the town and the base. The Second World War saw the port and coast fortified by the Germans with many blockhouses of the Atlantic Wall, of which quite a few still remain.

In recent years there has been a great deal of new building and the town has expanded well beyond its 1918 boundaries. But, here and there, the small bungalows, which were brought from England for the use of the camp and later by homeless local population, survive.

The **Colonne de La Grande Armée**, high above the town on N1 to Calais, was erected in 1804 to commemorate the nearby Camp de Boulogne. The original statue of Napoleon in a Roman toga was in bronze and was shot off its pedestal by the Royal Navy during the Second War! The head of the first statue can be seen together with other relics in the **town museum**.

The more interesting road to Calais is the coast road, the D940, on which, in 1 km, we reach **Terlincthun**. The **British Cemetery** here was one of the first to be completed with the well-known headstones and was visited by the King and Queen.

It is 5 kms to **Wimereux**. All along the coastal downs were hospitals and welfare establishments. Colonel John McCrae is

buried in the **British Communal Cemetery**. His headstone, close to the Cross of Sacrifice, is one of those lying flat due to the type of ground on which the cemetery is built. This is located behind the town cemetery.

For the next 36 kms, the road swings up and down just inside the coastal cliffs of **Cap Gris Nez**, through Wissant and up again over **Cap Blanc Nez**, with the **Memorial to the Dover Patrol**, and through the ramifications of the Channel Tunnel works to Sangatte and finally into Calais. At the major crossroads after Fort Nieulay, a left turn will lead to the complex of **Military Cemeteries**, French, German and Belgian, which lay behind the Communal Cemetery.

The Belgian Military Cemetery at Calais.

The funeral of the Red Baron. The firing party in Bertangles Cemetery, April 22, 1918. His body, transferred to Fricourt Cemetery after the war, was reburied in Berlin in 1925. In 1975, after several years of negotiations with the East Germans, a third move came when the remains were moved to the family vault at Wiesbaden.

St Pol-sur-Ternoise

Leave Amiens by the N25 to **Poulainville** (6 kms) and in 2 kms turn left for **Bertangles**. Near this village was the RFC aerodrome. The village was also a base for other units including the artillery. Time seems to have stood still, for the village and its magnificent château have altered little since 1918; only the old army hutments and the airfield have gone, replaced by modern villas. It was here that the body of Manfred von Richthofen was buried on April 22, 1918 with full military honours. The **small communal cemetery** — with one British war grave — is down a lane to the west of the village. The **château** used by the British is now open to the public at certain times.

Take the D97 for **Villers-Bocage** (5 kms) and rejoin N25. In 3½ kms turn left onto the D60 to **Naours** (3 kms). The first turning on the right as the village is reached leads to the **Souterrains-réfuges de Naours**. These very extensive underground caves and connecting tunnels can house over 3,000 people and have been used for centuries. They are open to visitors and entry is via the pleasure park and the preserved windmills of Naours.

Return to the N25 in 3 kms, we reach **Vert Galant**. Take the D3l, to the right, for **Beauquesne**. The **Château of Val Vion**, used by Field-Marshal Haig as a headquarters, is some 1½ kms further east. The château is on the right up a long tree-lined avenue. Here King George V stayed on his visits to the front. The present building dates only from the post-1945 era as the original house was bombed by the Germans in 1940, killing a party of Belgian refugees. The house was rebuilt almost identically.

Take next left turning at the crossroads, the D11, 3 kms to **Marieux**. Then turn right on to the D938 for 5 kms to **Louvencourt**. On the Acheux road (D938) to the south of the village is a small **British Cemetery**. It was one of the first three to be completed in the early 1920s and was designed by Lutyens. Among those buried here is Lieutenant

Château Val Vion where King George V stayed with Sir Douglas Haig during his visits to the front.

For many years the plot at Bertangles still bore the outline of the excavated grave.

Roland A. Leighton, Vera Brittain's fiancé who died of wounds on December 3, 1915. There are a number of unusual French grave markers.

Take the small road to the left of the church for **Bus-lès-Artois**. This is one of the concentration areas used for the divisions before July 12, 1916.

On leaving the village by the D176e, which shortly becomes the D25, we enter the Département of the Pas de Calais. The next village is **Couin**. At the bottom of the hill before the village note the **notice on the brick barn** on the right. This direction sign for a water point was there in 1916, when the 63rd Division were gathering here, and it is thought to have been placed there by the 94th Brigade.

Continue through **Pas-en-Artois**, in 5 kms turning left onto the D6 for **Mondicourt**, another staging area, and then left onto N25 for Doullens, 8½ kms. A turning to the left just before the railway arch leads up in 1 km to the **Foch Calvary** from where there are magnificent views. **Doullens** is an industrial town of the Authie valley and the steep hills around it. In 1916 it was the BEF base and concentration area previously being Foch's HQ. On March 26, 1918, the momentous meeting attended by Lord Milner, Poincaré, Clemenceau, Foch, Haig, Wilson and Pétain was held in the **Council Chamber of the Hôtel de Ville** at which Foch was appointed Supreme Allied Commander. The room is open to visitors.

At **Gézaincourt**, a village beyond the Citadel, is a **British Cemetery** of which there is a model in the Imperial War Museum in London. It is reached from N25 and is signposted through **Bagneux** reached in 3½ kms.

Leave the D925 for **Risquetout** (3 kms) then onto the D938 for **Wavans** (11 kms). In **Wavans Military Cemetery**, a small, lonely little graveyard on a narrow road on the right, just beyond the D117, lies Major J. McCudden, VC, DSO, MC — after so many combats killed while taking off from Auxi-le-Petit, not far away.

In 4 kms at **Auxi-le-Château** turn right on to the D941, through the **Bois d'Auxi** and over the plain to **Frévent** (15 kms). Frévent is an industrial town amid hills which was used considerably by the British.

Continue via the D916 to **St Pol** (12 kms). This small bustling town was a British base for most of the war. Third Army had its

Couin. One of the few original signs to be seen . . . and the water-point is still there!

Gézaincourt Cemetery clings to the hill above Doullens.

headquarters here in 1916 and it remained GHQ until 1921. The Army Graves Registration Service (later the Imperial War Graves Commission) HQ was here at St Pol. The choice of British Unknown Warrior was made here (in a hut near the **Cemetery of St Pol-sur-Ternoise**) by Colonel Wyatt in 1920 from bodies brought in from various battle areas.

A detour can be made from the N39 at **Humières**, 10 kms from St Pol, to go via **Blangy** on the D104 to **Tramecourt** to visit the **site of the battle of Agincourt** (Azincourt) 11 kms. Approaching the village, one of the two **memorials** is passed on the left. A plan of the battle is provided at this and other major positions relative to 1415, whilst others recall the Tramecourt family, a member of which was present, and his descendants who died in concentration camps in the Second World War. Their **château** is amid the avenues of huge trees. An **RFC aerodrome** was located here from 1916-18. The D71 passes through **Azincourt** and goes on to the D928 and in 12 kms to Hesdin.

The Council Chamber in Doullens Hôtel de Ville retains the original furniture in use at the meeting on March 26, 1918.

After his crash near Auxi-le-Petit, Major McCudden, the famous flying VC, was buried in the tiny cemetery at Wavans.

126

INSET PAGE 130

INSET PAGE 133

INSET PAGE 136

INSET PAGE 128

SCALE 1:1 000 000 1cm–10km

St Quentin to Reims

This extension to the main itinerary includes the areas of British involvement in 1914 and 1918 in the regions south of St Quentin and part of the American battlegrounds in 1918.

Leave St Quentin southwards via the N44, 21 kms to **La Fère**. Continue on the N44 10 kms to **Crépy**. As the road slopes down towards a bend, take the road on the left, the D26, for 1½ kms. On the left are woods and on the right, a little way from the road, will be seen a cluster of houses on the railway line. This is the **site of one of the huge German guns** which fired on Paris in 1918. The monster, which fired its first round on Paris on March 23 at 7.16 a.m., was hidden amongst the trees in the wood. Four minutes later the 210mm shell burst in north-west Paris. The distance was 74.12 miles. Today, little remains of the site of the huge railway gun with its three-part barrel, in all some 34 metres in length, weighing over 300 tons. The railway siding can still be traced across the road, along a track to the main line, and into the wood where it becomes a glade through the trees which has rather unusual ridges across it — the sleepers. There are bunkers and the mounts for the base plate but nothing more.

Return to Crépy and the N44. In 5 kms the lone hill of **Laon** comes into view and the spires and towers of the old fortress town can be clearly seen soaring 300 feet above the plain.

After another 4 kms, turn right on to the N2. Drop down 9 kms to cross the Canal de l'Oise. Then 3 kms further on, on the left, are the ruins of the **Fort de Malmaison** and it is from here that the **Chemin des Dames** commences. The **calvary** is a memorial to the defence of the fort in 1917.

It is another 15 kms to **Soissons**. This is one of the oldest cities in France which has been a fortress for many centuries. The Romans were defeated here by Clovis in 486. At the end of August 1914, the BEF, retreating from Mons, crossed the Aisne west of the city. The Germans held Soissons until September 12 before they retired after having blown all the bridges. On September 13 the Battle of the Aisne began. The Germans were dug in amid the hills and quarries on the north bank and the British divisions fought their way back across the river at a number of points east and west of Soissons. The 1st Division crossed at Bourg, the 2nd at

Traces still remain of the railway line which carried the Paris guns.

Eric Kennington's figures on the centrepiece of the Soissons Memorial to the Missing, which commemorates the missing of the British IX and XXII Corps.

ROUTE CONTINUED ON MAP ON PAGE 130

SCALE 1:200 000 1cm—2km

SOISSONS

Reproduced from Michelin Sheet No. 56 28th Edition 1989

Chavonne, the 3rd at Vailly, the 4th at Venizel, the 5th at Missy and the Guards Brigade at Chavonne and at Pont Arcy. They crossed in boats and rafts, by pontoons, and by using the girders of wrecked bridges. The crossing was successful and the force moved forward only to be checked in the Chemin des Dames region. In October the BEF were relieved by the French.

Counter-attacks by the Germans were repulsed in 1915 and 1917 but in May 1918 Soissons fell. On August 2 the city was recaptured only to be ruined further by the artillery bombardment which followed.

The **Soissons Memorial to the Missing** is just below the cathedral facing the Pont d'Anglais. The memorial commemorates the missing of the British IX and XXII Corps which fought during the July and August 1918 battles alongside the French Army. There are 3,987 names engraved on the panels. The memorial is unique for the sculptural group. Three soldiers in their greatcoats stand shoulder to shoulder, two of them with their gas masks in the alert position. In front of the middle soldier is a rifle butt planted in the ground with a helmet on it. The sculptor was Eric Kennington.

Buzancy lies 13 kms south of Soissons off the D1. This little town clings to the hills which were the scene of hectic fighting in the summer of 1918 and the drive there gives a good idea of the difficulties of the opposing armies. To reach the **British Cemetery** turn left off D1 and in the village turn left again up a narrow lane. The cemetery was created in July 1918 by the 15th Scottish Division who fought here with great distinction. Their courage so impressed their French comrades that at the close of the battle they erected a **cairn** to their honour with the inscription: 'Here for all time the glorious Scottish thistle will bloom amid the roses of France'. Some

Pont Arcy. A bridge still crosses the Aisne at the place where the BEF crossed in September 1914.

years ago the rough-hewn cairn was removed to the cemetery for safety.

Leave Soissons by the D925, travelling eastward along the pretty banks of the river on the northern side. Views of the area held by the BEF and the places at which they crossed in September 1914 can be seen all along this road. **Missy** (10 kms), **Vailly** (7 kms), **Chavonne** (4 kms), and **Pont Arcy** (4 kms), where there is still an iron bridge similar to the one blown by the Germans.

In 2½ kms we reach **Bourg-et-Comin**. Turn left onto D967 to climb up the hills to the ridge of the Chemin des Dames. Attractive and beautiful as these hills and valleys are, they show the difficulties the armies must have faced.

To the south at **Braine** on the N31-E46 Allenby's cavalry fought a delaying action in

September 1914, and in 1918 it was the Americans who were in action here. In the **town cemetery** is a **small British plot** where lies Captain Harry S. Ranken, VC, RAMC, attached to the KRRC. He was mortally wounded at Hautes Avesnes in the conflict of September 19-20, 1914, suffering ghastly wounds before he would relinquish his task of tending other comrades, and he did not live to know that he had won the decoration announced with the first awards. He was also Mentioned in Despatches and created a Chevalier of the Légion d'Honneur. He died here at Braine on September 25.

Vendresse is 5 km further on. On the slope above the village is a **British Cemetery**. This is the route of the I British Corps (Haig) in September 1914, and also in the sector of the 8th, 21st and 50th Divisions in May 1918.

Left: **Both in 1914 and later in 1918, the fighting swept over the wooded slopes at Vendresse as the graves in the cemetery indicate. Over the hill is the Chemin des Dames.** *Right:* **Rather unusual, the tall grey column at Cerny is a British Memorial to the 1st Bn. Loyal North Lancashire Regiment which fought here in 1914.**

Cerny-en-Laonnois (1½ kms) is a cross-road village on the crest of the ridge of the **Chemin des Dames**. On the left is a tall Greek pillar, the **Memorial of the 1st Bn. Loyal North Lancashire Regiment**; the 1st Brigade of the 1st Division fought here in 1914. In front of you as you reach the crossroads is the **Memorial of the Chemin des Dames**, a small elegant chapel with a modernistic column before it. Inside the chapel, in gleaming white stone and marble, are the memorials to the French units which fought here. The altar is a striking centre-piece being formed of rows of crosses in perspective. To the left of the chapel on the south side of this famous road are large **French** and **German cemeteries**.

Turn right along the Chemin des Dames, the D18, stretching straight and narrow along the ridge high above the surrounding country. The road owes its name to the daughters of Louis XV as it was constructed to ease their journeys between Compiègne and the Château de la Bôve situated in the upper valley of the Ailette which belonged to their great friend the Duchess of Narbonne.

The ridge is riddled with caverns and quarries which were used by both armies in the conflict. It is still possible to see the effects of the bombardments on the area in the shell-pocked chalky fields. The French gained a foothold on the ridge in April 1917 during Nivelle's offensive and the Germans fell back to Ailette. As with Vimy Ridge, this was considered to be a very strong position and very severe casualties were suffered by both sides in repeated attacks and counter-attacks for possession of the ridge.

In 5 kms on the right **a group of guns and a 1939-45 tank** come into view with several **memorials**. They mark the entrance to one of the fortified quarries known as the **Grotte or Caverne du Dragon**. The memorials are of the **4th Zouaves**, the **164th French Infantry Division** and the **41st Batallion de Chasseurs à Pied** — the last unveiled as recently as May 1982. The complex is now a museum open daily during the season. Unfortunately the collection has suffered from a number of burglaries in the past but new measures have been taken to ensure that this cannot happen again. The entrance is now through a recently erected building to the left of the steep path down the hillside — decorated with battlefield debris — and in through a foyer decorated with crests and banners of French units and photographs. Access to the underground caverns is via a steep stairway from which the visitor is transported into the chalk rooms and passages. The museum exhibits are displayed in cases representing the men of the French, British and German Armies who fought here. Relics include uniforms and badges, weapons and equipment, and the ephemera of war. In one room a cinema show is given telling the story of the history of the ridge through the ages. Clever lighting

Left: **Two large cemeteries dominate the Cerny-en-Laonnois crossroads, one French and one German. Over the plastic crosses of the former, the grey granite of the latter can be seen.** *Right:* **A striking marble altar in the memorial chapel.**

enhances the dread gloom of those who lived and fought below ground. Here the Germans set up a command post and stores depot for the troops who held the line. They had a huge arsenal and large numbers of men were housed in the various chambers. Water came from a deep well. Lighting was meagre and the modern guides depict the ink-black darkness by blacking out the whole suddenly for a moment and then relighting the area, section by section, in multi-coloured lights. Each time I visit the cavern I am amazed by the lack of graffiti on the walls, which are all rough and devoid of other markings save the soot from a candle or two. A car park is provided on the north side of the Chemin.

A French field gun and a tank of 1939 vintage at the Caverne du Dragon — a memorial to French Colonial Regiments.

The interior of the Caverne Museum — once a German command post.

ROUTE CONTINUED
ON MAP ON PAGE 133

FROM MAP
PAGE 128

Reproduced from Michelin Sheet No. 56 28th Edition 1989

A matter of some hundred metres further along is one of those places which prove the adage 'Once a good battlefield, always a battlefield.' This is **Hurtebise**. A rather striking **group in bronze** commemorates the Battle of Hurtebise Farm in 1814 and the 1914 battles; a **plaque on the wall of the farm** recalls the victory of the 4th Zouaves in 1914 and 1917 and one to the 4th Division Cuirassé in their armoured battle in 1940.

Take the D895 for **Craonne** (4½ kms). In this area there are a number of French memorials relating both to Napoleon's victory over the Allies in March 1814 and to the 1914-18 battles. One is a statue of the Emperor. Around Craonne, amid the pine-covered hills, several French positions are indicated, often with car park and picnic areas. Just above the village is the **California position** used by Napoleon in 1814 and which figured again in 1914 and 1917. An **orientation table** is set on the right above the precipitous hill with a magnificent view towards Reims and refers to the 1917 actions.

Towards the end of April 1918 five British Divisions were put into the lines between Soissons and Reims to enable them to enjoy a comparative 'rest cure' after the ravages of the German advance on the Lys and Somme fronts earlier in the year, and for them to refit after the tremendous battles. They formed the IX Corps and were to support the French Sixth Army. To replace casualties incurred in March and April, the units had been reinforced with young and often only partially-trained drafts direct from England. The blow fell on May 27 when the Germans opened the Champagne offensive. The corps was assaulted by a fierce mortar, gas and artillery attack and, with many casualties, fell back across the rivers Aisne and Ardres. On May 28 the Kaiser came to California to view the victory of his troops and is said to have looked out from the site of the orientation table at the utter devastation.

From Craonne take the D984 to **Craonnelle** (about a km of difficult road) and rejoin the D89 to descend into the valley near **Pontavert** with its important bridges over the Aisne. At the edge of the village (note the bunkers on the roadside to the right) take the left turn after the church. This is again the D89 and after traversing some open country the road curves into the notorious **Bois des Buttes**, still threaded with crumbling trenches and shell-holes. Current tree clearance and coppicing of an area marked by warning

Battles a century apart are remembered at Hurtebise.

The California position — used by Napoleon in 1814 and the Kaiser in 1918.

notices of the danger of flying bullets (from the game hunters) is making it easier to pick out the lines of battle where the 2nd Bn. Devonshire Regiment fought a defensive action until almost being annihilated by a numerically superior force on May 27. Incidentally, there is a picnic area on the right about ½ km in the wood. Not far from the woods, as they give way to orchards, the village of **Ville-aux-Bois-les-Pontavert** is reached. There are still a few concrete bunkers in the area. The road curves into the village and the simple stone cross of the **2nd Bn. Devonshire Regiment Memorial** comes into view in front of the mairie and church. The story of their gallant action is graphically told on the plinth of the cross in the words of the commander of the French Sixth Army under whose orders they fought. These words form the citation for the **Croix de Guerre** awarded to them and to the 5th (Gibraltar) Battery of 45th Brigade, RFA, also destroyed in the action. A plaque to the battery is on the wall of the mairie.

At the crossroads turn right to join the N44 in a few hundred metres at La Musette crossroads — the original site of the 2nd Devons' memorial before it was moved.

Bois des Buttes — the crumbling trench lines where the Devonshires fought a bitter holding action, virtually to complete annihilation, in May 1918.

Left: **Their memorial stands nearby in the little village of Ville-aux-Bois-les-Pontavert, its inscription recalling the 'ungrudging sacrifice to the sacred cause of the Allies' and 'in the face of an intense bombardment . . . though isolated and without hope of assistance held on to their trenches . . . and fought to the last with an unhesitating obedience to orders'.** *Above:* **The plaque recording the award of the Croix de Guerre to the 5th (Gibraltar) Field Battery who fought with them, can be seen on the wall of the mairie.**

Ville-aux-Bois. Here the Commonwealth War Graves Commission cemetery contains possibly the greatest proportion of unknown graves to any of those to be found on the Western Front: over eighty percent of the dead being unnamed. As many such headstones include the regimental badge, this would appear to indicate partial identification from shoulder strap titles or collar badges. Here, too, can be seen graves bearing the Royal Air Force crest — the new aviation service having superseded the Royal Flying Corps when the RAF came into being on April 1, 1918.

The D89 continues straight ahead to **Juvincourt-et-Damary** over part of the old **Berry-au-Bac airfield**, used in both wars by aviators of the French, British and German air forces. Now it has returned mostly to agricultural land, through which the overgrown runways can be discerned, and one section is maintained as a driving school.

Turn right on N44 and almost immediately on the right is **Ville-aux-Bois British Cemetery** with some concrete shelters on the north side of its boundary. The cemetery was made after the Armistice and, to my mind, is one of the most poignant I ever visit. Of the 540 buried here, 413 are unknown. Many are from units of the 8th, 21st and 50th Divisions, the unnamed headstones bearing the badges of several regiments and corps: the Devons, Durham Light Infantry, Middlesex, Machine Gun Corps, Artillery, and so on who bore the brunt of the German surge forward during the second battle of the Aisne. The 8th Division alone lost 7,000 out of 8,000 men, killed, wounded, missing or prisoners of war. In all, by the time IX Corps was withdrawn in July, it had lost 15,000 dead. The Germans claimed to have taken 45,000 British and French prisoners and 400 guns. Others buried in this cemetery include three airmen: two killed in July 1918 (one of whom is an American who joined the RFC in February 1917) and another, a New Zealander, who died in November 1943.

Proceed south to **Le Choléra crossroads** in 3 kms. On the left is the **Memorial to the French Armoured Forces of 1917-1918** and their commander, Général Estienne, while on the right are two examples of more modern **armoured vehicles** and an old crucifix on whose plinth are affixed various **commemorative plaques**.

The memorial at Le Choléra crossroads which commemorates the French Armoured Forces of 1917-18 and their commander, Général Estienne.

132

Turn left onto D925 for **Guignicourt**, crossing the route of the autoroute to Reims, and in 6 kms reach the village on the north bank of the river and canal, passing **Neufchâtel-sur-Aisne** (7 kms). Turn right and take the D926 to **Rethel**, 34 kms along the pleasant Aisne valley which has a number of hotels — quite a rarity in this area. It is an ancient town which, after the fighting in 1914, was behind the German line for the

rest of the war. It was badly damaged in 1940. It is also hilly and the **ruins of the castle** of the Counts of Rethel are on the high ridge to the north.

Climb out of Rethel crossing the Aisne on the N51 and almost immediately take the left fork of the D946 and then the right fork, the D985. The road passes a small airfield as it rises onto the plateau, broken only by the small town of Perthes.

In 15 kms, at a road junction, turn left onto the D925. These are the battlefields of **Champagne** fought over in July 1918 by the Americans.

At **Mazagran** (15 kms), turn right on to the D977. The long straight road, with few bends, sweeps southward across the rolling plain. Drive for 12 kms and, directly after entering the Département of the Marne, take the right-hand road which goes up 2 kms

SCALE 1:200 000 1cm=2km

Sommepy, where the American Monument now stands, was once a look-out of Kaiser Wilhelm.

Around the Sommepy Memorial, the ground has been left as it was and is complete with grassy trenches and shell-holes.

to the **American Sommepy Monument** on the Mont Blanc ridge. The tall, severe stone tower rises from the pine covered crest of a hill attacked and captured by the US 2nd Division in October 1918. All around there are vestiges of the bunkers and trenches and shell-holes in which they fought. The monument is only open on Sundays. Inside there is the usual explanation of the operations in the region which one comes to expect from the American Battle Monuments Commission. Each face of the monument bears the badge of a division with its battle honours — the 2nd, 36th, 42nd (the 'Rainbow' Division) and the 93rd. A stairway leads to the top to give an excellent view of the battlefield.

Take the D320 for **Sommepy-Tahure** (4½ kms). On the highest point of this road, 3½ kms south, is the **Monument de La Ferme de Navarin**, one of the principal positions in the Champagne battles of 1914, 1915 and again in 1918. The pyramid is surmounted by a

Below: **With unlimited views over the battlefield, the memorial at Ferme de Navarin marks one of the main positions.**

Above: **The Ferme de Navarin Memorial of the Battle of Champagne rises above the tomb of Général Gouraud, GOC Fourth French Army. This area was one of the principal positions in the Champagne battles of 1914-15.**

vigorous group of three soldiers. One is an infantryman charging; the second is a machine-gunner with his weapon over his shoulder as he presses forward whilst the third, with his right hand raised, urges them on. This is the work of the sculptor Maxime Real del Sarte and is a memorial to Lieutenant Quentin Roosevelt, the son of President Theodore Roosevelt, and to Général Gouraud, the GOC of the French Fourth Army. The Général is buried in the **crypt**, a small chapel lit by a stained glass window bearing the likeness of him. Steep steps lead to the foot of the statues from which views of the battlefield are aided by four orientation diagrams. In the immediate vicinity, the ground has been left as it was at the end of the war, complete with trenches and shell-holes. Lieutenant Roosevelt was killed in 1918 in the Tardenois battles.

We continue on the RD77 through this huge agricultural plain, descending to **Souain-Perthes-lès-Hurlus** in 4 kms. Here there is a **German Cemetery** containing 13,783 graves. On the right is a **French Cemetery**.

Turn right on the D19 for 7 kms to **St Hilaire-le-Grand**, a small town on the northern boundaries of one of the huge military camps and training grounds associated with this part of Champagne. Take the Mourmelon road, the D19, skirting the edge of a tank training area.

In 7 kms there is a sharp fork going off on the right, the D21. Five hundred metres along this road, on a slight incline, can be seen a group of pine trees and on the left, and most unexpectedly emerging from the trees, is the bulbous dome of a tiny **Russian Orthodox church** and beside it a **Russian Cemetery**. Here are buried Russian soldiers who fought for France in both wars with a separate enclosure for civilians. Two mass graves lie in the centre of the military graveyard.

Remain on this road for another 6½ kms and, at the **l'Espérance** crossroads, turn left onto the RD31. This highway crosses the battlefields of 1915 and 1918 as indicated by the **Franco-German Cemetery** near l'Espérance and **various French memorials** along the wayside.

In 21½ kms, the road joins the major highway to Reims, the N44, near an airfield and, on the rise in the ground as we turn right for Reims, the car park for **Fort de la Pompelle** is indicated. Access to the fort from the car park is through a narrow tunnel under the road. One emerges in a shattered landscape of torn chalk with the battered north-east face of the fort on the left.

Set amid the pine trees, the Russian Memorial church guards Russian graves from both world wars.

As one of the forts encircling the city of Reims, it was in the line throughout the war. Bitter fighting took place in and around it and it changed hands several times but always the French retook it. Today it is a national museum with a small military garrison. A varying collection of artillery pieces and equipment are displayed in front of the fort but most items are in the casemates. The internal galleries are well laid out recording the history of the fort, Reims and the Champagne district. Photographs and documents play a large part. Representative collections concerning Guynemer and other French heroes and a good selection of the uniforms and equipment of the Allies are displayed. The amazing Charles Friese collection of Imperial German Army headdresses occupies a whole gallery. One sub-gallery has been filled with battle debris and in another transport is shown.

After another 5 kms **Reims** is entered. This is a very ancient city which has played many rôles in the history of France, religious and secular, military and political. It is a great industrial centre and famous for its art and learning. Here, in the massive **cathedral**, so badly damaged during the bombardments but now repaired, the Kings of France were crowned.

In September 1914 the Germans occupied the city and ransacked it for a week. On September 15 the German Crown Prince made the **Grand Hôtel** his headquarters. Prince August Wilhelm was already there and, shortly, the Kaiser's brother joined them. However their stay was brief as the French Fifth Army under Général Franchet d'Esperey arrived and drove them out. For the next four years the city was in French hands but, always in artillery range, it was constantly shelled or bombed. By 1917 the city was almost surrounded but in 1918 the French gradually forced the Germans back until, in October, the retreat became a rout.

For those interested in the arts there are several fine galleries; there are collections of Roman remains and of course the priceless treasures of the cathedral which were saved from devastation. The **Porte du Mars** is a fine Roman triumphal arch near the Place de la République, and not far from this at **No. 10, rue Franklin-Roosevelt** is the **war room** which is preserved as it was left on May 8, 1945 after General Eisenhower had accepted the German surrender. It is open every day.

A splendid museum is located in Fort de la Pompelle — still lying in ruins almost as if time has stood still since 1918.

FROM REIMS 65 kms

SCALE 1 : 200 000 1cm–2km

The Verdun Battlefield

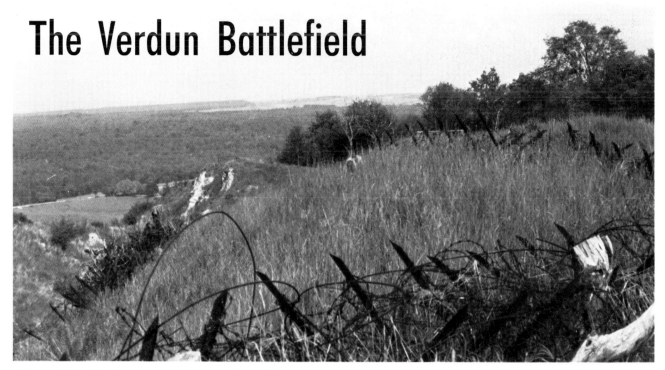

Beyond Reims lies the most sacred battle-field of France — Verdun — and the regions of the greatest American contribution in 1918 — the Meuse, Argonne and Château-Thierry fronts. This is a route for visiting those areas east and south-east of Reims. The southern and south-western region is covered in the final itinerary.

Leave Reims by the N44, branching off to the left onto the RD31 after passing Fort de la Pompelle. After 42 kms **Suippes** is reached after traversing the huge plain of almost uninterrupted grain fields, among which are occasional **forts and military establishments and war cemeteries** of France, Germany and Poland.

In 23 kms at **Orbeval**, turn left onto the N3 and travel 8 kms to **Ste. Menehould**. This ancient fortress town was occupied by the Germans in September 1914 and great destruction was wrought before they were driven out. Thereafter the town was a busy French HQ in the Argonne front battles over the next four years.

In another 9 kms we reach **Les Islettes**. Turn left on the D2. Then 10 kms to **Le Four de Paris**. Turn right onto the D38 for 5 kms through the **Bois de la Gruerie**. A small road on the left leads into the forest; it is straight and has a good surface for approximately

One of the last places where metal Frise de Cheval entanglements can still be seen as they were in the Great War — on the mine-riven hill of Vauquois.

1 km. Where it peters out into a number of mud tracks, a grubby notice will be seen on the right pointing to the **Abri du Krönprinz**. This unusual concrete shelter, built into a deep trench not many yards off the road, was erected for Crown Prince Wilhelm in 1915 and was used by him for quite a time. It has a front portal and large windows but is gradually disintegrating. Much of the surrounding woodland is cordoned off by barbed wire and entry into the trenches is forbidden.

Return to the D38 and continue to the left to **Varennes-en-Argonne** (4 kms). Before 1914, when the town was captured by the Germans, Varennes was only remembered in the history books as the town where Louis XVI and Marie Antoinette were arrested to be taken back to Paris and the guillotine. Now the town is dominated by the **Pennsylvania State Memorial** to her sons who died in the battles to recapture this region in September 1918. The memorial consists of a double colonnade surrounding a paved courtyard with a central monument in Grecian style. In the hillside below are a number of bunkers and concrete shelters which originally led into subways.

On the right of the main street (which is the D946) is the road leading to the monument and a little further up is the modern **Musée d'Argonne** where there are ethnographical and art collections, documents relating to the arrest of Louis XVI in June 1791, and the **Museum of Mine Warfare** with some interesting dioramas showing how mines were bored and blown. There are many relics of the American activities in the region and the personalities who fought here, including Harry S. Truman.

Remain on the D946 for **Boureuilles**, some 3½ kms to the south. There, turn left on D212 for **Vauquois** and the famous **Butte de Vauquois**. To visit this mine-riven hill, 290 metres high, requires a short steep walk from the car park. This was once the site of the village of Vauquois but now it is a grassy desert of barbed wire and mine craters. On the summit is a **memorial** to those who died and close by is one of two excellent orientation tables and also a machine which for a franc gives an explanation of the scene and its history in four languages. A map shows a route recommended for a comprehensive visit and each salient position is identified.

Entrance to Abri du Krönprinz, headquarters dugout of Crown Prince Wilhelm.

Bunker entrance beneath the Pennsylvania State Memorial at Varennes-en-Argonne.

The Angel of Victory surmounts the Missouri Memorial near Varennes.

The imposing memorial lantern to 'Les Combattants' amid the barbed wire on the summit of the Butte de Vauquois.

Return to the modern village at the foot of the butte and take D38 to the left to return to **Varennes**, noticing the **Memorial to the Men of the State of Missouri** on the outskirts. **Apremont** is reached in 6 kms. From here a detour into the forest along D442, with the **German Cemetery** on the hillside, will in 3½ kms arrive at the **ravine** where the **Lost Battalion** disappeared for several days having become cut off from their comrades of the US 77th Division between October 2-7, 1918. A marker on the roadside up the hill indicates the valley down very steep slopes.

After 4½ kms we reach **Fléville**. Take D4 to **Sommerance** and in 3 kms the D54/D123 to **Romagne-Gesnes**, 7 kms away, driving through more of the American battle zones to the **Meuse-Argonne Cemetery and Memorial** on the far side of the town. In this huge peaceful park 14,000 men lie buried on the gentle slopes of the valley. The administrative block looks out over the vista of gleaming white crosses, lawns and trees, to the memorial chapel on the opposite crest.

Leave the park by the Cunel road. In 3 kms take the D15 to the right. **Nantillois** is 5 kms. Soon the **Butte de Mont Faucon** is in sight and is reached in 2 kms. This outstanding ridge is capped with **Hill 336** from which

The central avenue of the American Meuse-Argonne Memorial and Cemetery.

rises the elegant Doric column of the **American Memorial**. Shallow steps lead to the entrance and an internal and very graceful stairway up to the observation balcony below the Statue of Liberty from where the view is spectacular. This was the site of an ancient monastery and hamlet which the Germans heavily fortified after its capture in 1914 and it was used thereafter as an OP, particularly in 1916. They built bunkers in the ruins. In

1914 the Crown Prince had his HQ on this prominence. It fell to the Americans on September 27, 1918 in their attack on the **Kreimhide Line** which ran east to Grandpré.

Leave by D15/D18 for **Malancourt**, 5 kms, and in 3 kms the Dl8bis on the left leads up to **Côte 304** with its **monument**. Over 19,000 men were killed fighting in this hilly wooded area in 1917-18. Survivors of 17th French Division erected the memorial in 1934.

Left: **A German observation post in the ruins of Mont Faucon monastery.** *Above:* **American monument on Mont Faucon.**

An apt memorial on summit of Cote 295, Mort Homme: 'They Shall Not Pass'.

Return to D18 and continue to **Esnes-en-Argonne** (3 kms), and join the D38 to the left for **Chattancourt** (5 kms). The infamous hill of **Mort Homme** is reached by taking the D38bis at the approach to the village. **Côte 295**, the highest in the **Forêt de Mort Homme,** has a very sombre **memorial** on its summit. This was the scene of intensive tunnelling by both sides, particularly by the Germans. Their longest subway, named after the Crown Prince, was some 3000 metres long and others were of 1500 to 2000 metres. These connected the three most important hills in the neighbourhood and provided support for the mine warfare, a predominant factor in this region.

From Chattancourt take the D38 for Verdun via **Charny-sur-Meuse** in 14 kms.

Verdun is a city with a violent history and, despite the terrible destruction of 1916 and the attacks in the Second World War, still retains the atmosphere of an ancient town. There are many monuments recalling its struggle for survival, being the hub of a circle of forts built in the surrounding hills after the war of 1870. In 1914 Général Sarrail saved the city and its military establishments from capture although it was frequently under fire. In February 1916 the Germans made fierce attacks on the fortifications and Fort Douaumont fell on the 24th. Fort Vaux held out until June when it also was overwhelmed. The next nearest fortress at Souville almost followed but, although completely ruined, the garrison held out and the city was saved. In July the German attacks eased as the Battle of the Somme began. In the autumn, Général Mangin's massive offensive regained all the ground lost and Verdun was relieved.

Before visiting Verdun itself or the surrounding battle zone, a call at the excellent Office du Tourisme is advised. Literature is available in several languages, including compact little guide books and leaflets outlining tours. The famous Michelin Guide, first produced in 1919, is obtainable in a reprint in English and French. The office is in the Place du Nation across the River Meuse from the handsome Porte Chaussée. From the bridge, the Avenue Général Mangin emerges and opposite the Syndicat d'Initiative is the impressive **Monument to the Fallen** — five figures represent the different corps of the French Army standing shoulder to shoulder above the columns of names. On either side are fragments of old fortifications landscaped into public gardens; a **memorial plaque for Général Mangin** is on one wall. Verdun has many very fine memorials and

A tall cross rises above the seven Unknown Warriors in Verdun Cemetery; the eighth lies in Paris, beneath the Arc de Triomphe.

buildings of interest but the **Victory Monument**, which towers over the rue Mazel and Avenue de la Victoire, dominates all. In the crypt are kept the Golden Books recording the many medals awarded to the city. The memorial, up steep steps, is flanked by two Russian guns.

An **avenue of huge statues of the Maréchals and Généraux of France**, beneath the Vauban ramparts, leads to the Porte du Secours entrance to the **Citadel**. As Verdun is still a major garrison, the Citadel remains active but certain sections are open to visitors below its imposing walls and ramparts. Much of the fortress is underground — in fact there are 4000 metres of tunnels which were of vital importance during the war. In one of the large chambers the selection of the French Unknown Soldier was made from eight bodies and this room is one of those open to view. The **museum** in a further chamber is confined mainly to small items and documents. There is another **museum in the Hôtel de Ville**, an Italianate Louis XIII-style building, once a small palace, where documents and decorations and flags are shown. Four old cannon flank the zero kilometre borne and a large shell or two can be seen in the Court of Honour through which access is gained to the museum.

In the cathedral crypt, the capitals of a number of the pillars represent various aspects of the Battle of Verdun, the sculptor,

Symbolised in stone on the Monument to the Fallen at Verdun — the graven figures representing the five French Army corps.

Le Bourgeois, depicting scenes of trench life and horrors in a simple, realistic style. There are many statues and memorials in the city but perhaps one of the most evocative is that by Rodin which is to be found in front of the

Porte St Paul in the Place Vauban. It was presented to the city by the Dutch nation. There are numerous hotels in the city and nearby towns such as Etain and several camp sites provide for battlefield visitors.

Towering above the French Cemetery at Douaumont is the great ossuary.

ROUTE I

Leave Verdun by the N3 pausing perhaps to visit the **Cimitière de Faubourg Pavé** —the military cemetery where lie the seven unknown soldiers not chosen. Note also the group of captured field guns in the entrance park. In 5½ kms, turn left onto the D913. Then in 1½ kms take the right fork for **Fort Vaux**, 2½ kms up the wooded slopes. Halfway up is the **Monument des Fusilées de Tavannes** for members of the Resistance executed here in 1944. Fort Vaux was the north-eastern bastion and one of the many which surrounded Verdun. Externally it is a battered crumbling heap of stones and the advent of thousands of visitors has ruined the immediate area and has given the fort an even more desolate appearance. The iron turrets still crown the grassy cover above it. Internally the galleries, through which the guides lead parties, drip with damp and present a very sombre and chilling aspect of the life of the men who lived and died here during the bombardments. It was gallantly defended but eventually the garrison was

The Lion Memorial at the Chapelle Sainte Fine crossroads commemorates the French 30th Division and its allies.

A monument to André Maginot, once a sergeant in the 44th Territorial Regiment, near Fort de Souville.

overcome in June 1916 only to be recaptured again by the French in November 1916. A **memorial to the pigeon** which carried the last message from Commandant Raynal is to be found with others on the outer walls.

After visiting the fort return to the D913 and turn right arriving in 2 kms at the crossroad of **Chapelle Sainte Fine**. The road to the left, the D122, is the direct one from Verdun; it passes **several monuments** including that of André Maginot, Minister of War responsible for the famous line of forts which bears his name. He fought at Verdun as a sergeant.

The **Lion Monument** which commemorates the **French 39th Division and Allies** also marks the limit reached by the Germans. **Fort de Souville** lies in the trees behind the lion, a ruined heap amid the craters.

Proceed straight ahead to **Douaumont**. In a short distance, on the site of the old railway station of **Fleury**, one of the nine villages obliterated by the battles and now marked only by name boards and a chapel, stands the **Mémorial de Verdun**. This is a magnificent museum where the history of the battle is fully explained in well-designed displays of documents, photographs, exhibits of battlefield equipment and relics found in the region. Captions are in three languages as are the excellent guide books. All the displays are set around a life-size representation of a sector of the battlefield beneath a huge animated map. Films are also shown continuously during opening hours.

Across the forest can be seen the tall tower of the **Ossuary of Douaumont** and, although there are many memorials and monuments in the region, this is the dominant one. The **Jewish Memorial** is on the left as the Ossuary is reached. A large car park is behind the building. The Ossuary was built between 1922 and 1932 and contains the remains of over 130,000 men, both French and German. Another 15,000 identified dead lie in the cemetery in front of it. The building, which is 137 metres long, was inaugurated by President Lebrun in August 1932. There is a small chapel under the tower and the long aisle is divided into 18 sections or chapels, each dedicated to a different département or city of France with other apses for the Allied nations. Services are held regularly in the chapel and the tower itself can be visited. The exterior of the building is decorated with the crests of the towns of France and others overseas which contributed to the cost of this enormous memorial. At the rear of the building the bones of the unknown can be viewed through ground-level windows. Temporary exhibitions are staged from time to time in rooms at the rear.

André Thome — the Soldat du Droit.

The Mémorial de Verdun stands on the site of Fleury railway station.

A path from the car park leads to the ruins of **Fort Thiaumont**. Resume your journey by turning left when leaving the car park and skirt the huge cemetery to take the D913b on the left for Fort Douaumont. At the roadside is the recumbent figure of **Le Soldat du Droit**, the memorial to André Thome who was killed in March 1916.

141

Fort Douaumont on Hill 388 was the most important of the arc of forts built in the last century. The exterior is similar to Fort Vaux with untidy paths and grassy tufts covering it. Here again the turrets remain and there is also an observation post looking out over the panoramic view. The German attack came from the region of the military camp to the north. Inside the fort, groups are conducted through the galleries and casemates, although most of the guides only speak French or German. English visitors are given typed translations.

Another interesting complex to visit is the **Ouvrage de Froideterre** on **Côte 345**. It is reached from the Ossuary by the D913b beside the Jewish Memorial. About 1 km down through the forest is the **Abri Caverne des Quatre Cheminées** on the slope which falls away to the left of the road. This bunker, with others at Command Post 118 and 119 near Thiaumont, were linked. All are now under the care and control of the Association Nationale du Souvenir de la Bataille de Verdun et la Sauvegarde de ses Hauts Lieux (ANSBV) which is based at the Mémorial de Verdun at Fleury. All their sites are well labelled with good explanatory notices, plans and orientation tables.

Above: **Battered Fort Douaumont surmounted by steel cupolas.** *Below:* **Several memorial plaques line the walls of Fort Vaux.**

Below: **The Ouvrage de Froideterre on Hill 345. Designed by the French army engineer Laurent in 1895, it withstood prolonged shelling during the Battle of Verdun.**

Just past the Four Cheminées complex, the approach road to Froideterre climbs up on the right. **Froideterre** was in action right through the Battle of Verdun, was subjected to heavy bombardments, and was partially occupied by the 10th Bavarian Regiment. However the garrison ejected the invaders, due in no small part to the effectiveness of the 75mm turret and its machine guns. Along the D913b and the fort road the trees are being cleared so that it is possible now to see the incredibly shell-torn ground, hitherto completely hidden.

Return to the D913 and turn left before the Ossuary to visit the **Tranchée du Baïonnettes** which is on the right of the road a little way down the hill. The entrance is through a massive gateway with intricately carved heavy metal doors. Beyond, after passing a disintegrating monument, the great bulk of the concrete canopy and pillars enclosing the famous trench comes into view. This was a front line trench of the Ravine de la Dame sector in which were buried men of the 137th Régiment d'Infanterie as they struggled through the trench. They were found in 1919 when it was noticed that a line of rusting bayonets and rifles was protruding from the ground in an area where men of the regiment were known to have disappeared. Today there are few bayonets or rifles visible; in fact every time I visit the monument I see a difference. Only 17 unknown soldiers remain buried here, marked by the wooden crosses. The other 40 who were identified were reburied in Fleury Cemetery.

The D913 winds down into the Meuse valley to reach **Bras** in 6 kms and Verdun in 7½ kms south on the D964. A detour can be made northwards to visit the **Bois de Caures** made famous by the resistance of Colonel Driant and his Chasseurs à Pied. Turn right on to the D964 to **Vacherauville** (2 kms) and then take the D906 up into the woods. Here in a glade are the **regimental and individual memorials** to the gallant colonel and his men of the 56th and 59th Bataillon Chasseurs à Pied. His grave and command post are nearby. Colonel Driant, who was the Deputy for Nancy, was the author of the bill which culminated in the institution of the Croix de Guerre.

In many of the clearings in the forests, and at numerous salient positions, the ANSBV have installed boards indicating interesting walks and drives. The whole region is signposted well, and places where it is not wise to penetrate are clearly shown. The paths are labelled and the trees are marked with the relative plot number in strategic spots. All

The successful defence of the Froideterre Casemate de Bourges was largely due to the turret-mounted 75mm cannons giving covering fire to the flanks in concert with the strong point at Charny.

are shown on the map 'Forêts de Verdun et du Mort Homme — Champs de Batailles de Verdun' issued in the 1/25,000 scale by the Institut Géographique National for the Office National des Forêts. The map sheet has translations in English and German. There are indeed many points of interest which are only accessible on foot and the map is invaluable for anyone studying the region in depth.

Memorial to Colonel Driant, who resisted the Germans from February to July 1916 in the Bois de Caures.

Rusty bayonets emerge beneath a concrete canopy — the infamous Tranchée du Baïonnettes at Douaumont. Only 17 unknown soldiers remain buried beneath the bayonets; the other 40 who were identified were interred in Fleury Cemetery.

143

ROUTE II

Take the D903 out of the city and then branch off to the right on D964. This pleasant road follows the valley of the Meuse and the hills which surround it. At intervals signposts point to the various forts such as **Fort du Géniecourt** (1 km south of Dieue) and **Fort du Troyon**, 2 kms south of the village of that name.

After 23 kms we reach **St Mihiel**. The Germans captured this pleasant town in September 1914 and the St Mihiel salient was formed. In September 1918, French Colonial troops with General Pershing's First Army made attacks on the flanks. Within three days they had reduced it, taking thousands of prisoners, many guns and much equipment, capturing 200 square miles of enemy-held territory.

Take the D907 towards Apremont-la-Forêt and the Forêt de Gobesart. In 2 kms, a small road on the right leads up to **Ailly-sur-Meuse** from which the **Bois d'Ailly** and the **Tranchée du Soif** and the **Monument of the French VIII Army Corps** is reached. Hidden in the woods behind this monument is an extremely interesting and extensive trench

A path leads from the obelisk of the French VIII Corps to the Tranchée du Soif.

A typical bunker entrance in the Tranchée du Soif.

The American Memorial on Mont Sec.

system with many bunkers and concrete shelters, some of which, no doubt, once led into subways. It is wise to keep to the path as subsidence has created gaping holes into the underground workings.

In **Apremont**, take the D12 to **Montsec** and climb up to the **American Memorial** on the crest of the **Butte** by a well-made road which ends at the wide stairway to the colonnade. The circular memorial can be seen for miles around and provides a good lookout point for the Meuse battle area. Within the pillars is a large bronze relief map of the region and orientation points between each pair.

Return to the valley and take the D119 to **Richecourt** (4 kms) and there turn left onto D33/D28 to **Essey-et-Maizerais** (6 kms). Cross the D904 and head for **Bouillonville** and **Thiaucourt-Regniéville**, 7 kms. Turn left on the D67 and on the outskirts of the town the **St Mihiel American Cemetery** is located. The dominating monuments in this cemetery of 4,152 graves are a large eagle sundial, a chapel and a museum connected by a graceful colonnade. There is also a handsome statue of a young American officer in field uniform.

The direct road back to Verdun is the D904 via Fresnes. However it is interesting to leave this road at **St Benoit-en-Woëvre** taking the D901 to the left. In 6 kms is **Vigneulles-lès-Hattonchâtel**, an important position in the St Mihiel salient. On the rocky ridge above is **Hattonchâtel** with an **interesting old church** and a **château**, rebuilt after the war by an American, Miss Skinner. These heights with their extensive views over the region were of great significance as observation posts.

Take the DSt31 going west of the village through the beautiful **Forêt de la Montagne** for 7 kms. At the crossroads turn right on the D154, leaving the long straight **Tranchée de Calonne** ahead. This road, built by Louis XVI, traverses the forest which formed an obstacle in the Eparges sector. **Dommartin, St Remy-la-Calonne** are passed and **Les Eparges** is reached in 7 kms. A road leads up to the **Crête des Eparges** with its **cemetery**, several monuments and huge craters to the right of the D203 to Fresnes (5½ kms). Turn left on the D904 for Verdun.

To return to Reims from Verdun take the N3 for 8 kms, when we reach the **Voie Sacrée** turning to the left. This was Verdun's lifeline in 1916 to **Bar le Duc** and 11 kms to the south it passes through **Souilly** which was Pétain's and later Pershing's headquarters. We continue straight ahead along the N3. In 36 kms we reach **Ste Menehould** and 42 kms further on **Chalons-sur-Marne**. Turn right onto the N44 to Reims which is 44 kms away.

Above: **St Mihiel American Cemetery and Memorial.** *Below:* **The French Memorial to the Missing on the summit of the Crête des Eparges.**

Reims to Compeigne

Leave Reims by the RD380 and in 17 kms we are once more in British lines. XXII Corps were in action in this region in July 1918 and the 9th Scottish Division had a fierce struggle in the **Montagne de Bligny** sector in June.

We leave the main road, turning right down the RD386 5½ kms to the village of **Marfaux**. Here is a small **British Cemetery** containing 1,129 graves and a **Memorial to the New Zealand Missing**. Among those buried here is Sergeant J. Meikle, VC, MM, of the Seaforth Highlanders, killed in action on July 20, 1918. A **German Cemetery** is close by.

The shelter at Marfaux Cemetery cloaks the New Zealand Memorial to the Missing in the attacks of 1918.

Grave of Sergeant Meikle, VC, MM, in Marfaux British Cemetery. The German Cemetery lies in the background.

One of two Italian cemeteries in the region is at Chambrecy.

Returning to the RD380, we climb up the hill towards **Chambrecy**. On the crest, an **Italian Memorial Garden** lies on the right and an **Italian Cemetery** on the left. These men, including their general, lost their lives fighting with the French armies in the defence of Reims. It is interesting to note that the graves are in order of rank although the crosses are uniform. The broken column in the Garden of Remembrance is a genuine Roman one from Italy.

The road now goes down a steep slope and, almost at the bottom, is the **British Cemetery** of Chambrecy where men of the 9th Scottish, 51st Highland and 62nd Divisions lie buried.

Theodore Roosevelt (a relative of Franklin Delano) was American president from 1901 to 1908). All his four sons fought in the Great War, Quentin being shot down just outside Chamery. This plaque still marks the spot where his aircraft crashed.

146

Ville-en-Tardenois, 2 kms further on, was one of the centres of the British defence in June 1918. In 4½ kms leave the main road taking the D2 to the right to travel across the battle area of both 1914 and 1918. It is a pleasant drive through pretty country with villages typical of the region. **Goussancourt** (3½ kms), **Coulonges-Cohan** (8 kms).

At the crossroad go left on the D14. As the road straightens out the ground rises on both sides. On the left, some ½ km further along, there is a grass track. Should the visitor be interested in the story of **Quentin Roosevelt**, the son of President Theodore Roosevelt, this is the way to reach his **crash site**. The young man was a pilot in the 95th Squadron, 1st Pursuit Group, of the American Air Service, and was killed on July 14, 1918. Legend has it that not for the first time this short-sighted man was up on patrol and, instead of rejoining aircraft of his own squadron after an engagement, he tacked on to those of the enemy — who promptly shot him down. The actual site is marked by two memorials and is about ¾ km from the road, up the track and along under the hedgerow to the right. It can just be seen from the village of **Chamery** where there is also a **large fountain** in his memory. This is of cream stone with an ever-flowing water supply, and is near to the farm where the body was brought. He was later buried in Oise-Aisne American Cemetery but now lies with his brother in Normandy.

In Chamery take the right turn — just before the fountain — to return to the D2 and then turn left. In 2 kms we reach **Nesles** with its rather attractive feudal castle and in 1½ kms through the front line area of the US divisions in July and August 1918 approach

the **Oise-Aisne American Cemetery**. It is the second largest of the WWI American cemeteries and lies on the right of the road with the offices and reception room and car park on the left. On the gentle slope up to the attractive, rose-coloured memorial colonnade over 6,000 lay buried beneath the glistening marble crosses and the smooth green lawns. Below the avenue of plane trees leading to the memorial are box trees cut into shell shapes. In the chapel panels record the names of 241 men with no known graves

'Only those are free to live who are not afraid to die.' The fountain memorial to Quentin Roosevelt in the village.

and in the map room the engraved wall map explains the actions of 1918.

Continue 2½ kms to **Fère-en-Tardenois**, a pleasant little country town on the banks of the Ourcq which has a place in history as British GHQ from September 12 to October 8, 1914, when it was moved to Abbeville. The town was then used by the French until

The Oise-Aisne American Cemetery. Here 6,012 lie buried in the 36½-acre plot to the north of the D2.

Buildings used as headquarters by three of the protagonists still remain to be seen at Fère-en-Tardenois. *Right:* General John French commanded the British Army in France from the outset until relieved of his command after the Loos battle in December 1915 and replaced by General (later Field-Marshal) Haig. This house was his HQ for a month in 1914.

they were ousted by the Germans in their May 1918 offensive. It was liberated on July 28 and, soon after, General Pershing established a headquarters here. In 1914 General French conferred with President Poincaré here and the **house** they used is still today much like it was then. It stands behind a high wall on the far right of the large central square. Years later it was used by General Pershing as well. He lived on the other side of town at 2 rue du Gres, having his desk in the bay window of the first floor front room. In the summer of 1918 the Kaiser visited his troops in the area, using the cellar of the bank, Crédit Agricole, as his office. The tables he used are preserved beneath the ancient vaulting and are used at the meetings often held here.

After the United States declared war on Germany in April 1917, General John Pershing became American Expeditionary Force Commander. Nicknamed 'Black Jack' after his reputation for stern discipline, he took over this house at No. 2 rue du Gres.

The German Emperor, Kaiser Wilhelm II, son of Frederick III and Victoria, eldest daughter of Britain's Queen Victoria, used this room beneath the present Crédit Agricole bank after the Germans captured the town in 1918.

Turn down the D967 to **Château-Thierry** (22 kms). The name comes from the castle on a hill on the northern side of the Marne which, legend says, was built by Charles Martel for the King of the Franks, Thierry IV. The site of the castle is now a public park where the ruined walls are still visible.

On September 9, 1914, a most important date in the first battle of the Marne (when the Allies began to advance), the British I Corps (Haig) crossed the Marne here and moved forward to Fère-en-Tardenois. Château-Thierry remained far behind the line until the German advance in May 1918. As it had been with the British in 1914, Château-Thierry was to be the scene of the first American offensive. Despite many attacks the Allied line held and the town, which had fallen to the Germans on May 31, was retaken on July 21, with the American

Theodore Roosevelt was US president from 1901-1908. His son, Quentin, served in the air arm and his aircraft was shot down in July 1918. These relics from the machine are now preserved in the old Hôtel de l'Elephant, now the Maison Amitié Fraternelle Americaine.

FROM PAGE 146

CONTINUED PAGE 152

Divisions pushing forward into the wooded hills north of the town. Near the bridge over the Marne is the Place des Etats-Unis (a useful car parking area). One of the old buildings salvaged from the destruction of the town in the battles of 1918 was the **Hôtel de l'Elephant**. This house overlooks the car park and in it was established the Maison Amitié Fraternelle Americaine — the initial letters are on the façade — by the American Methodist Church in 1919. A social centre and school for the benefit of local people, it is still a municipal institution with language and other courses and a good library. Until the bombardment of the Second World War the façade was decorated by bas reliefs of American soldiers but these have not been replaced. In the courtyard under the balcony are preserved **relics of Lieutenant Quentin Roosevelt's aircraft** — part of the engine and the propeller — together with **photographs of the battle area**. Dominating the town from the summit of **Hill 204** is the huge **American Memorial**.

To reach the memorial, leave the town by the N3 and climb up a fairly steep hill. In 3 kms, on a corner, the two stone pylons marking the entrance to the memorial will be seen on the left. The drive up to the memorial is about 1½kms. The memorial is immense and consists of a double colonnade above a paved terrace framed by an arc of fine trees. On the west face are two heroic figures representing the two countries, France and the USA. On the eastern side, a huge eagle perches above a map of the area of the American operations with an orientation table on the floor of the terrace.

Return to the main road and, with care, take the road on the far side, the D9 for **Belleau Wood**. In 7 kms we reach the village of **Belleau** and the **American Cemetery**. This is the Aisne-Marne Cemetery. The graves fan out on a curve on either side of a central lawn at the end of a tree-lined drive. Above the slopes of the cemetery, under the hill, is

the chapel with its imposing tower. Here there are 2,288 graves and the names of 1,060 who have no known grave are inscribed on the walls of the chapel. There is an observation platform high in the tower giving a fine panoramic view. From the chapel paths lead up into the wood.

Opposite the gate is the **Demarcation Stone** and the **reconstructed village church**, the work being paid for by the veterans of

the 26th US Division. A key of the church is held by the cemetery superintendent. Within are memorials and flags of the US forces and commemorative stained-glass windows. Down the village street is a **drinking trough**, filled with flowers, the gift to Belleau from the Belleau Wood Memorial Association in memory of the soldiers of Pennsylvania who lost their lives. At the bottom of the street is the **château stables** where the Americans

The magnificent American Château-Thierry Memorial is set on Côte 204, giving fine panoramic views over the plain below. Château-Thierry was the scene of the first American offensive.

Above: **Captured artillery pieces in a clearing in Belleau Wood.** *Right:* **This is the Belleau Wood Chapel surrounded by woodland.**

Memorial to the US 4th Marine Brigade.

were housed. The road to the left takes one back to the D9. Turn left to the gates of the American Cemetery passing the large **German Cemetery** where there are 8,625 graves.

Leave the American Cemetery and turn right and take the first right and the first right again thus entering the wood. The park road climbs up to the centre of the wood where a flagpole and a **Memorial to the 4th Marine Brigade** of the US 2nd Division which took the entire wood on June 25, 1918 after having withstood many attacks since June 1. The memorial states that, by order of the Commanding General of the French Sixth Army, the wood be officially renamed Bois de la Brigade de Marine. Placed around the clearing are various artillery pieces and mortars captured by the Marines and in the wood are vestiges of the trenches and craters. Down the glade towards the cemetery is the **ruined chapel** on which is a **plaque commemorating the 2nd Division**.

Leave the wood via the road to Lucy-le-Bocage and, in 4½ kms, reach the N3. Cross this and take the D82 to **Coupru** and then the D11 for **Domptin** and **Charly** (9 kms). Turn right on the D969 to follow the course of the Marne through very pretty scenery although difficult fighting country. The river winds in large loops between steep banks with hills covered with trees.

A few hundred metres away from the American Cemetery with its 2,288 graves is the German burial ground containing 8,625.

The BEF crossed the Marne in 1914 between Luzancy and La Ferté.

In 8 kms we arrive at **Luzancy**. Near the entrance to the village the road crosses the river close to the **site of the weir** over which the British infantry crossed as the bridge had been blown. A more modern weir is further up stream.

We then reach **La Ferté-sous-Jouarre** (7 kms), an attractive town at the junction of the Marne and the Petit Morin rivers. The BEF, which began to advance on September 6, 1914, arrived at La Ferté to find the Germans well placed on the northern banks and the bridges blown. The British artillery dealt severely with the enemy guns and the 4th Division Engineers built a floating bridge to enable the left wing of the BEF to cross. This bridge was built close to the ruined one on the main Paris road. At the southern end, today, is the **British Memorial to the Missing** who fell in the battles of Mons, Le Cateau, the Marne and the Aisne 1914. The names of 3,888 are recorded on the panels of the memorial which stands in a small park presented by the family of Monsieur Bernard de Jussieu. Constructed of white Massangis stone, the monument is surmounted by a sarcophagus on which are laid trophies — ensigns, magazines, bayonets and a tin hat. Four columns stand at the corners of the terrace supporting urns and bearing the arms of the UK. The memorial was designed by G. H. Goldsmith and was unveiled on November 4, 1928 by General Sir William Pulteney in the presence of Maréchal Foch, Field-Marshal Milne and Général Weygand.

On the riverside, by the bridge, the **position of the floating bridge** is marked on each shore by rectangular pylons crowned with the grenade of the Engineers mounted on a circular paving.

The road bridge at La Ferté. The monument records the building of an assault bridge by the 4th Divisional Engineers close to this spot whilst under fire in September 1914.

La Ferté-sous-Jouarre British Memorial to the Missing who fell in the battles of Mons, Le Cateau, the Marne and Aisne in 1914.

SCALE 1:200 000 1cm=2km

FROM PAGE 149

One wonders where the connection is in the massive American statue to French soldiery to be seen in a park outside Meaux. Possibly the most unusual of all war memorials.

From here Paris is a mere 65 kms along the N1 and it is on this road we leave La Ferté following the river to **St Jean-les-2-Jumeaux**.

In 11 kms we arrive at **Meaux**. The BEF reached this town on September 3, 1914 and, after crossing the river, blew the bridges and retired to the Fôret de Crécy some 18 kms to the south (on the N36). There they halted and on the 6th they began the return march.

From Meaux we turn north on the D405 for 1½ kms. As the road climbs out of the town there is a park to the right. Soaring above it is a huge group of sculpture which is the **American Memorial to the French Combatants of the Marne**. The figures are massive and are depicted in a fantastic pose. In 1 km turn left for Chambry on an unnumbered road and, at the edge of the village, turn left on to the D140 for 1 km then right onto D38 at the crossroads. Here is the **Monument des 4 Routes**. We now pass through the area of the French Sixth Army of Maunoury which was reinforced by 11,000 men from Paris in taxicabs. In 10 kms the road becomes D51, then D18. In Reez-Fosse-Martin take D332 for **Betz** (6 kms) across the plateau past one of the **Memorials to the Army of Paris**.

Take the D332 for **Crépy** (10 kms), occupied briefly by the Germans as they advanced on Senlis on September 1, 1914.

Turn left on the N324 for Duvy (2 kms) and in 3 kms turn right on D98 for Trumilly. In 7 kms turn right on D113 to enter **Néry** 1 km ahead.

Memorial to the 'Army of Paris' at Betz.

152

Néry church stands close to the site of one of the glorious feats of arms of the British Army. Earning three Victoria Crosses in almost as many minutes, 'L' Battery of the Royal Horse Artillery fought their famous rearguard action against German advance guards on September 1, 1914. Those who lost their lives lie in Néry Communal Cemetery.

In this small village was fought a brief but glorious rearguard action in the mist of the morning of September 1, 1914. 'L' Battery, Royal Horse Artillery, won lasting fame and three VCs when they (and the Cavalry Brigade) were surprised by the advancing German cavalry and artillery. In the action which followed, 'L' Battery lost two guns and their crews and, in a matter of minutes, 5 officers and 49 men were killed or wounded. Five were left to man the one remaining gun: Captain E. Bradbury, BSM G. Dorrell, Sergeant D. Nelson, Driver Osborne and Gunner H. Darbyshire. Captain Bradbury, although mortally wounded, continued to direct the fire until he died, propped up against the gun which Dorrell and Nelson kept firing, supplied with shells by the other two. The 1st Bn. the Middlesex Regiment and the 1st Scottish Rifles arrived and charged the enemy, recovering the guns and capturing eight of the German field pieces. The **gun position behind the church** is now overrun by shrubs but the **farm**, in which they had sheltered, has probably changed little. Recently a new **plaque** commemorating **'L' Battery** has been erected at the entrance to the village. Those who died are buried in **Néry Communal Cemetery** to the north of the village.

In 3 kms at **Vaucelle** turn right on the D123 for 24 kms and **Villers-Cotterêts** is reached through the attractive Automne valley. The delightful old town is now encircled by a ring road which relieves the traffic problems in this the birthplace of Alexander Dumas, which is also an ideal base for visiting the huge **Forêt de Retz**. It was in the forest that the 4th Guards Brigade fought a desperate rearguard action on September 1, 1914 after the Germans had entered the town. They were pushed out and away in the Allied advance ten days later, not to return until June 1918 when they got into the forest some 8 kms distant. In July, Généraux Mangin and Dogoutte gathered an Allied force in the forest and attacked on July 18, capturing 20,000 prisoners and some 400 guns as they overwhelmed a surprised enemy.

A circuit of the forest is not only very enjoyable but interesting and can be made by taking the D231 out of Villers-Cotterêts and, almost immediately as the forest is entered, the D80 to the right. After 5 kms **Fleury** and then turn left along a typical forest road to the D2 in 2½ kms. In places the forest is really dense and in others the enormous beeches soar over a clear forest floor and it is no wonder that an army could hide here. Turn left and carry on for 2 kms and then left again onto the N2 for 1 km before taking the second right exit from the carrefour to once more enter the cathedral of huge trees. In 1 km, where the beeches seem even more massive, hidden on the right is a track leading up to the **Mangin Memorial** marking the site of his OP. Here he watched his troops from the eminence of a forest fire-watchers' tower.

For a further km the road dips and rises and curves through the forest and then descends to join the D811 where there is a **private British memorial** to a fallen Guards officer. Turn right and soon the **Cross of Sacrifice of the Guards' Grave** comes in sight. Here 98 officers and men of the Guards Brigade are buried in a single grave below the level of the road. The ring-road is gained 2 kms further along, and a right turn and yet another right reaches the D973 for **Pierrefonds** via **Taillefontaine**.

Left: **Carrefour de la Reine — memorial to a Guards officer in the Forêt de Retz.** *Right:* **Guardsmen at rest in a French forest — 98 men out of the 1,114,744 British Great War dead. Casualties from the United Kingdom and Colonies totalled 888,367 (including 412,991 missing); Australia 61,860 (23,397 missing); Canada lost (64,665 (19,507 missing); Undivided India 72,407 (64,518 missing); New Zealand 18,148 (6,299 missing) and South Africa 9,297 (2,815 missing).**

The famous photo taken on November 11, 1918. The signatories descend from the Armistice coach; Admiral Wemyss flanked by Général Weygand (left) and Maréchal Foch (right).

A replica of the original coach preserved as a museum piece. The original was taken to Berlin after the 1940 Armistice and was last seen 80 kilometres south of the city in April 1945.

If a visit to Villers-Cotterêts is not required, after Vaucelles turn left off the D123 at **Elincourt** and onto the D335 and **Pierrefonds** which is 17 kms. The **fairy-tale castle** stands out as the town is approached; it was reconstructed in the 19th Century by Viollet Le Duc and is considered the finest example of his work. Continue through the town on the D335 to turn left onto N31 in 7 kms. Then 8 kms later take a right turn signposted for **Carrefour de l'Armistice**.

Here is the famous clearing where the Armistice was signed on November 11, 1918 in the Wagon Lits Company coach No. 2419D, which, with another train bearing the German plenipotentiaries, was drawn up on the two sections of railway line from Rethondes. These spurs were originally laid down for heavy artillery firing on Noyon. The two trains stopped there for the first time on November 8 when the terms were put before the Germans by Maréchal Foch and Général Weygand. Admiral Wemyss led the British delegation. They returned on the 11th and the Germans signed just after 5.10 a.m., the cease-fire sounding at 11.00 a.m.

After the war, the marshy area where this event had taken place was transformed and the Glade of the Armistice was laid out in the circular fashion it still retains. The opening ceremony was performed on November 11, 1932 by Millerand and Poincaré. The coach used by Foch had been returned to normal service but it was then taken to the Invalides where it became a popular exhibit. In 1927, it returned to the forest where it was housed in a special shed and the interior laid out as it had been nine years previously. A monument to the Armistice was erected in the avenue and in 1937 the statue of Foch was unveiled.

In June 1940 the coach was brought out of its shed and, amid much pomp and splendour, Hitler reversed the rôles. The Germans then took the coach to Berlin where it went on display. The coach disappeared between Elsterwerda and Grossenhain in April 1945.

On November 11, 1950, the carrefour having been repaired and a new shed built (the old one had been destroyed during the Occupation when the Germans defaced the whole area), a railway carriage, similar to the original, was run into the shed and fitted out with replicas of the documents, furniture and pictures. The monument of the eagle being struck down by a sword, which had been smashed in 1940 and taken in pieces to Germany in packing cases, was found after the war and was repaired and replaced on its own site. The railway lines into the shed have now been removed just outside the doors to prevent further removal of the coach!

Armistice at Compiègne. The memorial slab marking the exact spot where the coach stood on November 11, 1918.

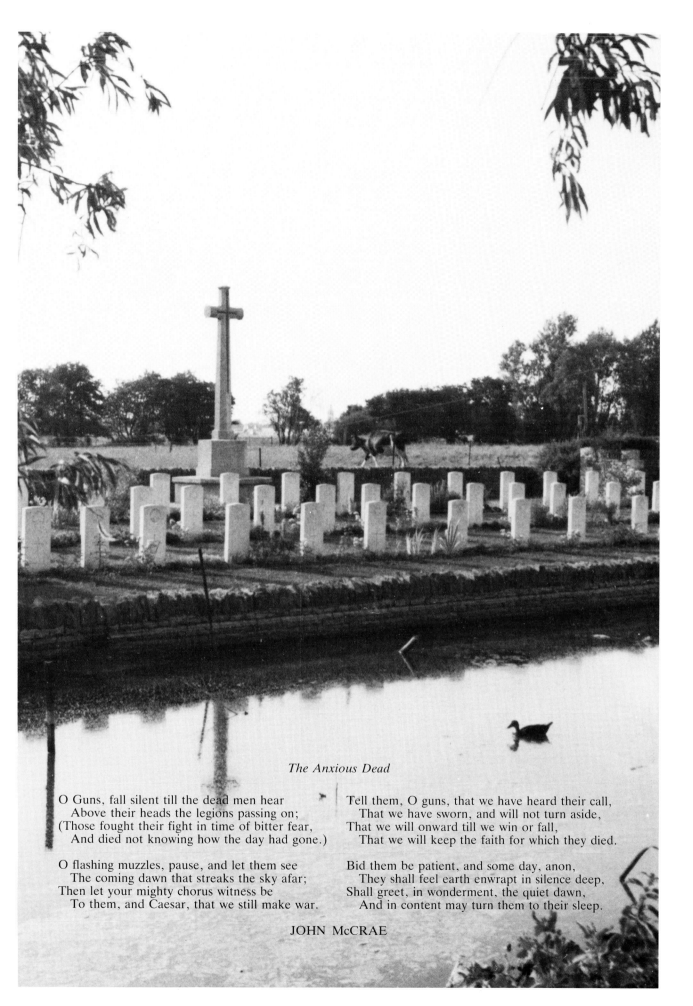

The Anxious Dead

O Guns, fall silent till the dead men hear
  Above their heads the legions passing on;
(Those fought their fight in time of bitter fear,
  And died not knowing how the day had gone.)

O flashing muzzles, pause, and let them see
  The coming dawn that streaks the sky afar;
Then let your mighty chorus witness be
  To them, and Caesar, that we still make war.

Tell them, O guns, that we have heard their call,
  That we have sworn, and will not turn aside,
That we will onward till we win or fall,
  That we will keep the faith for which they died.

Bid them be patient, and some day, anon,
  They shall feel earth enwrapt in silence deep,
Shall greet, in wonderment, the quiet dawn,
  And in content may turn them to their sleep.

JOHN McCRAE

155

The Commonwealth War Graves Commission

The origins of the Commission go back to 1914 when a British Red Cross unit headed by Fabian Ware went to France in September. It was a Mobile Ambulance Unit working with the French Army. In October, Ware visited Béthune cemetery with Dr Stewart, a Red Cross medical assessor. The latter, on seeing a number of British graves with their plain wooden crosses, suggested that although they were adequately marked, there seemed to be no evidence that they had been recorded or registered and that the unit should undertake this work when and where it was able.

From that day onward, the unit searched for, located, identified and registered thousands of graves. Gradually this task superseded the medical side as the Army's medical services improved and the need for the work on graves was appreciated by the authorities. In March 1915, it became the Graves Registration Commission and was attached to the Adjutant General's department.

Major Ware, as he had then become, made one of his first tasks that of negotiating with the French government for the permanency of the cemeteries. This led to the passing, in December 1915, of a law that the French nation would acquire the necessary lands and make a free gift of them to the British Empire, in perpetuity, and the British would be responsible for their maintenance.

Early in 1916, a National Committee for the Care of Soldiers' Graves was established with the Prince of Wales as its President. With representatives from the Dominions and India, one of its aims was to deal with the question of permanent memorials to be erected after the war.

In February 1916, the Commission had become the Directorate of Graves Registration and Enquiries and was an integral part of the Army. This Directorate was the sole unit with authority to negotiate between the French military and civil authorities in all matters relating to graves. Similar arrangements were soon made with the Belgians.

In May 1916, Colonel Ware moved his headquarters to London as the horizon of the department widened beyond the Western Front with the huge task of registering, burying and recording the dead. An early result of the work of the Directorate was the introduction of a double identification tag made of compressed fibre in place of the old oblong metal plaque or glazed linen tunic label.

Long before this, Colonel Ware had realised the need for photographs of graves for relatives who frequently contacted the unit for information. He organised the systematic photography of the graveyards and, by April 1917, some 12,000 photographs had been sent to relatives. By that date 150,000 graves in France and Belgium, 2,500 in Salonika and 400 in Egypt had been registered.

The horticultural work on the cemeteries began in 1916 when the aid and advice of the Royal Botanic Gardens was sought and plants and seeds from Kew were sent to France through funds supplied by the Red Cross. The flowers and shrubs were chosen with considerable care. The graves at the time were either individual mounds or long trenches, being planted with flowering annuals with grass paths separating them. Characteristic plants from overseas were planted to provide a more local atmosphere for the graves of the men from Canada, Australia and New Zealand. Care was taken with Indian and Chinese graves only to use plants which those nations regarded as sacred and suitable for cemeteries. Nurseries were set up but in 1918 some of these as well

as many cemeteries were overrun and all the work was destroyed. In time, of course, this was repaired.

The moral advantage of these almost English gardens was recognised from the beginning as oases of peace and quiet amid the hurly-burly of the battle area or the large base camps and hospitals. Men found the pleasant, colourful graveyards ideal for spending short periods to read letters from home — or to write them.

On May 21, 1917, the Imperial War Graves Commission was created by a Royal Charter with the duties of marking and maintaining the graves of all members of the Services of the Empire who died during the First World War. They were also to construct cemeteries and memorials, to keep registers and records, and to publish them. The principles which guided the Commission all those years ago have been maintained to this day. To quote from a recent Commission report:

'That each of the dead should be commemorated individually by name either on the headstone on the grave, or by an inscription on a memorial; that the headstones and memorials should be permanent; that the headstones should be uniform and that there should be no distinction made on account of military or civil rank.'

The whole cost of the work is shared by the partner governments — the United Kingdom, Canada, Australia, New Zealand, South Africa. India and Pakistan — in proportion to the numbers of their graves.

Each headstone bears the badge of the service, corps or national emblem; the name rank and number and decorations with, at the base, an inscription chosen by relatives. The headstones are 2ft 8in in height and 1ft 3in wide. The appropriate religious emblem is also included. Normally the top of the stone is gently curved but variations exist to identify foreign nationals or civilians. Headstones of soldiers awarded the Victoria Cross bear the emblem of the decoration in place of any other cross. Until recently Portland or Hopton Wood quarries provided the stone used for headstones but now Botticino limestone is being used as it requires less maintenance. The headstones stand in narrow borders planted, where conditions allow, with roses and perennials offset with lawns, shrubs and trees.

Where some doubt exists as to the exact location of a grave in a cemetery the words 'Believed to be buried in this cemetery' prefix the inscription. In places where the graves were destroyed by later battles. 'Known to be buried in this cemetery' or 'Buried near this spot' are used.

Graves of the unidentified bear the inscription chosen by Rudyard Kipling: 'Known Unto God'. He also suggested the wording inscribed on the Stone of Remembrance found in all but the smallest cemeteries, 'Their Name Liveth for Evermore' (Ecclesiasticus, Apocrypha 44:14). The Stone of Remembrance was designed by Sir Edwin Lutyens and the beautifully proportioned Cross of Sacrifice, found in all the cemeteries, by Sir Reginald Blomfield.

Immediately after the war ended, work on the permanent cemeteries began and, within a few years, these beautiful gardens of rest appeared in the once devastated regions. The first three were completed in 1920 and included two in the battle zones: Forceville and Louvencourt,

The pilgrimages, individual and collective, had also commenced and the Commission began its close contact with the British Legion and with travel agents Thomas Cook which organised cheap trips to the battle-

fields. Throughout the years the Commission's offices have been offering a first-class service with help and advice to those wishing to visit the cemeteries and memorials.

In the 1920s work commenced on the erection of the memorials to the missing at certain selected sites. These ranged from the gigantic Thiepval Arch and the Menin Gate to the smaller ones such as that at Zeebrugge or Nieuwpoort. The countries of the Empire also had their memorials and, at home, the Naval and Mercantile Marine memorials were erected at the naval ports of Portsmouth, Plymouth, Chatham and on Tower Hill in London.

The Commission also undertakes to care for, on a repayment contract, private Service memorials and certain individual graves of officers and men buried before the Commission came into being.

Almost every cemetery has a small bronze door let into a wall behind which will be found a copy of the cemetery or memorial register. There is also a book for visitors to sign before leaving the cemetery.

In March 1960, the title of the Commission was changed to The *Commonwealth* War Graves Commission and in June 1964 its terms of reference were further defined by a supplemental Charter.

A series of international agreements protect the Commission's work in foreign countries and many Governments have generously purchased land at State expense and given it for perpetual use as cemeteries by the Commission.

Copies of the Registers are published for the Commission by Her Majesty's Stationery Office. They can be seen at all the main offices abroad. The area offices in France and Belgium are:

France:
Rue Angèle Richard
Beaurains
62012 Arras, Cedex
Telephone: (21) 230324

North-West Europe:
Elverdingestraat 82
B 8900 Ieper (Ypres)
Telephone: Ypres (057) 200118

The Headquarters of the Commission are at
2 Marlow Road,
Maidenhead,
Berkshire, SL6 7DX
Telephone: Maidenhead (0628) 34221

For further, more detailed reading on the work of the Commission, I recommend *The Unending Vigil*, a history of the Commonwealth War Graves Commission, 1917-1967, by Philip Longworth, published by Constable of London in 1967. A new edition has recently been published.

I cannot, however, close this account without expressing my very deep gratitude for all the advice, encouragement and friendly help I have always received from the staff of the Commission over many years.

Addresses of the headquarters of other War Graves Commissions in Europe are:

FRANCE
Secretariat d'Etat Chargé des Anciens
    Combattants et Victimes de Guerre,
139 rue de Bercy, Paris (I2c), France.

GERMANY
Volksbund Deutsche Kriegsgräberfürsorge,
Werner-Hilpert-Strasse 2, Kassel 35,
West Germany.

USA (European Office)
The American Battle Monuments
    Commission,
68 rue 19 Janvier, 92 Garches, France.

INDEX

A

Nine villages were totally destroyed in the battles around Verdun. This is the site of Bezonvaux, ten kilometres north-east of the city, completely obliterated and never rebuilt.

One of the many plaques in the cathedral at Amiens.

The Canadian Memorial at Dury Crossroad near Vis-en-Artois on the road between Arras and Cambrai.

Memorial at Notre Dame de Lorette to the glory of Général Maistre and the French XXI Army Corps.

London Cemetery on the eastern side of High Wood.

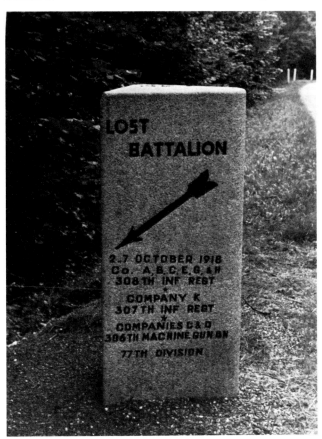

The US 77th Division's 'Lost Battalion' ravine near Apremont.

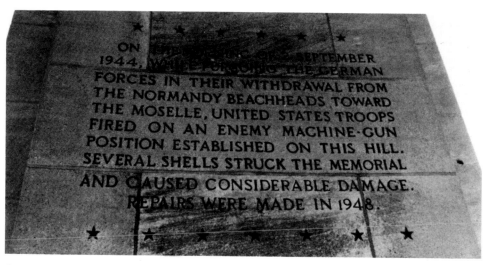

Second War damage to the American Memorial at Monsec now repaired.

The impressive village war memorial at Proyart on the Somme.

These enchanting beavers guard the twin flagpoles at the Canadian memorial on Vimy Ridge.

U

V

W

Y

Z

Buzancy. 'Here for all time the glorious Scottish thistle will bloom amid the roses of France.'